THE MANY LEGENDS OF JESSE JAMES

ALSO AVAILABLE FROM PJM PUBLISHING

NON FICTION

The 'Real' Wild West

The Technique of the Mystery Story

'I Do Solemnly Swear' Presidential Inaugurations from George Washington to George W. Bush

Complete Hypnotism

Getting The Scoop – A Manual of Newspaper Writing and Correspondence

FICTION

Southern Gothic Shorts

The Lodger by Marie Belloc Lowndes

Nightmare Town by Dashiell Hammett

The Evil Guest and Other Tales by J. Sheridan LeFanu

Sax Rohmer's Fu Manchu

Collected Screenplays of Phillip J. Morledge

Deadeye - The True Story of 'Private Lives'

VIEW THE FULL CATALOGUE ONLINE AT
WWW.PJMORLEDGE.COM

THE MANY LEGENDS OF JESSE JAMES

EDITED BY

PHILLIP J. MORLEDGE

PJM PUBLISHING
WWW.PJMORLEDGE.COM

THE MANY LEGENDS OF JESSE JAMES
© Copyright PJM Publishing 2009

ALL RIGHTS RESERVED

NO PART OF THIS BOOK MAY BE REPRODUCED IN ANY FORM,
BY PHOTOCOPYING OR BY ANY ELECTRONIC OR MECHANICAL MEANS,
INCLUDING INFORMATION STORAGE OR RETRIEVAL SYSTEMS,
WITHOUT PERMISSION IN WRITING FROM BOTH THE COPYRIGHT
OWNER AND THE PUBLISHER OF THIS BOOK.

COVER DESIGN © COPYRIGHT PHILLIP J. MORLEDGE 2009
PHOTOGRAPH'S FROM PUBLIC DOMAIN COLLECTIONS

FIRST EDITION PAPERBACK 2009

This Edition First Published April 2009
PJM Publishing Sheffield, England

ISBN 978-0-9559765-7-5

Printed in Great Britain for PJM Publishing

Contents

THE BORDER BANDITS
J.W. BUELL

DEEDS OF DARING
JAMES EDGAR

JESSE JAMES, MY FATHER
JESSE JAMES, JR.

THE
BORDER BANDITS

AN AUTHENTIC AND THRILLING HISTORY OF
THE NOTED OUTLAWS.

JESSE AND FRANK JAMES
And their Bands of Highwaymen

COMPILED FROM RELIABLE SOURCES ONLY AND
CONTAINING THE LATEST FACTS IN REGARD TO THESE
DESPERATE FREEBOOTERS.

BY

J W BUEL

FRANK JAMES

JESSE JAMES

NOTICE - These portraits were engraved from late photographs, obtained at some expense and danger; and having been copyrighted for this book all persons are warned against using them elsewhere.

PREFACE

The career of Jesse and Frank James has been as checkered as the sunlight that streams through a latticed window, and their crimes are a commentary upon the development of intellectual America. No one can afford to ignore the lesson which the lives of these outlaws teach, and therefore a correct history of their desperate deeds becomes necessary as a part of the country's annals, in juxtaposition with the commendable heroism of our brightest characters. So many improbable and romantic incidents have been credited to these noted brothers by sensational writers ; so many dashing escapades and hair-breadth escapes attributed to them, which they never even dreamed of, that thinking people, especially in the East, have begun, almost, to regard the James Boys as a myth, and their deeds as creations of sensational dreamers.

It has been my purpose for more than three years to prepare a true history of these noted outlaws, and during that time material has been collecting which is now given to the public entirely free from fulsome description or elaborated sensation. In the main essentials the James Boys themselves will confirm the truthfulness of this narrative, which has been written with a special regard for candor and indisputable facts only.

During several years of the most exciting period in the career of these noted bandits, I was engaged as reporter for the Kansas City press, and not only became acquainted with many of their relatives and friends who reside in that section, from whom were obtained numerous facts and incidents never before published ; but my duties as a journalist gave me many excellent opportunities to learn the real truth in regard to many of their most daring adventures, to one of which (the robbing of the cash-box at the Kansas City Fair) I was an eye-witness. As time unfolds the mysteries which have gathered around the names of these desperate outlaws, it will be seen that this is the most faithful history of their exploits that has ever been presented to the public.

J. W. B.

St. Louis, December 15, 1880.

THE BORDER BANDITS

JESSE AND FRANK JAMES - THEIR YOUTH
Career as Guerrillas
First Skirmishes
Desolation of Lawrence
Desperate Fighting by Squads
Direful Massacre at Centralia
Fortune Turning Against the Guerrillas
The Whirlwind of Destruction Changes
Jesse James' Career in Texas
Robbery and Murder
Plundering a Kentucky Bank
Bank Robbery and Murder
Mysterious Hiding Place in Jackson Co.
Terrible Fight in Mexico
Plundering an Iowa Bank
Another Bank Robbery in Kentucky
Robbing the Cash Box at the Kansas City Fair
Plundering the Ste. Genevieve Bank
Wrecking and Plundering a Train
The Stage Robbery near Hot Springs
Train Robbery at Gad's Hill
Wicher's Unfortunate Hunt for the James Boys
Murdering Cow Boys and Driving off Cattle
The Attack on the Samuels 'Residence
Assassination of Daniel Askew
The San Antonio Stage Robbery
The Great Train Robbery at Muncie

The Huntington Bank Robbery

The Rocky Cut Train Robbery

Fatal Attack on a Minnesota Bank

At Glendale — the Last Great Train Robbery

Shooting of Jesse James by George Shepherd

Why did Shepherd Shoot Jesse James?

Robbing of the Mammoth Cave Stage

Personal Characteristics of the James Boys

The Union Pacific Express Robbery

An Interview with the Younger Brothers

Anecdotes of Jesse and Frank James

THE BORDER BANDITS

JESSE AND FRANK JAMES
THEIR YOUTH

Strangely, and yet a not uncommon circumstance, Jesse and Frank James were the sons of a respectable Kentucky minister of the Baptist persuasion. Rev. Robt. James, " in the good old times," as he was wont to call the early days of his ministry, was a great camp-meeting exhorter, and many of the rock-ribbed hills of middle Kentucky have been musical with the echoes of his strong voice. Like many other pastoral exhorters and close communionists, the Rev. James was illiterate so far as "book learning" was concerned, but his sincerity was rarely debated. It has been asserted that he passed an academic course at Georgetown College, but the records of that institution show the name of no such person. Zerelda Cole, (the mother of the noted outlaws,) was married to the Rev. Robert James in Scott county, Kentucky, the same county in which Georgetown College is located; this fact, added to the desire to heroize, to the largest possible extent, the paternity of the James boys, is doubtless the reason for ascribing to the father "a finished education and unusual ability."

"Like father, like son," is a very ancient oriental adage; but it does not apply to Jesse and Frank James, though it is true that their dispositions are due to maternal inheritance. In fact, the wife's strength of will and uncompanionable traits of character resulted in a final separation a few years after their removal to Clay County, Missouri, in 1843. The Rev. James, in 1849, joined in the pilgrimage to California, from whence he never returned; and, in 1857, Mrs. James took another husband, in the person of Dr. Reuben Samuels. It is quite unimportant to follow the domestic career of Mrs. James, now Mrs. Samuels, and what has been related is merely for the purpose of defining the inherited bent and inclination of the parents of the great outlaws.

Jesse James was born in Clay County, Missouri, in 1845, while Frank's nativity is Scott County, Kentucky, where he was born in 1841. At an extremely early age they displayed traits of character which have ever since distinguished them. Their hatreds were always bitter and their cruelty remorseless. They manifested especial delight in punishing dumb animals, which is evidenced by their cutting off the tails and ears of dogs and cats, burying small animals alive, and diversions of every kind which would inflict the most grievous pains. Among other boys they were domineering and cruel, and would rarely participate in innocent amusements. They were never subjected to parental restraint and their youth was passed in the most perfect indulgence. At the age of ten and fourteen years, respectively, the boys were provided with fire-arms, in the use of which they readily became proficient, and were no less expert in throwing a bowie-knife which they could send quivering into a two-inch sapling, at the space of fifteen feet, almost without fail.

- *THEIR CAREER AS GUERRILLAS* -

When the tocsin of war sounded, and the feverish thrill of excitement ran through the nation, boys though they were, Jesse and Frank James were electrified with the ominous news and longed to participate in the affray where human blood might be drawn until, like a fountain, it would swell into a gory river. Soon the unmerciful Quantrell, that terrible wraith of slaughter, came trooping through Missouri upon an errand of destruction, and attracted to his banner many impetuous youths of the West, among whom was Frank James; Jesse being the junior brother, and but little more than fourteen years of age, was rejected by Quantrell, and returned home to his farm labors with sorrow. But he did not remain inactive. The family being in- tensely Southern in their political predilections, all possible aid and sympathy were given to Quantrell. Many dark nights Jesse would mount his best horse and ride through the gloomy wilderness of Western Missouri until he gained the guerrilla haunts, where he would deliver important information concerning the movements of Federal troops.

The part played by Jesse and the open and decided expressions frequently made by Dr. Samuels and his decidedly demonstrative wife, greatly excited the Federal soldiers, and it was determined to make an example of the family. Accordingly, in June, 1862, a company of Missouri militia approached the Samuels' homestead, which is near Kearney, in Clay County, and first meeting Dr. Samuels, they soon gave him to understand that their visit was made for a purpose decidedly unpleasant to him.

A strong rope was produced with which he was securely pinioned and then led away from the house a distance of about one 'hundred yards. Here the rope was fastened in a noose around his neck, while the 'other end was thrown over the limb of a tree, and several men hastily drew him up and left him suspended to choke to death. Mrs. Samuels, however, had followed stealthily, and the moment the militia had departed she rushed to the rescue of her husband, whom she hastily cut down, and by patient nursing saved his life. The enraged troops decided also to hang Jesse James, whom they found plowing in the field, but his youth saved him from any other violence than a few cuffs and the production of a rope with a suspicious noose which they threatened to ornament his neck with if he again visited the guerrilla camp.

Instead of producing the desired effect, this act of the militia only excited Jesse the more, and led him to deeds of graver importance. He continued to communicate almost daily with Quantrell, which so exasperated the militia that they paid a second visit to the Samuels' residence, decided upon killing both Dr. Samuels and the daring Jesse. When they reached the place, however, they found their intended victims absent, but, determined not to return without some trophy of their revengeful sortie, they took Mrs. Samuels and her daughter. Miss Susie, captive, and carried them to St. Joseph, where they were kept confined in jail for several weeks. This last act greatly inflamed Jesse's passions, and he immediately mounted his horse and again rode to Quantrell's camp, where, after detailing the particulars of this last outrage, perhaps exaggerating the facts some in order to make his appeal more effective, he begged the guerrilla commander to accept his services as a private. So hard did he plead for permission to join the ranks that marched under the shadow of the black flag, that at length the barrier which' his youth imposed was overlooked and the terrible Quantrell oath was administered to him.

- THE FIRST SKIRMISHES -

Up to this time the guerrillas had been engaged in but few skirmishes, their services consisting chiefly in small foraging expeditions, making themselves thoroughly acquainted with the topography of the country preparatory to engaging in more effective measures. There was a slight brush at Richfield, in which Captain Scott, with twelve of Quantrell's men, surprised thirty militia whom they captured, after killing ten, and in this attack Jesse James participated. Upon his return to camp he was sent out with orders from Quantrell to scour the counties adjoining Clay and locate the militia. After passing through Clinton County he paid a short visit to his mother, who received him with many manifestations of pleasure, and then began to unload herself of the valuable information she had gathered for the benefit of the guerrillas. She told him that the attack on

Richfield had resulted in massing the militia for a determined stroke, and that the troops were concentrating near that point; that Plattsburg had been almost entirely relieved of its garrison and would fall an easy prey to the guerrillas if they chose to profit by the opportunity. Jesse lost no time in communicating the situation to Quantrell, and, accordingly, three days after the capture of the squad of militiamen at Richfield, Captain Scott took fifteen men and silently stole upon Plattsburg, which he found defended by less than a score of Federals, under the command of a lieutenant. The guerrillas dashed into the town about 3 p.m. (August 25th), yelling like a tribe of Comanche Indians. The citizens fled into their houses with such fear that few ventured to look into the streets even through key holes. The Federal lieutenant chanced to be in the public square when the charge was made, and Jesse James had the honor and credit of capturing him. The rest of the militia gained the court-house, where it would have been impossible to dislodge them, and to have attacked the building would have exposed the guerrillas to the fire of the enemy. It was here that Jesse James' strategy and military tact were first manifested. Turning his prisoner (the lieutenant) over to Captain Scott, he said in a loud voice: "Captain, there is no use parleying with these cut-throats; shoot this fellow if he don't order his men in the court-house to surrender immediately."* Captain Scott replied that he would if the court-house was not surrendered in two minutes. The result was that Plattsburg fell into the hands of the guerrillas, who pillaged the town and gathered booty, consisting of two hundred and fifty muskets, several hundred rounds of ammunition, ten thousand dollars in Missouri warrants, besides a large quantity of clothing, etc. The money was divided among the participating guerrillas, each of whom received nearly one thousand dollars in warrants besides clothing and other articles of value. The guerrillas compelled the landlord of the principal hotel to prepare them a good supper, to which they invited their prisoners, whom they paroled; and after feasting until 9 o'clock p.m., they withdrew to the cover of the forest.

After raiding Plattsburg, Quantrell broke camp and moved southward, passing through Independence, and bivouacked near Lee's Summit. The residents of that section suffered pitilessly from the sack and pillage of both Federals and Confederates. They occupied a middle ground which was subject to the incursions of both armies, and what was left after the forage of the Union forces was remorselessly appropriated by the guerrillas. There were skirmishes almost daily, and every highway was red with human blood. The James boys, young as they were, became the terror of the border; the crack of their pistols or the whirr of their pirouetting bowies daily proclaimed the sacrifice of new victims. The sanguinary harvest grew broader as the sickle of death was thrust in to reap, and the little brooks and rivulets that had babbled merry music for ages and laved the thirst of man and beast with their crystal water, suddenly became tinged with a dye fresh from the fountain of bitterest sorrow. And thus the days sped on heavy with desolation. Quantrell and his followers were scarcely interrupted by the militia, who never attacked them except at the price of terrible defeat, until at length a direful scheme was proposed in which the desperate character of these free riders was manifested in its blackest hues.

- THE DESOLATION OF LAWRENCE -

Lawrence, Kansas, a thrifty town located on the Kaw River, was selected by Quantrell as the place upon which to wreak a long-pent-up vengeance. Sitting around the camp fire on the night of August 18th, 1863, the chief of the black banner held a consultation with Frank and Jesse James, the Younger boys, the Shepherd brothers, and others of his most daring followers, as to the next advisable move upon a place which would furnish the best inducements for their peculiar mode of war. There was a concert of opinion that Lawrence was the most available place. The point having been selected, Quantrell did not neglect to inform his followers of the danger such an undertaking involved; that their road would be infested with militia, the forces of which would be daily augmented when the first intimation of the purposes of the guerrillas should be made known; that it would be ceaseless fighting and countless hardships, and many would be left upon the prairies to fester in the sun. He then called his command to arms and acquainted every man with the decision in the following speech:

"Fellow soldiers, a consultation just held with several of my comrades has resulted in a decision that we break camp to-morrow and take up a line of march for Lawrence, Kansas; that we attack that town and, if pressed too hard, lay it in ashes. This undertaking, let me assure you, is hazardous in the extreme. The territory through which we must pass is full of enemies, and the entire way will be beset by well armed men through whom it will be necessary for us to carve our way. I know full well that there is not a man in my command who fears a foe; that no braver force ever existed than it is my honor to lead, but you have never encountered danger so great as we will have to meet on our way to Lawrence; therefore let me say to you, without doubting in the least your heroism, if there are any in my command who would prefer not to stake their lives in such a dangerous attempt, let them step outside the ranks."

At the conclusion of Quantrell's remarks a shout went up from every man, "On to Lawrence! " Not a face blanched, but on the other hand there was but one desire, to lay waste the city on the Kaw.

On the following day the order was given to "mount," and with that dreadfully black flag streaming over their heads the command, two hundred strong, turned their faces to the west. As they crossed the Kansas line at the small town of Aubrey, in Johnson county, Quantrell compelled three men, whom he found sitting in front of a small store kept by John Beeson, to accompany him as guides. The command passed through Johnson county midway between Olathe and Spring Hill, and through the northern part of Franklin county. When they reached Cole creek, eight miles from Lawrence, the three guides were taken into a clump of thick woods and shot by Jesse and Frank James. One of the party, an elderly man, begged piteously to be spared, reminding his executioners that he had never done them any wrong, but his prayers for mercy ended in the death rattle as a bullet went crashing through his neck.

Quantrell had been agreeably mistaken concerning the resistance he expected to encounter. Not a foe had yet appeared, but he never permitted a per- son to pass him alive. No less than twenty-five persons whom he met in the highway, after getting into Kansas, had been shot, and yet he avoided the public roads as much as possible.

Early in the morning of August 21st Quantrell and his band came in sight of the fated town. The sun was just straggling above the undulations of the prairie and the people of the place were beginning to resume the duties of a newly-born day. With a cry which froze the blood of every one in the town who heard it, Quantrell and his two hundred followers descended upon the place with pistol, sword and firebrand.

The prime object of the guerrillas was to capture Gen. Jim Lane, who resided at Lawrence, and retaliate upon him for the burning and sacking of Osceola, Mo., which had been accomplished by men under his command. But Lane fled on the first alarm, and concealed himself in an adjacent cornfield. Foiled in their desire to capture him, the enraged guerrillas turned their vengeance loose upon the ill-fated town, killing every man who came within range of their deadly revolvers. Quantrell's orders were to kill all the men, but to spare the women and children. By accident, however, — possibly by design of some drunken privates — several women and children were shot; and this fact was made use of in subsequent reports of the affair to greatly exaggerate its barbarous details. It was certainly sufficiently inexcusable and barbarous without exaggeration. The torch was applied to the light frame buildings as the killing progressed, and the beautiful little city was soon enveloped in a sheet of flames. Stores and saloons were broken into and robbed of their contents, and the guerrilla band soon became a howling mob of drunken madmen. The dreadful harvest of death and destruction lasted nearly all day, and when the guerrillas took up their line of retreat toward the borders of Missouri, the city of Lawrence had disappeared from the face of the earth. In this affair Jesse James is said to have killed thirty men and Frank thirty-five. They seemed to take a sort of devilish pride in numbering their victims.

Quantrell and his men hastily retraced their steps, but they were terribly harassed during the entire return march by the Kansas militia and Federal troops that hurriedly concentrated and went in pursuit of them. This force has been reliably estimated at fully seven thousand, and nothing but hard marching, determined fighting, and an endurance that has never been equaled saved the guerrillas from total destruction. At Black Jack, about fifteen miles from Lawrence, a stand was made and some brisk fighting occurred. The guerrillas took to cover in a large barn which stood at the edge of an orchard. Several assaults were made to dislodge them but in vain. The horses of the guerrillas were suffering severely, however, and realizing that without horses they would be unable to get out of Kansas, the guerrillas made a desperate charge in which thirty-two of the militia were killed and a panic was the result. But the guerrillas did not care to follow up the victory, as every moment was precious. The militia were swarming and closing in upon them rapidly, and it was only by the rarest stroke of fortune that Quantrell and his men ever escaped from Kansas; this rare fortune was due entirely to the unparalleled cowardice of three hundred well armed and mounted men who had been organized into a militia force near Spring Hill, Kansas. These men exhibited remarkable bravery until the enemy appeared in sight, when they immediately retreated and never halted until they were ten miles from the place where they saw Quantrell. Had they engaged the enemy, which was one-third less in number, besides badly fatigued, they could either have beaten Quantrell or held him at bay until enough reinforcements were received to have annihilated every one of the guerrilla band.

It was a continual fight, however, and as Quantrell predicted, many of his followers were left dead and unburied on the hot prairies, where they became the prey of carrion birds. At Shawnee, in the northern part of Johnson county, the last stand was made, but the fight lasted only a few minutes, for the guerrillas, appreciating the critical position they occupied, with nearly five thousand militia gradually surrounding them, in the manner of early settlers who join in general hunts for the destruction of obnoxious wild animals, Quantrell soon ordered a charge and retreat. After breaking through the lines the guerrillas disbanded and each one then considered alone his own safety; this rendered a general pursuit impossible, and with a total loss of twenty-one men the bands reached the coverts of Jackson and Clay counties, where they were comparatively safe.

- DESPERATE FIGHTING BY SQUADS -

After spending a month in apparent leisure, during which time Jesse and Frank James were frequent night visitors to their old home, Quantrell again called his command together for the purpose of resuming active hostilities, but he changed his tactics and added new terrors to the border counties of Missouri. The command was divided into squads of twenty and thirty, by which means they could make bold dashes at various points almost simultaneously and so confuse their enemies as to make pursuit futile. Indeed this peculiar and remorseless warfare gave rise to the strange superstition that Quantrell was some spirit of darkness who could transport himself and troops from place to place in the twinkle of an eye. He became no less dreaded by the Federal troops than by Union citizens, and day and night non-combatants as well as armed militiamen fell victims to the terrible guerrillas.

In the early part of October, Jesse James, in charge of a squad of twenty-five men, learning of the movements of a company of Federal cavalry under command of Capt. Ransom, who was marching toward Pleasant Hill, made a rapid detour and flanked the Federals five miles north of Blue Springs. Jesse selected a place near the road which was well screened by a dense thicket; here he stationed his men, and when the Federals came riding leisurely by, unconscious of any lurking danger, suddenly a storm of bullets poured upon them from the thicket and men fell like leaves in an autumn gust. The entire company was immediately thrown into the greatest confusion. The youthful commander of the guerrillas made the most of his advantage and ordered a dash into the confused and stricken ranks of the enemy, which he shot down with as little resistance as is offered by dumb animals. The havoc was terrible, for out of nearly one hundred Federals less than one-third the number escaped, while the loss of the guerrillas was only one killed and three slightly wounded.

On the following day another squad of Quantrell's men ambushed a body of militia who were returning from a forage in Lafayette county, and mercilessly annihilated nearly every one of the unfortunate command. One week later Frank and Jesse James, with fifty men, suddenly appeared in Bourbon county, Kansas, five miles south of Fort Scott, and swooped down upon Capt. Blunt and his company of seventy-five mounted infantry, and with a yell of rage and triumph swept with deathly missiles the astonished Federals, leaving forty of them to bleach in autumn rains.

The next attack Was upon Lieut. Nash's command, three miles west of Warrensburg, Missouri, which was surprised by the guerrillas and cut to pieces. Following close upon this came the furious desolation of Camden. This little town was garrisoned by a small company of Federals, who, upon the day in question, were in the midst of bacchanalian revels and unable to offer any resistance. This fight was a slaughter, in which the drunken soldiers were shot down without compunction, and the riot of murder was a pastime of sport for the guerrillas. After completing the harvest of death the town was pillaged and fired, and when the guerrillas rode out of the place they left its ruins in charge of the dead.

Another squad, under command of George Todd suddenly encountered the Second Colorado cavalry, under command of Capt. Wagner, and a desperate fight ensued. The Colorado troops understood guerrilla warfare, and Wagner was as brave a man as ever mustered a company. The guerrillas made a furious charge, but the onslaught was met with such resistance that the opposing forces mingled together in a hand-to-hand contest. The fight was terrible, the rattle of revolvers being at times almost drowned by the clash of sabers. Jesse James fought like a hungry tiger, and his death-dealing pistol made terrible inroads among his foes. Singling out the Captain, who was fighting with wonderful desperation, Jesse rode by him at a furious pace, and, discharging his pistol with remarkable accuracy, he sent a bullet through the brave Captain's heart. This act sent consternation through the ranks of the Colorado troops, and a retreat, in confusion, was soon begun. Those that were wounded received no mercy at the hands of the guerrillas, but were shot or put to the sword and then left unburied.

Every attack made by the guerrillas added new terrors to the neighborhood ; there was a concentrating of militia at every available point and a thousand schemes proposed by which to surprise and bring to punishment the desperate band; but the guerrillas were kept thoroughly posted and continued their reckless mode of warfare with varying success.

In the early part of 1864 Frank James was sent out by Bill Anderson to locate and number the Federal force at Harrisonville. The duty was fraught with much peril, but it was danger the James Boys courted as the spice of existence. He rode straight for the town, until within sight of the picket lines. He then hitched his horse in the closest thicket he could find, after which he approached with great care, and at night succeeded in passing the pickets. Very soon after reaching the outskirts of Harrisonville he met a negro from whom he obtained what information he desired and then crept back again through the lines and mounted his horse. At this juncture he was spied by two of the picket guards, who commanded him to halt. The reply came from his pistol, and though the night was without moonshine he sent a bullet through the brain of one, and another shot tore through the body of the other picket. The camp was speedily in arms but Frank rode rapidly out of harm and delivered the information he had gained with such risk to Anderson.

On the second day thereafter the plan of attack on Harrisonville was consummated and a hard fought battle was the consequence, but the guerrillas were forced to retire, and they turned their attention to a company of Federal volunteers who were encamped on Grand river at Flat Rock Ford. These they attacked with determined fierceness, but they were met with equal force and were again compelled to retreat. In this fight Jesse James was badly wounded, a musket ball having passed through his breast, tearing away a large portion of his left lung and knocking him from his horse. Notwithstanding the rain of bullets, Arch Clements and John Jarrette rode back, and gathering up their wounded comrade they bore him to the house of Capt. John M. Rudd, where for several days his death was hourly expected. Careful nursing and the best surgical skill, however, saved his life, and in one month's time he was able to resume the saddle, and in six weeks he again went on active duty.

On the 16th of September, 1864, Jesse James concluded to pay another visit to his mother, but the road thence was beset with a thousand dangers which very few men could be induced to encounter. During the ride he came suddenly upon three uniformed militia, who ordered him to halt, but instead of obeying the summons he whipped out two pistols and in a moment the three men were struggling in the throes of death. Jesse met with no other adventure on the journey, and after spending two days with his mother returned to the camp of the guerrillas. Immediately upon his return he was informed of the plans conceived during his absence, of attacking Fayette, Missouri. On the 20th the attack was made, and charge after charge, with all the force the guerrillas could command, was hurled against the stockades which protected the Federals, but every onslaught was firmly met and left a trail of dead and wounded guerrillas. Lee McMurtry, one of the bravest of Anderson's forces, fell dreadfully wounded directly under the Federal parapets. Jesse James was an intimate comrade of McMurty and he determined to rescue his friend. What a nature is that which can rush up to the very blazing muzzles of deadly rifles to drag away a wounded friend! But Jesse James seemed to court death without the ability to win it. He braved that lurid stream of fatal fire and drew away the gasping form of his friend, and yet escaped unscathed. This battle also resulted adversely to the guerrillas, and they were driven with great loss from Fayette. Leaving this place they rode west again and went into camp near Wellington.

- DIREFUL MASSACRE AT CENTRALIA -

Quantrell continued to direct the movements of the guerrilla bands, but he was rarely engaged in any of the battles; the active service he delegated to the most strategical and unmerciful members of his command. Bill Anderson, a human tiger in disposition, was placed in charge of the full force when it was decided to move upon Centralia, a small town in Boone county, on the Wabash, St. Louis & Pacific Railway. On the 27th of September, one week after the attack on Fayette, the guerrillas, numbering one hundred and fifty men, headed by Anderson and that most ominous of banners, the black flag, with skull and cross-bones, marched upon Centralia, which they took possession of without resistance. After pillaging the place the guerrillas took up their station at the depot and awaited the coming of the train. They had not long to wait, for soon the shrill whistle of the engine, as it came thundering through a cut, drawing five passenger coaches loaded with soldiers and citizen travelers, announced the coming of the prize. The moment the train stopped the dreadful black flag was flung out and with the exchange of a few shots the messengers of death boarded the cars. Everyone on the train was ordered out and made to form in line, after which the thirty-two soldiers were separated from the other passengers and all disarmed. Now the breathless suspense, the terrible forebodings and the anxiety as to the fate that would be meted out to them! Every soldier was shot as unmercifully as if they had been obnoxious beasts or poisonous snakes. The passengers were relieved of whatever valuables they possessed, after which they were permitted to proceed on their journey.

In the afternoon of the same day and before the guerrillas had departed from Centralia, a body of Iowa volunteers, one hundred strong, under the command of Major J. H. Johnson, rode into the town and in the space of a few hours the two forces met and engaged in a terrible conflict. Again Jesse James, who was the best pistol shot in the guerrilla service, made a furious dash at Major Johnson and planted a pistol ball almost in the center of the brave Major's forehead. The guerrillas now rushed upon the terrorized volunteers with such resistless impetuosity that they broke in confusion. The fight became a massacre, and but very few of the brave volunteers escaped to convey to anxious friends the dreadful fate that had befallen their comrades. One of the militiamen had a very remarkable escape. Being badly wounded, in the early part of the fight, he remained unconscious, with the blood streaming from a saber gash in his head, until the foe had departed.

When the fight was over the guerrillas went among the wounded and shot them with their revolvers, determined that not a soldier should escape. This single exception to the consummation of guerrilla vengeance was supposed to be dead, and he therefore escaped the crowning feature of that day's massacre. When consciousness was regained he found himself alone, among the dead bodies of his comrades, and his shouts for help brought to his assistance the services of a kind old negro woman who took him to her house and obtained surgical aid, so that in two week's time he was able to return home.

The result of the fight at Centralia was not such as brought great encouragement to the guerrillas; the victory they gained was at the cost of nearly fifty of their number, whom it would be impossible to replace, because men of their bold, reckless and desperate character are rarely to be found. It was therefore determined to again divide up into squads and renew the warfare which they had waged so successfully in the previous year. But the guerrillas never fought again as they had at Fayette and Harrisonville; their courage to meet an armed force seemed to have vanished.

- FORTUNE TURNING AGAINST THE GUERRILLAS -

The numerous and desperate deeds of the guerillas received the earnest condemnation of the Confederate forces and for a time it was seriously considered, by many of the most distinguished Confederate officers, advisable to unite in the effort to rid Missouri of this terrible scourge. But their career was rapidly culminating. In attempting to cross the Missouri river in Howard county, a detachment of the guerrillas, headed by Bill Anderson, was attacked by a force of Federals under Montgomery, and in the fight which ensued Anderson and five of his men were killed, while the others escaped to the hills. They were again surprised while in camp on the Blackwater and several more were killed, and Jesse James was badly wounded in the leg, besides having his horse killed under him. In another fight which followed soon after, on Sugar creek, George Todd, one of the most daring and shrewd of Quantrell's old comrades, was shot to the death, and in the latter part of 1864, in order to save themselves from capture or annihilation, the guerrillas concluded to disband finally. Jesse James joined his fortunes with George Shepherd and went to Texas, while Frank James followed Quantrell to Kentucky.

- THE WHIRLWIND OF DESTRUCTION CHANGES -

In January, 1865, Quantrell collected together nearly fifty of his old followers, among whom was Frank James, and started for the hills of Kentucky, where he expected to continue his warfare. Their route lay southeast, and before they got out of Missouri they came very near falling into the hands of Curtis, who pursued them hard almost to the Arkansas line, where the trail was lost. The guerrillas crossed the Mississippi river at Gaine's Landing, nearly twenty miles above Memphis, and made their way through Tennessee, entering Kentucky from the south. At Hartford, in Ohio county, the command met a squad of thirty militia under command of Capt. Barnett, whom they readily deceived into the belief that they were Federal troops searching for guerrillas, and that Quantrell was a Federal captain. Indeed the deception was played so successfully that Barnett was induced to accompany them upon an expedition. Quantrell managed to communicate with each of his men, whom he instructed to ride beside the Federals, and when he should draw his handkerchief and throw it over his shoulder it was the signal -for the slaughter. At about five o'clock in the afternoon Frank James rode up beside Capt. Barnett, while Quantrell moved forward, and as his horse stepped into a shallow branch where all his men could see him, he drew the fatal handkerchief, and without looking back he waved it and then threw it over his shoulder. Their was a rattle of pistol shots and Capt. Barnett and his men fell dead under their horses.

Near Hopkinsville the guerrillas met twelve Federal cavalrymen who sought the shelter of a barn and gave battle. The fight lasted for more than an hour, and until the barn was fired, when the twelve brave fellows were forced from their defense and were shot as they rushed from the flames. Their horses then became the property of the guerrillas. Frank James stopped one day with an uncle, who lives about fifty miles from Hopkinsville, and thus permitted the command to get so far ahead of him that he did not engage in any more skirmishes in Kentucky; for, two days afterward, Quantrell was driven into a small village called Smiley, where, finding escape impossible, he made his last stand. It was forty against nearly three hundred, and Quantrell knew that it was a fight to the death. Bleeding almost at every pore, the black-bannered bandit fought like the gladiators, until, blinded by his own blood, and with a score of gaping wounds, he fell mortally wounded, with an empty pistol in one hand and a bloody sword in the other. It was thus that the entire force of Quantrell's guerrillas died, excepting Frank James, whose life was spared for darker deeds.

- JESSE JAMES' CAREER IN TEXAS -

As previously stated, Jesse James left Missouri in company with George Shepherd and forty or fifty guerrillas, for Texas, where they spent the winter of 1864-5 without special activity, and in the spring it was decided to return to Missouri, although such a decision was pregnant with a renewal of all the dangers from which they had just escaped. Upon reaching Benton county Jesse James, Arch Clements and another comrade proceeded to the farm-house of James Harkness, who was known as an uncompromising Union man. They decoyed him a short distance from his house by requesting him to direct them to a spring which they knew was in the neighborhood. When out of sight of the house Jesse James and his comrade caught Harkness by the arms and held him firmly, while Arch Clements drew a large bowie-knife with which he cut the throat of the defenseless farmer, almost severing his head. Fresh blood being upon their hands, they rode into Johnson county to the house of Alien Duncan, another Union man, and finding him chopping wood in his yard, Jesse James first accosted him and then sent a bullet into his brain.

The guerrilla band, now numbering scarce a score, before getting out of Johnson county were surprised by a company of Federal volunteers and almost annihilated. Jesse James had his horse shot under him and a musket ball went crashing through his lungs. Supposing him dead, the Federals gave pursuit to the fleeing guerrillas and chased the remaining few for nearly fifty miles. The wounded guerrilla lay for two days where he fell, in terrible agony, and would have died except for the kindly ministrations of a farmer who chanced to find him. The care he received, after weeks of suffering, enabled him to again resume the saddle, and he went to Nebraska, where his mother was temporarily living and where he remained until the return of Frank James from Kentucky late in the following summer.

Before Frank left Brandensburg, however, he met with an adventure which nearly cost his life. The vicinity of Brandensburg was infested with horse thieves, and suspicion was directed against Frank as one of the guilty band. It was determined to arrest him, and for this purpose a posse of six men went to the house where he was stopping, and after charging him with horse-stealing, demanded his arms. The response was most unexpected, for, with an oath, he drew his pistol and shot three of the party, and in re- turn was badly wounded in the thigh. The other three fled, but a large crowd soon collected, to intimidate which Frank backed up against the house and threatened to shoot any one who made the least motion to harm him. A horse was standing hitched conveniently near, and, compelling the crowd to fall back, he drew his suffering body up into the saddle and made his escape. The wound proved a very serious one and kept him confined to his bed at the house of a friend, where he found refuge, nearly seventy-five miles from Brandenburg, for several months.

- ROBBERY AND MURDER -

It is a trite old saying that "one crime begets another," and in the life of Jesse and Frank James it is well illustrated. When the war closed and the occupation of the guerrilla, under color of authority, was gone, the James Boys were loath to change the exciting and dangerous vocation to which they had become inured by nearly four years of almost ceaseless activity. Other guerrillas, who had been their comrades in so many desperate struggles, which had made their very names a terror, had surrendered themselves when the bond of national union had been repaired, and returned to peaceful pursuits; but Jesse and Frank James affected to despise the ordinary walks of life and refused to tread other than paths which bristled with danger and anxiety. Both were sorely wounded, and a period of recuperation was necessary; and this respite from the turmoil's of bandit life was employed in the conception of bold schemes by which to enlarge the notoriety of their names and to accumulate wealth.

When they had somewhat recovered from their wounds, Mrs. Samuels returned to her old home, in Clay county, while the boys paid her occasional visits as opportunity offered, but generally keeping themselves well hidden in the fastnesses of Jackson county. In the latter part of 1866, Jesse James was attacked with a severe type of malarial fever, which the exposure he had to endure so intensified that he determined to secretly visit his mother and place himself under her immediate care. The record which he had made during the war rendered him amenable to the vengeance of a large number of the residents of Clay and adjoining counties, who had suffered by his desperate acts. Consequently, Jesse knew that eternal vigilance was necessary, but hoped to so conceal his presence at the Samuels' homestead that no one would suspect his location or condition. But in this he was deceived, for only a few days had elapsed after his arrival at home when, by some means unknown to the writer, it was discovered that Jesse had taken up at least a temporary residence with his mother.

It was a bitter cold night in the month of February, 1867, that a band of six persons, each of whom had a special grievance to revenge, knocked at the door of Dr. Samuels' residence and demanded immediate admittance. Jesse was in a bed up stairs, but he was the first to hear and understand the peremptory challenge, as it were, of the men outside. Hastily drawing on his pantaloons and boots, he grabbed his two heavy pistols and looked out of the window where, by the light refracted by the snow, he saw six horses and only a single man. He knew then that the house was surrounded and all chance of escape lay in a bloody fight. He silently descended to the first floor, where Dr. Samuels was rattling the door and explaining to those awaiting admittance that the lock was out of repair so that the key would not work readily. This was a ruse, however, to secure time for Jesse who. Dr. Samuels hoped, would be able to escape through a back window. Locating the voice of one of the men who was threatening to break in the door, Jesse fired through the panel and a stifled groan told him that his aim had been perfect. On hearing the shot, the other five rushed to the front of the house. Jesse threw the door partly open and the light from the snow made the men outside easy targets for his unerring aim, while he was so hidden by the door and darkness within that the attacking party could not fire with the least accuracy. In half the time it has taken the reader to even scan this report three of the six men were lying dead in the snow and two others were desperately wounded, while the other fled in mortal terror.

Suffering, as he was, from a very high fever, Jesse lost no time in mounting his horse, and with a hurried good-bye, he again rode into the wilderness, leaving his mother and her family with the dead and wounded. It was a ghastly scene, there upon the white-shrouded ground, one man dead on the doorstep, two others stiff and frozen in their own blood which crimsoned the yard, while the groans from the wounded made the place more hideous. Dr. Samuels notified his nearest neighbor as soon as possible and with the assistance he secured, the two wounded men were taken into the house and cared for, while a lonely vigil over the dead was kept until morning. A large crowd collected at the homestead on the following day and removed the bodies, while more than fifty well mounted citizens went in pursuit of the youthful desperado, but after a week's fruitless search they returned to their homes and quiet again brooded over the distressed neighborhood.

- PLUNDERING A KENTUCKY BANK -

The bloody record of the James Boys had been almost forgotten, for they had not been seen in Clay County for many months and no specially reckless deeds had been committed to bring back a remembrance of them; when, suddenly, the town of Russellville, Kentucky, was thrown into a greater excitement than it had ever before experienced. The James Boys had paid the place a visit and left a souvenir of their desperate valor. On the 20th of March, 1868, Jesse James, accompanied by four comrades, George Shepherd, Oll. Shepherd, Cole Younger and Jim White, dashed into the town like a hurricane, yelling and firing their pistols until every one was frightened from the streets. They then rode to the bank where four of them dismounted and entered, with drawn revolvers, so intimidating the cashier that he opened the safe to Jesse James, while Cole Younger gathered the money that was lying upon the counter. The amount appropriated by the bandits was ;^ 14,000, which they threw into a sack and then leisurely departed. Everything connected with the robbery showed thorough system and a management which could be attributed to none other than the fierce Missouri freebooters.

When the excitement and surprise had somewhat subsided the sheriff summoned twenty deputies and started in pursuit. The chase continued through Kentucky and western Tennessee. Telegrams were sent in every direction with the hope of intercepting the robbers, who, finding themselves close pressed, scattered, as was their custom, and all, save George Shepherd, eluded pursuit and gained the marshes and dense coverts of Arkansas, where it was impossible to trail them. Shepherd was captured two weeks after the robbery in a small drug store in Tennessee and taken back to Logan county, where he was convicted and sentenced to the penitentiary for a term of three years.

Oliver Shepherd, a brother of George, who was also connected with the bank robbery, was afterward found in Jackson county, Missouri, and a requisition being first obtained, a dozen men attempted his arrest. But OH., as he was called, was made of that sterner composition which would not brook a curtailment of his liberty, and he threw defiance at the officers of the law. Then began a battle of extermination. The officers had armed themselves with carbines because they knew that to come in range of the old guerrilla's pistols would be death to many of them. The hero of a hundred desperate conflicts felt that his time had come, so, bracing himself against a large tree, he stood and received the fire of his slayers at a range of nearly two hundred and fifty yards. His pistols were useless, although he fired every shot, fourteen rounds, at the officers, who, from behind trees, shot seven terrible slugs into his body before he fell; even then, like Spartacus, he struck out towards his foes in the last throes of death.

- BANK ROBBERY AND MURDER -

After the affair at Russellville the James Boys appeared twice in their old haunts in Missouri, but spent nearly a year in Texas and Mexico, in remote districts, where they were free from the interference of officers anxious for their capture. It was not until the latter part of 1869 that they resumed criminal operations, their plans being laid to rob the bank at Gallatin, Missouri. In this scheme they were assisted by the three Younger brothers, whose career for consummate daring and recklessness is fully equal to that of the James Boys.

It was on the 7th of December that a body of seven thoroughly armed men, superbly mounted, galloped into Gallatin and commenced firing their pistols indiscriminately, shouting most terrible oaths and fearful threats. After alarming the residents of the place and preventing resistance, Jesse James and Cole Younger dashed into the bank, and at the muzzles of drawn revolvers, they compelled the cashier, Capt. John W. Sheets, to deliver the keys of the money department of the safe, the main door being open. After rifling the bank of $700, Jesse and Cole whispered a few words together, put the money in a bag, and then one of them, but which of the two it is not known, deliberately shot Capt. Sheets dead. The reason given for the commission of this crime was that Capt. Sheets had, during the war, led a party of militia against the guerrillas, in which conflict Bill Anderson was killed, and that the killing of Sheets was in revenge for Anderson's tragic death.

Capt. Sheets was a very popular man in Gallatin and the surrounding neighborhood, and when the news of the terrible tragedy and robbery spread, nearly the entire county arose in arms and demanded the blood of the assassins. Several bands were organized and started in pursuit, each taking a different route, with the hope that one of them might be able to apprehend the bandits before they could get out of the county. One of these bands, numbering twelve citizens, overtook the robbers on the edge of Clay county and a running fight ensued, in which one of the citizens was wounded slightly and the horse of another killed. These casualties ended the pursuit and the bandits reached Jackson county in safety, where they disappeared.

- THE MYSTERIOUS HIDING PLACE IN JACKSON COUNTY -

In perusing books and newspaper articles recording the adventures of the James and Younger boys, the reader must have been impressed with the somewhat singular assertion that pursuit of the bandits generally ended by their sudden disappearance in Jackson County, Missouri. I will confess that I have often wondered how it was possible for a body of men to mysteriously disappear in a certain locality and thereby end a close pursuit. A gentleman who has been intimate with the James Boys for a period of nearly twenty years and with whom I am intimately acquainted, volunteered to me the long- wished-for information, which he gave as follows, omitting only the exact location. I will use his own words as nearly as possible :

"You know,'" said he, "that Jackson county is one of the most rugged and broken districts in Missouri ; it not only abounds with bluffs, but also, in at least a few places, with almost impenetrable thickets, fit only for the abode of catamounts and foxes. One day I was riding through Jackson county, I will not tell you where, when suddenly I was confronted by Frank James. He greeted me cordially and then said; ' , I have every confidence in you and I know you would not betray us to save your right arm; therefore I invite you to our retreat; come with me! I followed him in a bridle path for nearly a mile, when we came to a precipitous bluff, the base of which was completely hidden by a thick growth. There was an entrance between the growth and bluff, where any one would least suspect it, because, at the mouth are two bold rocks, which are apparently attached to the bluff itself; this delusion is accomplished by keeping the interstices filled with fresh brush so laid as to appear like a natural coppice. This passageway leads about fifty feet, to a large fissure in the side of the bluff, resembling a vestibule; from this we stepped into a large cave, quite roomy enough to contain comfortably more than a score of men and horses. I was astonished at the completeness of the arrangement of things in the cave. There was a cooking stove, the pipe of which extended up and was lost in the top of the cave. Frank

James told me that the smoke from the stove passed into a fissure of rock which evidently opened into another cave, as no smoke could ever be seen issuing from the bluff He then took me over to another part of the cavern, where there was a clear spring of beautiful water, and over this was another fissure from which there was a cool draft of air which thoroughly ventilated the entire cave. I could see that many of the conveniences of the place were due to no little labor. A part of the cave was ceiled nicely with grooved pine lumber so as to prevent dampness, and in this division was a large heating stove, and about a dozen beds, all supplied with neat bedding. In the rear of the cave, which was, perhaps, one hundred feet deep by sixty broad, were twenty-one stalls for the horses, and over the stalls was a large feed bin filled with oats and corn, but no hay, as the latter was too bulky to convey readily into the cave. But what surprised me most was the means of defense. There was an arsenal of fire-arms and a magazine for ammunition, while the approach to the cave was commanded by a fierce, breech-loading ten-pound cannon, which was kept constantly loaded with buckshot, and looked out towards the entrance in such a way that one man could defend the place against a hundred, for a discharge of that cannon would sweep everything out of the passage. The place is absolutely impregnable, even if it could be found, which it would be exceedingly difficult to do.

"I would not have told you this except for the fact that the cave is now abandoned and may never be occupied again, but yet there is a certain obligation, from which I do not feel myself wholly relieved, that causes me to keep the location of the cave a secret. Frank James is in the East, and Jesse James — well, I don't know what has become of him, but I hope he is living in safety and happiness, as I believe he is, because, with all their crimes, the James Boys have been good friends to me."

- A TERRIBLE FIGHT IN MEXICO -

After robbing the Gallatin bank, the James Boys left Missouri and went to Texas, where they remained a short time and then crossed the border into Mexico. It has been suspected that they drove a herd of cattle across the border with them, but of this there is no ready proof, and the crimes of some greasers may have been attributed to the bandits. In the month of May, 1860, Frank and Jesse James rode into Matamoras and, as there was a fandango advertised to take place at a public house on the night of their arrival, they decided to attend. Accordingly, when the night shadows fell, they paid the price of admission and entered the hall, which was rapidly filling up with swarthy senoritas and hidalgoes. From the belts of the latter protruded the glittering handles of bright, keen stilettos, in preparation for the affray which is always anticipated.

The dance began about eight o'clock, with much spirit, and the whirl of the graceful girls soon excited a desire on the part of Frank and Jesse to participate, although they were not familiar with the movements and figures of the Spanish dances. Nevertheless they essayed an attempt, which only served to excite the ridicule of the Mexicans who, by gesture and speech, went so far in their sport and mimicry of the outlaws that at length Frank James knocked down one of the boldest. This act came near proving disastrous to both the boys, for the moment the Mexican fell to the floor another powerfully built hidalgo struck Frank a blow on the cheek which sent him spinning into the laps of two girls who were seated on a bench awaiting partners. For a moment he was so stunned as to scarcely know what to do, but Jesse saw where his aid was most needed and the next instant the powerful Mexican fell with a bullet in his brain. A general fight then ensued in which Jesse and Frank rushed for the door, but their passage was impeded; so nothing remained for the boys except to clear a way by shooting those who stood before them. Frank received a thrust in the shoulder from a stiletto and Jesse's right fore-arm was punctured with a similar instrument, but the boys fired rapidly and with such effect that four Mexicans lay dead and six others were dreadfully wounded, some mortally. Jesse was the first to break through the doorway, and as he did so he turned at the very instant a dagger, in the hands of a strong Mexican, was directed at Frank's heart, but ere the hand fell to its purpose a bullet from Jesse's pistol entered the Mexican's eye and he dropped dead at Frank's feet, striking the dagger deep into the floor as he fell. This fortunate shot enabled Frank to escape from the building and as the Mexicans had no arms except stilettos, they were powerless to continue the fight, but many of them rushed to their homes to procure fire-arms and horses, and the place was swarming so rapidly with blood-craving hidalgoes and greasers that the only avenue of escape lay in the river. They accordingly rushed toward their horses which were hitched in the woods nearby, but just before reaching them three powerful Mexicans suddenly sprang upon Frank James, who was a little in the rear, and attempted to bind him with a stout cord which they threw over his shoulders. Fortunately, in running he had picked up a large bludgeon which lay in his path, and shaking himself loose from the grasp of his assailants he laid about him so briskly with this formidable weapon that in a moment the three Mexicans lay stunned on the ground at his feet, then hastily joining Jesse, who had already mounted and was holding his horse for him, he sprang into the saddle, and putting spurs to their restless steeds they plunged boldly into the Rio Grande and swam to the other side, while the Mexicans were riding about in every direction trying to find the bandits whom they did not imagine would dare to take to the river. The boys made good their escape, but the wounds they had received in the fight were of a most painful nature and required careful attention. Frank's was the most severe, and had not Jesse bandaged it with the greatest skill the outlaw must have bled to death before obtaining medical aid, for one of the veins in his neck had been severed. The two reached Concepcion, a small town in Texas, about one hundred miles from Matamoras, where they remained in charge of a surgeon for nearly three months before their wounds had healed sufficiently to permit them to travel.

- PLUNDERING AN IOWA BANK -

In the spring of 1871 Jesse and Frank James secretly returned to their haunts in Jackson County, Missouri, where they remained for some time arranging for an expedition into Iowa. Their plans being perfected, they, with five other bandits, started north, riding by night, until they reached Corydon, the bank in which place they had previously decided to rob. At ten o'clock in the morning the seven desperadoes made a furious charge into the center of the town and commenced a fusillade of firing, threatening to kill every person found on the streets within five minutes afterward. None of the citizens thought of offering any resistance, and dashing up to the bank, three of the robbers dismounted and rushed in with cocked pistols, and demanded of the cashier every cent the bank contained. Finding himself powerless, and realizing that death would be his certain portion if he refused to comply with the immediate demands of the desperate outlaws, the cashier opened the safe and permitted them to appropriate nearly; $40,000. The money was placed in a sack, which they invariably carried with them for the purpose, and then the seven desperadoes rode rapidly out of the city, firing their pistols indiscriminately as they swept through the streets.

The citizens were, of course, intensely excited, and after the disappearance of the robbers a hundred persons volunteered their services to the sheriff to assist in the apprehension of the bold plunderers. Efforts at capture were made by a large body of men, but like all similar attempts, the result was nothing. They were followed into Missouri and telegrams sent to every town in the State, but, like imps of darkness, the seven dare-devils disappeared and were not again seen for several months; but it is now known that they were lying quietly in their impregnable haunt in the eastern part of Jackson county, waiting for a return of quiet.

- ANOTHER BANK ROBBERY IN KENTUCKY -

In the latter part of 1870, Jesse and Frank James visited Kentucky, where they had a large number of friends and relatives, who admired their bravery and condoned their crimes. They remained here until in the early part of the spring of 1874, when they and the Younger boys conceived a plan for robbing the bank at Columbia, Kentucky. On the 29th of April of that year, the three Youngers and the two James Boys entered Columbia about the same hour from five different roads, so that there was not the least apprehension excited. Just before three o'clock in the afternoon the five desperadoes rode up to the bank together, while Frank James and Cole Younger leisurely dismounted and entered the bank, where they found the cashier, Mr. Martin, the president, Mr. Dalrymple, and another gentleman engaged in a conversation. Without losing any time or creating any suspicion from the citizens of the place, the two bandits drew their pistols and going behind the bank counter, leveled them at the heads of the cashier and president, and demanded the keys to the safe. Seeing, at a glance, however, that the safe was secured by a combination lock, they commanded the cashier to open it under penalty of immediate death if he refused. Martin was a brave man, and instead of being intimidated, tried to raise an alarm ; but at the first outcry Frank James thrust a heavy navy revolver into his face and fired, killing him instantly ; at the same moment Cole Younger fired at the president but, luckily, that gentleman struck up the pistol, and running into the back office, escaped with his life. The two robbers hastily gathered the money that was in sight, (about; $200,) and gaining their horses the five rode out of the town at a rapid pace.

Fifteen men, headed by the sheriff, went in pursuit of the desperadoes, and chased them hard into the eastern part of Tennessee, where the trail was lost in the Cumberland range. Again the bandits doubled on their tracks, after the pursuit was abandoned, and went into the western part of Texas, where they mingled with the lawless elements of the border.

Every attempt at their capture had proven fruitless, and for the time being, the provincial banks were kept well armed in anticipation of a raid. The James Boys were too crafty to appear again in the counties where their terrible deeds had excited the people to desperation. They waited until the memory of their crimes had been partially forgotten, and then planned new schemes of pillage.

- ROBBING OF THE CASH-BOX AT THE KANSAS CITY FAIR -

On the 26th of September, 1872, the people of Kansas City had an opportunity for considering the cunning and bravery of the James Boys, from immediate circumstances which suddenly involved the city in a furore of excitement. It was on Thursday, the " big day " of the Kansas City Exposition, when nearly thirty thousand visitors were assembled to see the races, and particularly to witness Ethan Allen trot in harness against a running mate. The crowd was immense and of course the gate receipts were correspondingly large. About four o'clock in the afternoon Mr. Hall, the secretary and treasurer of the association, counted up the receipts of the day, which were nearly ten thousand dollars, and placing the money in a tin box kept for the purpose, he told one of his assistants to take it to the First National Bank where, although it was after banking hours, arrangements had been made to make the deposit. No thought was entertained that any attempt would be made to steal the cash-box while so many people were constantly on the highway leading to the city, and the young man started off whistling gaily, carrying the treasure box by a wire handle in his right hand. As he reached the entrance gate, where more than a dozen persons were coming in and going out, three men on horseback (Jesse and Frank James and Bob Younger) dashed up to the young man with such reckless haste that a little girl was badly trampled by one of the horses ; at the same moment a pistol shot was fired and Jesse James jumped from his horse into the confused crowd and snatching the cash-box from the hand of the affrighted messenger, he leaped into the saddle again and the three highwaymen disappeared, with a clatter of fast-flying feet, like the sweep of a whirlwind. For several minutes it was thought that the little girl had been struck by a pistol ball, but after she was carried home it was ascertained that her injuries, which were not fatal, were caused by the horse of one of the robbers knocking her down and trampling upon her hips.

The news of the robbery spread over the city in a few minutes, and Marshal Shepherd sent out some of his detectives, while several gentlemen mounted fleet horses and used every possible endeavor to capture the robbers. The trail led over the hills east of Kansas City and about ten miles into Jackson county, where every trace was suddenly blotted out. The outlaws had reached their favorite haunt where no pursuer had ever been able to find them. The writer was a reporter on the Kansas City Journal at the time of the robbery and reported the details as here related.

- PLUNDERING THE STE. GENEVIEVE BANK -

The success of the bandits thus far greatly encouraged them in their lawless operations, and they were constantly planning new and still more reckless adventures. They remained in their secure hiding place during the winter of 1872-3, retiring upon their laurels and living royally upon their immense gains. During this period of jolly hibernation, schemes were proposed for wrecking railroad trains, and before the appearance of spring, Frank James and Jim Younger were sent into Nebraska for the purpose of gathering information concerning the express shipment of treasure from the west. Not hearing from the robber agents as soon as was expected, Jesse James, Bill Chadwell, Clell Miller, and Bob and Cole Younger decided to pay their respects to another bank before venturing upon their proposed railroad enterprise, and the Savings Association, at Ste. Genevieve, Missouri, was selected for the strike. Accordingly, early in the morning of May 27th, 1873, the five desperate free-booters appeared in the streets of that old-time Catholic town, and the moment that Mr. O. D. Harris, the cashier, accompanied by F. A. Rozier, a son of Hon. Firman A. Rozier, the president, entered the bank to begin the business of the day, the three daring bandits followed them into the building and presenting six pistols, demanded the immediate opening of the bank vault. Young Rozier, regardless of the danger, made a speedy exit, and as he ran down the street crying for help, a bullet from one of the outlaws' weapons went whistling through the tail of his coat, but he escaped. Mr. Harris, however, was covered by too many pistols to permit of his escape, and stern necessity forced him into a compliance with the wishes of the robbers.

He opened the vault, from which the sum of four thousand one hundred dollars was taken, a large part of which was specie, and shoving it speedily into the sack provided, the bandits mounted their horses and decamped. As they were riding out of the city, the bag containing the treasure was accidentally dropped, to recover which it was necessary to return, and one of the robbers had to dismount. In doing so his horse became frightened and broke away. At this juncture a German came riding by and the robbers compelled him to ride after and catch the fleeing animal, which was returned to the riderless bandit, only after such delay as permitted a hastily organized posse of the citizens to approach within pistol shot of the three highwaymen. An exchange of fire caused the posse to check their pace and the distance thus gained by the pursued, was never made up. The pursuit was continued for several days, but without result. The outlaws stopped at Hermann, Mo., two days after the robbery, but as usual, there was no posse there to apprehend them. Several well known detectives from St. Louis were sent out, and the sheriff of every county in Missouri notified and requested to keep a sharp lookout for the desperadoes; but though many suspicious characters were arrested the real culprits were never captured. The amount secured at Ste. Genevieve was a great disappointment to the robbers, for it was known that the bank usually carried from seventy five thousand to one hundred thousand dollars, but at this particular time, very fortunately, the association was winding up business, and had deposited the greater portion of its funds in the Merchants' Bank of St. Louis.

- WRECKING AND PLUNDERING A TRAIN -

In June following both the James Boys were seen in Kansas City by intimate acquaintances, and the night of June 27th was spent by both the bandits with their mother at the Samuels* residence. On the 15th of July, Bob, Jim and Cole Younger, Jesse and Frank James, Bud Singleton and two other bandits, whose names have never been learned by the authorities, left Clay county, Missouri, and rode northward to a spot which had been selected by Frank James and Jim Younger, on the line of the Chicago, Rock Island & Pacific Railroad, about five miles east of Council Bluffs. The reason for selecting this place and time was because of information received of an intended shipment of a large amount of gold from San Francisco to New York, which would be made over this route, reaching Omaha about the 19th of July. How this information was imparted was never ascertained, but its truth has led to the belief that the James Boys had confederates on the 'Pacific slope with whom they were in constant communication; On the evening of July 21st a formidable band of eight of the most desperate men that ever committed a crime, took position in a dense thicket beside a deep cut in the railroad. They hitched their horses out of view of passengers on the train and then, after a few minutes' work, displaced one of the rails. This accomplished, they waited the coming of the express train which was due at that point at 8:30p.m. From a knoll near the rendezvous Jesse James descried the blazing headlight of the coming train, and then made everything ready for their villainous work. A sharp curve in the track prevented the engineer from discovering anything wrong, until it was impossible to prevent the disaster which the banditti had prepared for. The screaming engine came thundering like an infuriated mammoth, which a reversal of the lever only began to check when it struck the loosened rail and plunged sideways into the bank, while the cars telescoped and piled up in terrible confusion. The engineer was instantly killed, and a dozen passengers were seriously injured, but the desperadoes did not stop to consider this terrible disaster. The moment the havoc was complete the bandits fell upon the excited passengers, whom they robbed without exception, both men and women, taking every species of jewelry and the last cent that could be discovered from the wounded as well as those who remained unhurt. The express car was entered and the messenger, groaning with pain from a broken arm, was compelled to open the safe, which was rifled of six thousand dollars and then the messenger was forced to give the robbers his watch and ten dollars which he had with him. Fortunately the desperadoes were twelve hours too soon for the train upon which the expected treasure was carried, as the express that went east on the morning of the 21st, carried gold bricks, specie and currency amounting to over one hundred thousand dollars.

The total amount secured by the train-wrecking band was about $2,500 each, which they carried off, as was their custom, in a sack, departing southward at a rapid gait.

The officers of Council Bluffs were soon notified of the robbery. The wounded and dead were taken to the city and cared for, and then another pursuit of the robbers was begun, which was united in by sheriffs and posses of other counties until the pursuing parties numbered nearly two hundred men. The desperadoes were traced over hill and prairie, through Clay county and into Jackson, where the trail was lost as effectually as if the robbers had mounted into space and fled behind the clouds. Reward after reward was offered until they aggregated more than $50,000; the most expert detectives from St. Louis and Chicago concentrated upon an effort to win the prize and rid the country of the most consummate highwaymen since the days of Rolla, the bearded Knight of the forests. But every clue proved deceiving, and the most cunning of detectives finally abandoned the chase, thoroughly confounded by the marvelous cunning of the bandits.

- THE STAGE ROBBERY NEAR HOT SPRINGS -

In December of 1873, a council was held in the haunt of the bandits, near the Big Blue, in Jackson County, in which it was decided to attempt a stage robbery, and the line between Malvern and Hot Springs, Arkansas, was selected for the first stroke in the inauguration of a new species of crime. Accordingly, on the 15th of January, 1874, five of the highwaymen, consisting of Frank James, Clell Miller, Arthur McCoy and Jim and Cole Younger repaired to the scene of their intended operations and secreted themselves in a dense covert on the south side of the stage road, five miles from Hot Springs, and awaited the coming of their victims.

The conception of this scheme manifested the judgment of the bandits, for they were influenced by the supposition that those who visited Hot Springs in search of health, were people of liberal means who would naturally carry with them a goodly sum of money with which to meet expected large expenses, and in this their judgment was correct.

It was after mid-day when the heavy Concord stage, filled with passengers, came rattling over the rough and stony road opposite the secret hiding place of the highway freebooters. Suddenly a shot startled the driver, and his surprise culminated when Jesse James arose from a clump of brush, and with a heavy revolver in each hand, commanded the driver to halt. The order was instantly obeyed, and as the passengers thrust their heads out of the vehicle they saw five fierce looking men, armed and spurred, whose purposes were at once divined. Frank James, who acted as leader, ordered the occupants of the stage to get out, which being complied with the passengers were formed into line and then submitted to a search by Clell Miller and Jim Younger, while the three other bandits stood guard with cocked pistols. The fright of the travelers was greatly intensified by the blood-chilling threats of the desperadoes. They jested with one another and made banters to test their skill as pistol shots oh the trembling and unarmed passengers. " Now," said Frank James to Cole Younger, " I will bet you the contents of that fellow's pocket-book," pointing to one of the travelers who was a small tradesman at Little Rock, " that I can shoot off a smaller bit out of his right ear than you can." "I'll take the wager," responded Cole, "but you must let me have the first shot, because my eyesight is not as good as yours, and if you should hit his ear first the blood might confuse my aim." Frank insisted on shooting first, and in the wrangle, the poor victim trembled until he could scarcely retain his feet, and with the most prayerful entreaties begged the robbers to take what he had but spare his life.

Mr. Taylor, of Massachusetts, a sufferer from rheumatism, then drew the attention of the bandits, and Jesse James offered to bet his share of the booty that he could throw his bowie-knife through Taylor's underclothing without drawing blood. It was thus the bandits jested with one another and in turn had each of the fear-stricken passengers praying for his life.

When the search was concluded, Frank James produced a memorandum book and took the names of all the travelers, saying: " I am like lightning, I don't want to strike the same parties twice."

The total amount of money and valuables taken approximated; $4,000, the heaviest loser being Ex- Gov. Burbank, of Dakota, from whom the robbers secured; $1,500. When the bandits left their victims, they graciously and with great punctilio, raised their hats and bade them a most courteous adieu, wishing them a pleasant visit at the Springs.

When the travelers reached Hot Springs they were in a sorry plight, not one of them having enough money to send a message home for additional funds, but the citizens kindly provided for their wants and exhibited much sympathy, but little or no attempt was made to capture the highwaymen. Indeed any such effort would have undoubtedly terminated fruitlessly, for, in addition to the cunning and bravery of the bandits, the inouiuainous nature of the country would have prevented a pursuing party from making up the time lost in reporting the circumstances of the robbery.

- THE TRAIN ROBBERY AT GAD'S HILL -

After leaving the scene of their Hot Springs adventure the five daring highwaymen, finding that they were not pursued, rode up into the northern part of Arkansas, where they had several friends, and there planned a scheme for plundering a train on the Iron Mountain Railroad. The place chosen for the purpose was Gad's Hill, a very small station in Wayne county, Missouri, which, in the summer time, is almost hidden by the copse of pine trees which surrounds it. The adjacent country was a very jungle in which it was easy to hide and elude the most determined pursuit.

On the last day of January, 1874, but little more than two weeks after their last successful robbery, the five bandits, with Frank James still acting as leader, rode into the station and made prisoners of every man in the place, consisting of the railroad agent, a saloon-keeper, blacksmith, two wood-choppers, and the son of Dr. John M. Rock. These were confined in the station house under threats of instant death if any attempt at escape were made. Having prevented every means of alarm, the desperadoes turned the switch in order to ditch the train if it attempted to run past, (as Gad's Hill was only a flag station,) and then planted a red flag in the track immediately in front of the station house.

The train was not due until 5:40 in the evening, at which time the shadows of twilight curtained the little place and prepared the approach of darkness. Promptly upon time the train came bowling along, and the engineer, seeing the danger-signal ahead, brought the engine to a standstill alongside the station house. No one was seen when the train stopped, but in a moment thereafter Cole Younger mounted the cab and, with drawn pistol, compelled the engineer and fireman to leave the engine and walk out into the woods. Mr. Alford, the conductor, was arrested by Jesse James as he stepped from the train to ascertain the cause of the display of the red flag. He was forced to give up his watch and $75.00 in money, after which he was placed in the station house. Then began a sack of the passengers. Clell Miller, Jim Younger and Frank James searched the affrighted people in the cars, while Jesse James and Cole Younger, taking opposite sides of the train, maintained a watch and kept shooting in various directions, while they uttered terrible oaths and threats, to keep the passengers in a state of constant trepidation.

After stripping all the passengers of every bit of valuables, the outlaws proceeded to the express car, where they broke open the safe and secured the contents. The mail car was next plundered and the letters cut open, one of which contained $2,000, and several smaller sums were obtained. The total amount of booty secured by the bandits was about $11,500. Having again successfully accomplished their criminal purpose without meeting any resistance, the five desperadoes released those confined in the station house; the engineer and fireman were recalled from their position in the woods, and the train was ordered to proceed. Then mounting their horses, which were hitched near by, the outlaws rode into the brush and disappeared in the darkness. When the train reached Piedmont information of the robbery was telegraphed to Little Rock, St. Louis, and all the towns along the road. On the following day, a large body of well-armed men started from Ironton and Piedmont in pursuit of the desperate outlaws, and soon got on their track. The pursuing party found where the bandits had breakfasted, sixty miles from Gad's Hill; following the trail closely on the second day the citizen's posse reached the spot where the outlaws had spent the night, and they were encouraged by the belief that a capture might be effected before the close of the day, but suddenly the party came to a low marsh through which it was dangerous to ride, and in searching for a pathway around the boggy district much time was lost and the trail of the robbers could not be found again; so the pursuit was abandoned.

- WICHER'S UNFORTUNATE HUNT FOR THE JAMES BOYS -

In the spring of 1874 John W. Wicher of Chicago, a brave, cool, cunning man, scarcely thirty years of age, connected with the Pinkerton force, appeared before his chief and asked to be sent out to discover the hiding place of the terrible brigands. He was fully informed of the dangers of such a mission, but his self-reliance and pride made him anxious to make the attempt which had already cost the lives of so many courageous officials. The chief gave his consent, and Wicher set out at once for the Samuels residence. In the early part of March the detective arrived in Liberty, where he soon laid his schemes before the sheriff of Clay county, and asked for assistance when the time and circumstances were ripe for a strike. The sheriff promised all needful aid and gave Wicher all the information in his possession concerning the habits and rendezvous of the James and Younger boys.

Changing his garb for the habit of a tramp, Wicher left Liberty on the 15th of March and arrived at Kearney on the same day, late in the afternoon. He took the road leading directly to the Samuels residence and had proceeded perhaps two miles on the lonely highway, when suddenly Jesse James walked out from behind a pile of dead brush and, with pistol presented, confronted the detective. Wicher's surprise was complete, but he manifested not the least excitement, his cool self-possession never deserting him for a moment.

" Where are you going ? " was the first remark made by Jesse James.

" I am looking for work," was Wicher's reply.

" What kind of work do you want, and where do you expect to find it ? " asked Jesse, his pistol still pointing full in poor Wicher's face.

"I have been used to farm labor, and hope to find something to do on some farm in the vicinity, " responded the detective.

Jesse James smiled contemptuously and then gave a sharp whistle, which brought to his side Clell Miller and Frank James, whose near presence Wicher had not thought of. The conversation then continued. Said Jesse:

"You don't look much like a laborer, nor is there any appearance of a tramp about you except in your clothes. Now I want you to acknowledge frankly just what your purpose is in this part of the country."

The detective began to realize how critical was his position, and that unless the most fortuitous circumstance should arise in his favor his chances of escape were exceedingly small. But with the same coolness he made reply :

"Well, gentlemen, I am nothing more than a poor man, without as much as a dollar in my pocket, and what I have told you as to my purpose is true. If you will be good enough to let me proceed, or furnish me with means by which I can secure work I shall be thankful."

At this the bandits laughed scornfully, while Jesse James proceeded with the examination : " I think you are from Chicago, and when you arrived at Liberty a few days ago you wore much better clothes than you now have on; besides, it seems that you and Moss (the sheriff) had some business together. Say, now, young fellow, haven't you set out to locate the James Boys, whom you have found rather unexpectedly ?"

Wicher then saw that he was in the hands of his enemies, and his heart beat in excited pulsations as he thought of the young wife he had so recently wedded, and from whom an eternal separation appeared certain. Dropping his head as if resigning himself to cruel fate, Wicher hoped to deceive his captors, and in an unguarded moment be able to draw his pistol and fight for his life. Like a flash from a hazy cloud, the detective thrust his hand into his bosom and succeeded in grasping his pistol, but before he could use it the bandits sprang upon him, and in the grip of three strong men he was helpless. He was then disarmed and firmly bound by small cords which Frank James produced. Clell Miller went into the woods and' soon returned leading three horses, on the largest of which Wicher was placed and his feet tied under the horse's belly. A gag was placed tightly in his mouth and Jesse James, mounting behind, the desperadoes rode into the deepening twilight of the woods with their victim. They crossed the Missouri river at Independence Landing, and just before day they halted in the black shadows of a copse in Jackson county. Here they prepared for the punishment and execution of their prisoner. Wicher was taken from his horse and bound fast to a tree; the gag was removed from his mouth and then the bandits tried to extort from him information concerning the plans of Pinkerton and the number and names of the detectives he had engaged in the attempt to capture the outlaws. Though they pricked him with their bowie-knives and bent his head forward with their combined strength until the spinal column was almost broken, and practiced other atrocious torments, yet Wicher never spoke. He knew that death was his portion and he defied the desperadoes and dared them to do their worst. Finding all their endeavors fruitless, Jesse and Frank James murdered their victim ; one of them shooting him through the heart and the other through the brain. The body was then carried to the nearest highway, where it was left to be found next day by a farmer who was driving into Independence.

- MURDERING COW-BOYS AND DRIVING OFF CATTLE -

The excitement following the murder of Wicher was so great that the James Boys, Clell Miller, Arthur McCoy, and the three Younger brothers quit Missouri and again visited Texas. After carousing around through the State until their pecuniary means were well nigh exhausted, they determined upon the commission of a new crime, stealing a herd of cattle. It was in September, 1874, that the seven brigands rode into the southwestern part of the State, where they selected a herd of five hundred of the finest beef cattle in Starr county, which were being tended by three cow-boys. The herders were cruelly murdered and the robbers drove the cattle rapidly toward Mexico with the design of selling them to the Mexicans who cared little for the real ownership of the cattle after they were upon Mexican soil. On the extensive plains of Texas where the large herds are left in charge of cow-boys to roam from season to season, subsisting entirely upon the rich grasses of the prairies, the owners often do not see their cattle for months, trusting them to the care of the herders. It is due to this fact, perhaps, that the bandits, after killing the cow-boys, were permitted to drive the herd over sixty miles and into Mexico without being pursued.

Reaching Camargo the bandits had no difficulty in disposing of the cattle, and with this money they went on a big spree, which terminated In a fight with fifteen gringos, who were saloon loafers and petty disturbers by profession. The result of this combat was the wounding of Clell Miller and Jim Younger and the killing of two Mexicans. The bandits would have fared much worse, however, had they not gained their horses and made rapid retreat, gaining the Rio Grande so far in advance of their pursuers as permitted them to cross the river before the Mexicans reached the bank.

The free-booters having eluded their pursuers stopped at Camp Hudson for several weeks, where the wounds of Miller and Younger were attended to, and in December the party returned to Missouri, thinking that, as had been usual, the excitement over their crimes had so far subsided as to permit them to visit their old homes and haunts. Their appearance in Clay county, at least the James Boys, was noted on the 20th of January, 1875, and report of their return was at once made to Allen Pinkerton, who, after some correspondence with county officials and others, formed a plan for capturing the outlaws.

- THE ATTACK ON THE SAMUELS RESIDENCE -

William Pinkerton, a brother of the chief detective, was sent to Kansas City immediately with five of the most trusted men in the force. Upon arriving at that place the sheriff of Clay county was sent for, after which twelve citizens of known pluck and reliability were engaged to watch the Samuels homestead and report from hour to hour by a rapid means of communication, which had been established. The greatest secrecy was enjoined upon all engaged in the undertaking and every possible precaution was taken to prevent any alarm reaching the bandits.

On the afternoon of January 25th, Jesse and Frank James were both seen in the yard fronting the Samuels residence and report of this quickly reached the sheriff and Mr. Pinkerton who were in Liberty. Arrangements were made for the immediate capture of the two bandits, who it was confidently supposed would spend the night in their mother's house. Accordingly the two officers rode to Kearney late in the afternoon, where they organized a party of twelve men who were to assist them, and preparing several balls of cotton saturated with turpentine and two hand-grenades, the well armed body of men proceeded to the Samuels residence, which they reached about midnight. A reconnaissance was first made with great care for indications of possible surprise, and after completely surrounding the house four of the men, with turpentine balls, were sent forward to open the attack. A window on the west side of the residence was stealthily approached, but in the act of raising it an old colored woman, who had for many years been a house servant in the family, was awakened, and she at once gave the alarm. But the window was forced up and the two lighted balls were thrown into the room, and as the flames shot upward, threatening destruction to the house and its contents, the family were speedily aroused and efforts were made to extinguish the fire. At the moment every member of the household, consisting of Mr. and Mrs. Samuels, a son eight years of age, and the daughter, Miss Susie, and the old colored woman, had partially subdued, the flames, one of the detectives, or at least one of the party leading the attack, flung a hand-grenade into the room among the affrighted occupants, and a heavy explosion was the prelude to the dreadful havoc made by that instrument of death. A scream of anguish succeeded the report and groans from within, without any evidence of the outlaws' presence, convinced the detectives and citizen's posse that they had committed a grave and horrible crime ; so, without examining the premises further the party withdrew, apparently with the fear that the inexcusable deed they had just committed would be avenged speedily if they tarried in the vicinity.

When the lamp was lighted by Dr. Samuels he found his little boy in the agonies of death, having received a terrible wound in the side from the exploded shell. Mrs. Samuels' left arm had been shattered, and hung helpless by her side; but she forgot her own misfortune in the anguish she suffered at seeing the dying struggles of her little boy. What a terrible night was that memorable 25th of January to the Samuels family! Alone with their dead boy, whom they worshipped, and with a desperately wounded mother, who would certainly have bled to death but for the thoughtfulness of the old colored servant who hastily bandaged the arm and staunched the flow of the crimson life-current.

The funeral of the innocent victim did not take place until the second day after the midnight attack, and then Mrs. Samuels, who had suffered an amputation of the injured member, was too greatly prostrated to attend and witness the last service over her darling boy, but the remains were accompanied to the grave by a very large body of sympathizing people of the neighborhood.

This unfortunate and indefensible attack, for a time allayed public animosity against the James Boys and turned the sympathy of people in western Missouri somewhat in their favor. Those who had been most earnest in their desire to see Jesse and Frank James brought to punishment, began to think more lightly of their crimes, attributing them partly, at least, to the manner in which they had been hunted and persecuted. It is a notorious fact that for some time this sentiment predominated in Clay and Jackson counties, and the same feeling extended to other parts of the State, and in March following led to the introduction of an amnesty bill in the Legislature, granting immunity for past offenses committed by Jesse and Frank James, Coleman Younger, James Younger and Robert Younger. The bill was introduced by Gen. Jeff. Jones, of Callaway county, and contained a provisional clause that amnesty would be granted the parties named in the instrument for all offenses committed during the war, provided they would surrender to the lawful authorities and submit to such proceedings as might be brought against them in the several States for crimes charged against them since the war. After a stormy debate the bill was defeated, although had it passed none of the bandits named would have accepted the terms, for surrender meant either execution or life imprisonment. A rejection of the terms of surrender, by the Legislature, afforded a fresh pretext, however, to the bandits to pursue their crimes of blood and pillage, and it was not long before the country was again startled by the daring deeds of the outlaws.

- ASSASSINATION OF DANIEL ASKEW -

Immediately after the defeat of the "outlaw amnesty bill," as it was called, the brigands planned the execution of new and direful schemes, one of which involved the assassination of a respectable citizen of Clay county.

The James Boys concluded, for reasons known only to themselves, that Mr. Daniel Askew was a member of the posse which made the attack on the Samuels residence, and this belief was justification sufficient, in their estimation, for murdering that gentleman ; but the plan of its execution was equally as dastardly as the casting of the hand-grenade blindly and savagely among the several members of Dr. Samuels' family. The circumstances of the assassination were as follows : Mr. Askew was an unpretentious farmer, living about five miles from Liberty, in a neat frame house, but with no neighbors nearer than one mile. He had returned home from Liberty, late in the afternoon of April 12th, 1875, and after eating supper took a bucket and went to the spring, which was fifty yards from the house, after water. This was about eight o'clock in the evening, but the moon was shining brightly and objects were plainly discernible. He returned from the spring with the water and sat the bucket upon a shelf on the porch, after which he proceeded to take a drink, but as he was in the act of lifting the cup to his mouth, three sharp shots rang out upon the still air and Mr. Askew plunged forward on his face dead, the three bullets having taken fatal effect upon his person, one entering the brain and the two others reaching vital spots in his body.

At the sound of the shots and the heavy fall on the porch, Mr. Askew's wife and daughter rushed out of the house just in time to see three men steal out from behind the cover of a large woodpile in front of the porch, and regain their horses and ride swiftly away. The three assassins were undoubtedly Jesse and Frank James and Clell Miller, for within an hour after the murder these three met a gentleman upon the highway and informed him of Mr. Askew's fate, and told him the murder was in consequence of the acts of Pinkerton's detectives.

This cowardly act, by which a peaceable citizen had been made to surrender up his life for the sake of a savage revenge, destroyed again every spark of sympathy for the desperadoes, and the determination for their capture was renewed. Armed posses of Clay county citizens set out in search of the assassins, but the pursuit was in vain, and after a week of earnest effort, finding no trace of the brigands, the party returned to their homes, each one reckoning how soon his turn might come to add to the gory record of the remorseless freebooters.

- THE SAN ANTONIO STAGE ROBBERY -

After the murder of Mr. Askew, the bandits, in anticipation of renewed efforts to effect their capture, left Missouri and visited their old haunts in the southwest. They spent several days in the Indian Territory for the purpose of learning with what persistency and the character of the search being made by the authorities. Finding that all effort at their apprehension was confined to western Missouri, the outlaws rode into Texas and soon formed a plan for robbing the stage running between San Antonio and Austin. To plan was to execute, and on the 12th of May, 1875, Jesse James, Clell Miller, Jim Reed and Cole and Jim Younger selected a spot on the highway, about twenty-three miles south-west of Austin, and there ambushed themselves to await the coming of the stage.

It was late in the evening, the sun just descending behind the hills and the chirrup of twilight insects had begun to echo in the solitude of the place. Eleven passengers, three of whom were ladies, were cheerily cracking jokes and relieving the discomforts of the journey by agreeable conversation. Suddenly the driver descried five horsemen riding out into the road one hundred yards ahead of the stage and advancing leisurely. Their appearance and conduct looked suspicious, but as no robberies had been perpetrated on the highway for many years, the driver did not realize what the act portended until, as the stage bowled up, the five men, drawing their pistols, commanded a halt. The order being accompanied by such persuasive authority of course the obedience of the driver was prompt. Then the passengers wondered what it meant, but before they could propound a question four of the brigands rode up on either side of the stage and ordered the inmates to get out. The women, seeing such cruel looking men and their fiercer looking pistols, screamed and scrambled over the male passengers with utter disregard of propriety, and created much confusion. Jesse James and Cole Younger did the talking for the bandits, and in courteous language assured the ladies they had nothing to fear provided the passengers acted with discretion. Soon the eleven but recently gay travelers were arranged in single file along the road behind the stage, and as not the slightest resistance was offered Frank James and Jim Younger had no difficulty in expeditiously relieving all the passengers of their money, watches and other valuables. Among the number was John Breckenridge, president of the First National Bank at San Antonio, from whom $1,000 were obtained; Bishop Gregg, of Austin, contributed his gold watch and nearly $50 in money, while from the other passengers sums from $25 to $50 were obtained. Having completed the personal plunder, the bandits cut open the two mail bags from which a goodly sum of money was secured, but the amount has not been estimated. The haul aggregated, perhaps, $3,000, which they placed in a sack carried for the purpose, and then, bidding the passengers adieu, the border desperadoes rode swiftly into the shadows, leaving the surprised party to resume their journey in a less amiable mood.

- THE GREAT TRAIN ROBBERY AT MUNCIE -

Nothing was heard of the bandits for several months after the stage robbery, and their crimes were again relegated to partially forgotten incidents of the past. In December following, however, another attack by the outlaws refreshed the memory of their deeds and threw Missouri and Kansas into a fever of intense excitement.

The band of desperadoes, by some means known only to themselves, learned of an intended large shipment of gold-dust from Denver, via Kansas Pacific Railroad, and that it would be carried by a train arriving in Kansas City on a certain day. The place selected at which to intercept the train bearing the valuable shipment, was Muncie, a little station six miles west of Wyandotte, Kansas. There was a water tank near the place, at which the engines almost invariably stopped to take a fresh supply of water. At this point six bandits stationed themselves and awaited the train, which was not due until after nightfall. Prompt upon time the engine blew its shrill whistle, and then rolled up under the tank and stopped. In a moment the brigands left their place of concealment and boarded the train, one of them, Bill McDaniels, being deputed to cover and remain with the engineer and fireman. The robbers rushed through the cars and commanded every passenger to remain quiet under penalty of death. Two of them stood on the platforms of the cars while the other three proceeded to the express car. The bandits presented their pistols at the head of the messenger and forced him to open the safe, from which the sum of $25,000 in money was taken and gold dust valued at $30,000. This total sum secured was so large that no attempt was made to rob any of the passengers, and after the valuable plunder was placed in a sack, Jesse James blew a keen whistle and a moment after all the free-booters abandoned the train and regained their horses.

Soon as the passengers reached Wyandotte, which was speedily, the alarm was given, which spread to Kansas City, and another large body of men was sent in pursuit of the daring highwaymen. They chased the fugitives southward into Indian Territory, but the pursuit was abandoned in the Creek Nation, where all traces were blotted out.

About one month after this great robbery a police officer arrested Bill McDaniels in Kansas City, for drunkenness, his participation in the train plundering not then being suspected. But when searched at the police station a sheep-skin bag was found on his person filled with gold-dust. In addition to this he had a large roll of money, and being known in Kansas City as a worthless fellow, suspicion was at once excited that he was a confederate of the train robbers. He was placed in the calaboose and allowed to sober up, and then taken upon a requisition to Lawrence, Kansas. On the following day after his arrest the city marshal and Con O'Hara, the detective, went into McDaniels' cell and spent two hours in a persistent endeavor to obtain a confession from him of his complicity in the robbery, or the names of those who committed the act. But he remained as silent as if he had lost the power of speech, and not a word concerning the robbery did the officers ever hear from him. Two months after his apprehension, in taking him from the jail for trial, McDaniels broke from the deputy sheriff and escaped. After a week's search he was found, but resisting arrest, he was mortally wounded by a member of a citizens' posse named Bauermann. McDaniels died, however, refusing to reveal anything in regard to his confederates. It has since been ascertained, however, that those engaged in the Muncie robbery consisted of Jesse James, Arthur McCoy, Cole and Bob Younger, Clell Miller and McDaniels, the latter only being captured.

- THE HUNTINGTON BANK ROBBERY -

After the train robbery the highwaymen separated, some going to Texas and others to Kentucky. In April, 1876, Frank James, Cole Younger, Tom McDaniels, a brother of Bill, and a small black-eyed fellow called Jack Keen, alias Tom Webb, confederated together for the purpose of perpetrating another bank robbery. Keen had been raised in the eastern part of Kentucky and was well acquainted with the mountainous regions of West Virginia and his native State. It was decided to attack and plunder the bank in Huntington, a town of 2,500 people, on the Ohio river, in West Virginia.

About the 1st of September the four bandits rode into the town under the leadership of Frank James and proceeded directly to the bank, which they reached at 2 p.m. Frank James and McDaniels dismounted, leaving Younger and Keen standing guard on the outside. When Frank and McDaniels entered the bank they found only R. T. Oney, the cashier, and a citizen who was making a deposit; these the robbers covered with their pistols and compelled the cashier to open the safe and deliver up all the money in the bank, amounting to $10,000. Having secured the booty the four outlaws rode rapidly out of town, not a single person in the place having the least suspicion of what had occurred until Mr. Oney spread the news.

A posse of twenty-five citizens, headed by the sheriff, set out in pursuit of the bandits at three o'clock, one hour after the robbery was consummated, and followed the trail with the greatest persistency. The officers in other counties were notified by telegraph, and armed bodies of men were sent out from a dozen towns. One hundred miles south-west of Huntington the robbers were sighted and in an exchange of shots McDaniels was killed. This encouraged the pursuing party, who pressed the bandits so hard that they were forced to abandon their horses and take to the mountain fastnesses of Kentucky. The pursuit continued unabated for four weeks, and at length the outlaws were driven out of Kentucky and into Tennessee; here Keen was captured and taken back to Huntington, where he made a confession and was sentenced to eight years imprisonment in the penitentiary. Frank James and Cole Younger eluded pursuit and returned to the Indian Territory, where they met Jesse James and his band of highwaymen, and forthwith new plans were laid for another big robbery.

- THE ROCKY CUT TRAIN ROBBERY -

Seven months elapsed after the Muncie robbery before the desperate brigands, under the leadership of Jesse James, made another attempt to increase their ill-gotten gains. But in the meantime the band of highwaymen was increasing and organizing for another bold stroke. Many outlaws who had found safety in the Indian Nation were anxious to attach themselves to the James and Younger brothers, but very few were received. The noted bandits were excellent judges of human nature, and they were exceedingly careful not to repose confidence in any one who did not possess indisputable evidence of cunning and bravery; men who, in the event of capture, would not betray their comrades at any sacrifice. In July, 1876, arrangements were completed for rifling another treasure-laden train and the Missouri Pacific Railroad was chosen as the line for their operations. The reorganized party of highwaymen, consisting of Jesse and Frank James, Cole, Bob and Jim Younger, Clell Miller, Hobbs Kerry, Charlie Pitts and Bill Chadwell, nine in number, left their rendezvous in the Indian Territory and, riding separately, reached Otterville, Missouri, by a preconcerted understanding, on the 7th of July.

The capture and confession of Hobbs Kerry enables the giving of a minute narrative of all the circumstances connected with the robbery about to be related.

About one mile east of Otterville, a small station in Pittis county, is a place called Rocky Cut, which is a deep stone cleft, from which the train emerges only to strike the bridge across Otter creek. On the south side of the cut is a heavy wood, and in this the robbers concealed themselves to await the train which was not due there until nearly midnight. A watchman was stationed at the bridge, whom Charlie Pitts and Bob Younger arrested and, after taking his signal lantern and placing it in the track at the bridge approach, they securely tied the helpless fellow and then joined the main party. Hobbs Kerry and Bill Chadwell were detailed to watch the horses and keep them prepared for sudden flight.

As the train came dashing through the cut the engineer saw the danger signal and at once concluded something was wrong with the bridge, and he lost no time in having the brakes set and the engine reversed. The train came to a stop directly in the cut, and as it slowed up seven of the dare-devils leaped upon the cars and with one at each door the robbers had no trouble in so intimidating the passengers as to prevent attack. Jesse James, the boldest of the bold, was the first to enter the express car, followed by Cole Younger. At the mouth of two heavy navy pistols the messenger was forced to open the safe, which contained fifteen thousand dollars in bank notes. This money was hastily thrown into a sack, and the shrill whistle was given by Jesse, which was the signal for the bandits to leave the train and mount. No effort was made to rob or harm any of the passengers, the single purpose of the bandits, agreed upon before the attack was to secure only the valuables of the express.

When the train reached Tipton, report of the robbery was telegraphed to every station along the line, and also to St. Louis and Kansas City, and from these points all over the country.

Hobbs Kerry's statement is, that after the perpetration of the crime, the bandits rode southward together very rapidly until nearly daylight, when they entered a deep wood and there divided the money, after which the band rode off in pairs, except the James Boys and Cole Younger, who kept together. Kerry soon separated from Chadwell, who was his companion, and went to Fort Scott, and from there to Parsons, Kansas, thence to

Joplin and then to Granby, where he remained for nearly a week, spending a great deal of money in gambling dens, and in his drunken moments let drop such remarks as led to the suspicion that he was a member of the gang that robbed the train. He next made a trip into Indian Territory, but after a short stay in that country he returned to Granby; there he was arrested in the latter part of August. The authorities had no difficulty in obtaining from Kerry the full particulars of the robbery and the names of his confederates. Detectives from all parts of the country, stimulated by the large rewards offered by the express company and Governor Hardin, set out in search of the bandits. Every State was penetrated, every suspicious character put under surveillance, and all the ingenuity that could be devised by experienced hunters of criminals was exercised.

The James and Younger boys and Clell Miller, finding the pursuit at an end, returned from the Nation, whither they had first fled, and by stealthy night marches succeeded in reaching Jackson county, where they retired to the robbers' cave and were there safe from pursuit.

- THE FATAL ATTACK ON A MINNESOTA BANK -

The efforts of the detectives to capture the outlaws seemed to be chiefly confined to the southwestern States, and learning this the bandits, after remaining within the seclusion of their undiscoverable haunts for a few weeks, grew tired of the inactivity such life imposed, and as Bill Chadwell was well acquainted in Minnesota, it was decided to send Bob Younger out to find him, and through him to perfect a plan for raiding one of the banks in that State. The means of communication between the bandits was such that Chadwell was soon found and brought into conference with the other members.

The purpose of going into Minnesota could not have been merely because of a supposition that a more ample booty might be secured in that State, for there were many richer banks much nearer.

One of the prime motives of the outlaws was undoubtedly to make a stroke in the far north which would confuse the officers in pursuit of them, and thereby draw the attention of the detectives away from the favorite haunts. Aside from this, no sufficient reason for the strange determination of the brigands is assignable.

A decision was soon reached, and it was decided to make an examination of the country, and raid the bank which gave promise of the largest reward with the least chances of surprise or capture. Cole Younger and Chadwell were accordingly dispatched as a reconnoitering party, and were to ride three days in advance of the others, take observations and make report by leaving certain pre-arranged signals along the route decided upon. Those engaged in the intended enterprise were the two James Boys, Cole, Jim and Bob Younger, Charlie Pitts, Clell Miller and Bill Chadwell. The expedition started for Minnesota about the 3d of September, 1876, proceeding by railroad directly to Mankato, the place appointed for a meeting with the two bandits sent in advance. A second consultation, held at that place on the 6th of September, resulted in a decision to strike the bank at Northfield, Rice county, a town of 2500 people, on the I. & M. division of the Milwaukee & St. Paul Railroad.

On the afternoon of the 7th the eight desperadoes entered Northfield at a furious pace, discharging their pistols and by direful threats endeavoring to so intimidate the citizens as to prevent resistance. They rode direct for the bank, which was located fronting the public square, and stopping in front of the institution. Frank and Jesse James and Bob Younger quickly dismounted and entered the bank while the other robbers were left to guard against attack from the outside. J. L. Haywood, the cashier, A. E. Bunker, teller, and Frank Wilcox, bookkeeper, were the only persons in the bank at the time of the entrance of the bandits. Jesse James drew a pistol and presented it at the cashier's head and commanded him to open the safe. Haywood promptly refused, and the next instant he lay dead at the bandit's feet, his brain pierced with a bullet. At this Bunker and Wilcox fled out at the back door, but as they reached the step a bullet from Frank James' pistol plunged through Bunker's shoulder, but it did not impede his flight. The robbers were left alone in the bank, but beyond a small amount lying upon the counter no money could be found, and the bandits, hearing firing in the streets, rushed out just in time to see Bill Chadwell fall from his horse, his heart pierced with a musket ball, and in a few seconds after Clell Miller received a bullet in his breast, and with a groan tumbled mortally wounded to the ground while his horse galloped riderless up the street.

By this time the citizens came rushing to the attack and the firing became general. Jim Younger was shot in the mouth and a horse was wounded. The effective shots were fired by Dr. Henry Wheeler from a second-story window in the Damphier House, facing the bank. The six unharmed bandits rushed for their horses and rode at their highest speed out of town, followed in fifteen minutes afterward by fifty well mounted citizens. Then succeeded a flight and pursuit which for persistency, endurance, courage and results is without a parallel.

Information of the murder and robbery was telegraphed in every direction and each hour the pursuing force was augmented by volunteers who sprang up in the pathways of the robbers and guarded every highway and bridle path. The chase led through Shieldsville and from there into LeSeur county where, being pressed closely, too Jesse and Frank James insisted on killing Jim Younger, the blood from whose wound was furnishing a trail for the pursuers. This proposition resulted in a separation of the outlaws, Jesse and Frank James remaining together and the Younger boys and Charley Pitts, (whose real name was Sam Wells), remaining in a body. The country was fairly filled with resolute men determined upon the death of the bandits. It was very soon discovered that the robbers had separated and the pursuing parties were divided and put upon the two trails.

About one hundred and fifty miles south-west of Northfield, near a place called Madelia, the Youngers and Charlie Pitts were surrounded in a swamp, and captured after a desperate fight with the citizens' posse Pitts being killed and all the Youngers receiving fresh wounds. Pitts was buried, and the Youngers, always under guard, after months of suffering finally recovered. After their recovery they pleaded guilty to the charges against them and were sentenced to prison for the term of their natural lives. They are yet in the Minnesota penitentiary at Stillwater. Jesse and Frank James were more fortunate; although so closely pressed that a hundred times they could see and hear the voices of their pursuers, yet they were not discovered. Day and night the James Boys continued their flight, unable to cook anything, subsisting on green corn and raw potatoes; never daring to show their faces, swimming streams, and confining their route to the least accessible sections of country. Extraordinary cunning, a knowledge of men and adaptability to circumstances, after ten days of a most remark-able pursuit, covering their tracks by wading for miles in streams of water, Jesse and Frank James eluded their pursuers and regained their secure haunts in Jackson county.

- AT GLENDALE— THE LAST GREAT TRAIN ROBBERY -

Three years elapsed from the time of the attack at Northfield until the James Boys were heard of again in connection with criminal escapades. Their names existed in tradition, and the horror which was once manifested at the mention of their savage natures had become dwarfed into mere expressions of surprise. It was reported that Frank James had died of consumption in the Indian Nation and that Jesse was living peaceably in one of the remote Territories, following the profitable occupation of cattle-raising. On the evening of October 7th, 1879, the people of Western Missouri were suddenly shocked by the intelligence of another great train robbery, committed in the old guerrilla haunts, where crime had held such high carnival during the dark period of the great rebellion. On the day in question Jesse James, Jim Cummings, Ed. Miller, a brother of Clell, Daniel (better known as Tucker) Bassham and seven others whose names are not known, appeared suddenly at the little station of Glendale, which is on the line of the Chicago, Alton & St. Louis Railroad, twenty two miles from Kansas City. The town consists of a post-office and store combined and a station house, and is a flag station only. About six o'clock in the evening the party of bandits rode into the place and proceeded at once to put every one present under arrest, which they readily accomplished, as there were but three men at the station, and these were locked in the station house. The train going east was due at 6:45 p. m., at a time when darkness clothed the scene, and the masked robbers compelled the station operator to display his signal to stop the train. Previous to this preliminary the masked bandits had piled a large number of condemned ties on the track only a few hundred yards east of Glendale, and had everything fully prepared to execute their purpose expeditiously. The train was on time, and seeing the stop signal displayed, the engineer obeyed its import, and in a moment the conductor, John Greenman, was facing an ominous pistol, while others of the robbers covered the engineer and demanded submission. Meeting with no resistance the bandits broke in the door of the express car, but in their efforts to break in the door, William Grimes, the messenger, hastily unlocked the safe and took out thirty-five thousand dollars in money and valuables, which he attempted to conceal. He was too late, however, for at the moment he was placing the money bag behind some boxes in the car, the door yielded and three robbers rushed on him. Refusing to deliver the safe-key, Grimes was knocked down and badly punished. The key was taken from him and the few remaining contents of value in the safe were appropriated, as was also the bag containing the money.

The haul was a Very rich one and the attempt having been successful the passengers were not molested, and the train was permitted to depart after a detention of no more than ten minutes.

The commission of this crime again aroused the officers, and as Glendale is in Jackson county, Major James Leggitt, the county marshal, took immediate steps to discover and arrest the perpetrators. Being a shrewd and fearless man, he went to work intelligently and unceasingly. He soon discovered who composed the party that committed the robbery, notwithstanding the fact that they were heavily masked.

Tucker Bassham, one of the robbers, who was raised in Jackson county, was suspected directly after the deed was accomplished. He left the county for a time, but returned and buried his share of the booty, which was one thousand one hundred dollars. Soon he began to exhibit an unusual amount of money, and a spy was placed upon him until enough information was obtained to conclusively establish his connection with the robbery. But Marshal Leggitt deferred the arrest with the hope that he might learn of some communication between, Bassham and other members of the gang, and accomplish their arrest. In June last (1880) deputy marshals W. G. Keshler and M. M. Langhorn, arrested Bassham and lodged him in the jail at Kansas City. Shortly afterward Major Leggitt obtained a full confession from his prisoner, which was reduced to writing and made in the form of an affidavit.

- SHOOTING OF JESSE JAMES BY GEO. SHEPHERD -

The pursuit of the Glendale robbers did not cease after a week's efforts, as previously, but Maj. Leggitt was determined to accomplish his purpose. He resolved upon an expedient which evidences his cunning and strategy: Living in Kansas City, at the time of the robbery, was George Shepherd, one of the most courageous men that ever faced danger. He was one of Quantrell's lieutenants and fought in all the terrible and unmerciful encounters of that chief of the black banner. He was at Lawrence, and rode beside the James Boys in that dreadful cyclone of remorseless murder. He had run the gauntlet of a hundred rifles and fought against odds which it appeared impossible to escape. After the close of the war Jesse James accepted Geo. Shepherd as a leader and followed him into Texas, and would still be following his counsels had not circumstances separated them.

Maj. Leggitt evolved a scheme out of his hours of study looking towards the capture of Jesse James. He sent for Shepherd, who was working for Jesse Noland, a leading dry goods merchant of Kansas City, and to the ex-guerrilla he proposed his scheme. It was this: Shepherd, being known to have formerly been a comrade of Jesse James, it was to be reported that undoubted information had reached the authorities establishing Shepherd's connection with the Glendale robbery. A report of this was to be printed upon a slip of paper having printed matter upon the reverse side, so as to appear like a newspaper clipping. Shepherd was to take this printed slip, find Jesse James and propose to join him, saying that he was being hounded by detectives, and, although innocent, he felt that his only safety was in uniting his fortunes with Jesse and his fearless band. This being accomplished, Shepherd was to find an opportunity for killing Jesse James, and the reward for him, dead or alive, was to be divided. In addition to this, Shepherd was to be provided with a horse and to receive $50 per month during the time of his service.

The conditions and terms were satisfactory to Shepherd, and in the latter part of October, about two weeks after the Glendale robbery, he started out in quest of Jesse James.

The plan of Shepherd's operations and the manner in which he accomplished his hazardous undertaking is herewith detailed just as he related the story to the writer, and other corroborative testimony establishes its truth:

When Shepherd left Kansas City he was mounted upon a sorrel horse and his weapons consisted of a thirty-two calibre single-barrel pistol and a small pocket-knife. He rode directly to the Samuels residence, which he reached at dusk, and tied his horse in a thicket about two hundred yards from the house. He found Mrs. Samuels and the Doctor at home just preparing to sit down to supper. The story that any enmity existed on the part of Jesse James against Shepherd is untrue; reports of this kind may have been circulated but there was not a semblance of truth in them. Shepherd was warmly received by Mrs. Samuels and her husband, and at their invitation he took supper with them. While they were eating, Shepherd explained that his life and liberty were in great jeopardy and that owing to reports, false as they were, of his connection with the Glendale robbery, he had been forced to flee, and for mutual protection he wished to join Jesse James and his confederates; thereupon Shepherd produced the apparently newspaper clipping already referred to, which Dr. and Mrs. Samuels both read. After finishing supper Dr. Samuels told Shepherd to ride to a certain point in the main highway where he would meet Jesse and some of his associates. The Dr. went out into the woods where he knew the bandits were concealed, while Shepherd mounted his horse and rode to the spot indicated, where, after waiting for less than five minutes, he was met by Jesse James, Jim Cummings, Ed. Miller and another party whom Shepherd did not know. Shepherd repeated his story to Jesse James and showed him the clipping, after which he was immediately received into the full confidence of Jesse and the band. Why should Jesse have entertained suspicions? Shepherd had been his intimate comrade for many years; the two had ridden and fought together in a hundred terrible conflicts, and were associated together in the Kentucky bank robbery. Shepherd was the very man of all others whom Jesse wanted for a companion in his daring deeds and it was unnatural, under the circumstances, for any of the bandits to doubt Shepherd's story.

The party remained all night at the Samuels residence and on the following day they proceeded to a spot in Jackson county called "Six Mile," which is eighteen miles from Kansas City, and spent the day at Benjamin Marr's. It was here a plan was laid for robbing the bank at Empire City, in Jasper county. After the scheme was fully understood Shepherd told Jesse that it would be necessary for him to procure a better horse and some effective weapons, which he could do at a friend's near Kansas City. Jesse urged Shepherd then to return at night to the friend's place, get a good horse and at least two heavy pistols and meet the party at Six Mile on the third night following.

Shepherd then rode back to Kansas City and imparted the information of his meeting and arrangements with

Jesse James to Maj. Leggitt, who provided Shepherd with a splendid horse and three large-sized Smith & Wesson pistols. But in order to prevent any possibility of deception, Maj. Leggitt took Shepherd to Independence and placed him in jail, and then sent three trusted men to Six Mile for the purpose of ascertaining if Jesse James and his party were really rendezvoused at that point. Maj. Leggitt soon learned that Shepherd had reported nothing but facts and he was then sent out, splendidly armed and mounted, for the meeting place. Shepherd did not reach the trysting spot until the morning after the time agreed upon, and he found Jesse and his followers gone, but the party at whose house the meeting was to occur — Benj. Marr's — gave Shepherd the following letter, which is herewith copied verbatim.

Friend Georg.

I cant wate for you hear, I want you to meet me on Rogs Hand, and we will talk about that Business we spok of. I would wate for you but the boys wants to leave hear, dont fale to come and if we dont by them cattle I will come back with you. Come to the plase whear we meet going south that time and stay in that naborhood untill I find you.

Your Friend.

J

Thus instructed Shepherd started for Rogue's Island, but met Jesse James at the head of Grand River. This fact furnishes one of the proofs of Jesse's anxiety to have Shepherd as a comrade, for he was so anxious lest Shepherd would not meet them, or fail to get the letter he left with Marr, that he returned to find him. Jesse and Shepherd returned to the camp, where they found Cummings, Miller and the unknown, and then the party rode directly for Empire City, the vicinity of which they reached about noon on Saturday, November 1, 1879. They went into camp on Short Creek, eight miles south of Empire City, and at four o'clock in the afternoon it was agreed that Shepherd should ride into the town and learn what he could respecting the surroundings and location of the bank. It was after dark when Shepherd reached the place, and, pursuing his story, he was astonished at finding the bank lighted up and a close inspection revealed to him a dozen men inside the bank armed with double-barreled shot-guns. Shepherd stated to the writer that Maj. Leggitt must have notified the bank officers of the intended raid, by telegraph, but Maj. Leggitt denies having done so, and says that Shepherd must have told some person who communicated with the bank. Anyhow the arrangement was that Maj. Leggitt was to be in Empire City with a good force of assistants and was to be aided by Shepherd in capturing the outlaws when the attack on the bank should be made. Circumstances prevented Maj. Leggitt from appearing in Empire City at the time agreed upon, but he sent word to the town authorities.

Finding everything in readiness to meet the intended attack, Shepherd went into a restaurant and while eating his supper, Tom Cleary, an old acquaintance, came in and greeted him. After supper the two went to Cleary's house and remained all night, and Shepherd told his friend the part he was acting in the effort to capture Jesse James. Ed. Cleary, a brother of Tom's, was also informed of the scheme and Shepherd asked their assistance, or to at least follow him the next morning to the camp of the bandits. The understanding was at the time Shepherd left the outlaws that he should return to the camp by nine o'clock Sunday morning and, if his report was favorable, the raid on the bank would be made Sunday night.

Shepherd kept the appointment and returned to the place where the bandits had encamped, but found the camp deserted. He thought this strange, but soon found the old sign of a "turn-out" had been made to let him know where they were. It is well known that the James Boys and their comrades frequently separate. They have a sign, however, by which it is not difficult for them to find one another. This sign is the crossing of two twigs along the highway, which indicates that one or more of the parties, according to the number of twigs, has turned out of the highway at that point. Shepherd saw the twigs and after riding about half a mile in the direction the branches lay he found the party, all of whom were slightly intoxicated. He knew they had no whiskey with them when he left on Saturday afternoon, and at once concluded they had been in town. Cummings was the first to speak. Said he :

THE BORDER BANDITS

"The bank is guarded; how is this?" Shepherd responded: "Yes, and I think the best thing for us to do is to separate and get out of this."

Cummings had ridden into Galena on Saturday night, where he had purchased some whiskey and there heard rumors of the intended bank raid.

The party agreed with Shepherd that it would be wise for them to get out of that section, and they mounted their horses and divided, riding southward. Ed. Miller's position was one hundred yards to the right while Cummings and the unknown rode at the same distance to the left of the center which was taken by Jesse James and Shepherd. The woods were open enough for all parties to remain in sight of each other.

When they reached a point twelve miles south of Galena, all parties maintaining their respective positions, Shepherd gave a smart jerk to the bridle rein which caused his horse to stop while Jesse rode on. It was the work of an instant, for as Jesse's horse gained two steps forward Shepherd drew one of his large pistols and without speaking a word fired, the ball taking effect in Jesse's head one inch behind the left ear. Only the one shot was fired, for Shepherd saw the result of the shot, and Jesse plunged headlong from his horse and lay motionless on the ground as if death had been instantaneous. Shepherd says he viewed the body for nearly one minute before either of the other outlaws made any demonstration. Ed. Miller first started toward him in a walking pace, and then Cummings, and the unknown drew their pistols and rode swiftly after him. Shepherd's horse was swift and he put him to the greatest speed, soon distancing the unknown, but Cummings was mounted on a superior animal and the chase for three miles was a hot one. Each of the two kept firing, but the rapid rate at which they were riding made the shots ineffectual. Seeing that he was pursued only by Cummings who was gaining on him, Shepherd stopped and wheeled his horse and at that moment a bullet struck him in the left leg just below the knee, producing, however, only a flesh wound. As Cummings dashed up Shepherd took deliberate aim and fired, and Cummings reeled in the saddle, turned his horse and retreated. Shepherd says he feels confident that he struck Cummings hard in the side, and that he killed Jesse James. He rode back to Galena where he remained two weeks under a surgeon's care, and after recovery returned to Kansas City.

That Shepherd told the truth there is no room for doubt, and he had the best reasons for believing that he had killed Jesse James; but two parties, at least, whose word is reliable affirm that they have seen Jesse James since the shooting and that Cummings has also been met by them, who stated that Shepherd did shoot Jesse, and that the bullet did strike him just behind the left ear, but instead of penetrating the brain it had coursed around the skull partially paralyzing the brain and spine. Cummings further stated that while Jesse James was still living his career as a bandit was ended forever by the bullet from Shepherd's pistol. In other words, Jesse's mind has been totally destroyed. How much truth there is in this report is left for conjecture. Mrs. Samuels says she believes that Jesse is dead, and a meeting which she had with Shepherd since the shooting was such as caused those who witnessed it, to believe the woman was earnest in that opinion.

- *WHY DID SHEPHERD SHOOT JESSE JAMES?* -

The prime motive which actuated George Shepherd in shooting Jesse James has never been suspicioned by more than one man, and acting upon suggestions made by that single person, the writer verified the theory. It is true that the rewards, amounting to nearly one hundred thousand dollars, for the apprehension or dead body of Jesse James, were a strong temptation, and it certainly had its influence with Shepherd, but there was a stronger motive.

Directly after the war Ike Flannery, a nephew of George Shepherd, reached the age of manhood and came into possession of five thousand dollars, a sum he had inherited from the estate of his deceased father. Ike was somewhat wayward and was well acquainted with the James Boys and the guerrillas. Jesse James and Jim Anderson, a brother of the notorious Bill, knew of Ike Flannery's inheritance, and they induced him to buckle on his pistols, take his money and go with them upon a pretended expedition. Near Glasgow, Missouri, the three stopped at the house of a friend where there were three girls the men of the house being away on business. After eating dinner the three started away, but they had been gone only a few moments when the report of two pistol shots was heard and Jim Anderson came riding back to the house where they had dined, and told the girls that his party had been fired on by the militia, and that Flannery had been killed. Jesse James and Anderson rode away while the girls notified some of the neighbors, and when the body of Flannery was found in the road, there were two bullet holes in the head and the five thousand dollars were missing. Shepherd did not learn all the circumstances connected with Flannery's death until sometime afterward, but when he was told how Anderson and Jesse James acted, he was convinced that they murdered his nephew and plundered his dead body.

It was more than one year after this tragic occurrence before Shepherd met either of the murderers. He was in Sherman, Texas, when Jim Anderson came up to him with a cordial greeting, little suspecting the terrible result of that meeting. The two drank together and appeared on the best of terms until the hour of eleven o'clock at night. The saloon was closing and the darkness without was most uninviting. Shepherd asked Anderson to accompany him over to the court-house yard as he wanted to talk secretly concerning a certain transaction.

When the two reached the yard, and about them was nothing but sombre shadow and the quiet of sleep, cautiously, yet determinedly. Shepherd drew from its sheath a long, bright, deadly knife, which gathered on its blade and focused the light unseen before, and then made ready for a horrible deed. Anderson had never thought of danger until the keen edge of the terrible weapon was at his throat.

Said Shepherd: "You murdered Ike Flannery and robbed his body of five thousand dollars. I have determined to avenge his death, and to accomplish my purpose I brought you here. What have you got to say ?"

Anderson had killed many men and he knew how to die. There was no begging, no denying, only a realization of what he could not avert; and he accepted fate with a stoicism worthy of a religious fanatic. Before receiving the fatal stroke, however, he told Shepherd that Jesse James was the one who proposed the murder and robbery of young Flannery, and that each fired a fatal shot and then divided the stolen money. When this admission escaped his lips, Shepherd sprang upon him like a tiger, drew the glittering blade of the terrible knife across his throat, and the spirit of the murderer and robber took its flight into the realms of the unknown.

On the following morning a dead body with a ghastly gash in the throat, from which the blood had poured until it dyed the grass a yard in diameter, was found and identified as that of Jim Anderson. DeHart, an old-time guerrilla, was in Sherman at the time of the murder, and was known to have a grudge against the murdered man, so suspicion attached to him so strongly that he had to leave Texas. No one ever suspected Shepherd of the murder, but his own confessions to the writer are given in this account of Anderson's execution.

Shepherd has longed for an opportunity to kill Jesse James, but the surroundings, even during a long association, were never sufficiently favorable. The opportunity was exceedingly unfavorable at Short Creek, but revenge and the promise of such an immense reward nerved him to the undertaking.

THE BORDER BANDITS

- ROBBERY OF THE MAMMOTH CAVE STAGES -

The James Boys, and especially Frank, nave remained in seclusion for a considerable period, and with the shooting of Jesse — whom many still believe to be dead — it was thought that the old remnants of guerrilla plunderers had entirely disappeared. It is positively known that Frank James resided in Baltimore during the winter of 1879-80, and his home was located on one of the principal resident streets. At that time he wore full whiskers which were very long, reaching to his waist. The name he bore while in Baltimore the writer has not been able to learn, for obvious reasons. He disappeared from that city in March last, and it is reported by Kansas City police officers that Frank was seen in Jackson county, Missouri, by two of his acquaintances in the latter part of July, 1880, and that his whiskers were cut short. The following account of the robbery of the Mammoth Cave stage again brings Frank James and Jim Cummings prominently into notice.

The Concord stage running between Mammoth Cave and Cave City, in Edmonson county, Kentucky, was captured by highwaymen on the afternoon of Friday, September 3rd, 1880, and the passengers despoiled of everything they carried.

At this season of the year Mammoth Cave is visited by thousands of tourists and sight-seers, who are usually people of means, furnishing fat pickings for the robbers. One of the routes to the cave, and the one selected by the large majority of its visitors, is by way of the Louisville and Nashville Railroad to Cave City, and thence by the Concord stages to the cave, which is about eight or ten miles distant. The stage road is through a lonely and rocky region, and about midway on the route it runs through a dense wood, which adds considerably to its dreariness. About 6 o'clock Friday evening, while the coach from the cave was coming to Cave City, it reached this wood, and while coming through the narrow road in a walk, two men, one mounted on a thin black thoroughbred horse, and the other on a fine sorrel, rode out of the dense forest, and, dashing up to the stage, covered the driver and passengers with their revolvers and called a halt. The stage was pulled up, the driver was ordered down and to the door of his vehicle, and then calmly dismounting and holding their horses by the bridle reins, the work of delivering the booty began. The rider of the black horse, a man about thirty-five years old, with a straggling red mustache and beard, was the leader and spokesman. He was rather small, not appearing to be over five feet six inches in height, and would weigh about 140 pounds. He had light blue eyes, a pleasant smile and distributed his attentions to the defenseless party of eight passengers with a sang froid and easy politeness which did much to alleviate their feelings. His accomplice was about the same age, with black whiskers and mustache rather ragged in trim, and had a pair of black eyes. He was rather slow in his movements, but the business in hand suffered nothing for that.

"Come out of the stage, please," said the spokesman, in a light, high pitched voice.

The passengers looked through the open windows and saw the muzzels of the impassive revolvers covering the whole length of the vehicle, and, as there was not a weapon in the party as large as a penknife, they could not resist or parley. There were seven gentlemen and one lady in the coach, and the lady naturally was nervous and alarmed. In the excitement and bustle attendant upon rising and leaving their seats, Mr. R. S. Rountree, of the Milwaukee Evening Wisconsin, who was making the trip with relatives, slipped his pocket-book and gold watch under the cushion of the seat.

Very few words were spoken, though the highwaymen seemed impatient and ordered them to "hurry up." As each gentleman stepped out he was covered with the muzzle of a revolver and told to take his place in line and hold up his hands. The lady, a daughter of Hon. R. H. Rountree, of Lebanon, Ky., was permitted to remain in the stage. After the passengers were all out the leader of the two villains tossed his rein to his accomplice, who covered the line while the spokesman proceeded to rifle their pockets, talking pleasantly as he went. J. E.

Craig, Jr., of Lawrenceville, Ga., lost $670; Hon. R. H. Rountree, of Lebanon, Ky., handed out a handsome gold watch, valued at $200, and; $55 in cash; S. W. Shelton, of Calhoun, Tenn., gave up about $50; Miss Lizzie Rountree, of Lebanan, Ky., lost nothing but rings, one of them a handsome diamond; S. H. Frohlichstein, of Mobile, Ala., lost $23, Geo. M. Paisley, of Pittsburg, gave up $33; W. G. Welsh, of Pittsburg, lost $5 and a handsome watch. R. S. Rountree, of Milwaukee, saved his money as stated. Hon. R. H. Rountree felt very sore over the loss of an elegant engraved watch, which was presented by Hon. J. Proctor Knott, the member of Congress from the Fourth District.

The spokesman of the marauders explained that they were not highwaymen, but moonshiners, and were pursued so hotly by the government officers that they were compelled to have money to get out of the country. He asked each passenger his name and place of residence, and noted them down, saying that some day he would repay them their losses. When he came to Mr. Craig, of Georgia, he remarked that he hated to take his money because he had fought in a Georgia regiment during the war, but the case was a desperate one and he was compelled to do it.

When Miss Rountree gave her name and place of residence at Lebanon, a pleased smile lighted up the robber's face, and he asked :

"Do you know the Misses of Lebanon?"

"Quite well," answered the young lady.

"So do I," he rejoined, "and they are nice girls. Give them my regards when you see them, and tell them I will make this right some day."

After getting all the valuables of the party the marauders returned the pocket-books with the railway passes and tickets, and giving the passengers orders to get in, mounted and rode off. They told the passengers, for consolation, that they had robbed the out stage, getting; $700 from Mr. George Croghan, one of the owners of the cave.

The rider of the black horse was Frank James, and his companion was Jim Cummings. These facts have been fully established by information of an indisputable character, which came into the possession of the writer since the robbery.

- PERSONAL CHARACTERISTICS OF THE JAMES BOYS -

Singular as it may appear, there is scarcely a single feature of similarity in the character of the James brothers. Frank James is a man of more than ordinary education, and his manners show some effort at refinement. He is very slim, and not more than five feet six inches in height, and weighs about one hundred and forty pounds. He has blue eyes, very light hair and usually wears a shortly cropped full beard and straggling mustache, of a pale, reddish color. His face is peculiar in shape, being broad at the forehead and tapering abruptly from the cheek bones to the chin, which is almost pointed. In his motions he is neither naturally slow nor quick, but at times he affects either. His cunning and coolness are remarkable, and to compare the two boys in this respect would be like comparing the boldest highwayman with the lowest sneak thief, so great is Frank's superiority. In the matter of education Frank has improved his opportunities and is a student, being a lover of books and familiar with the different phases of life. He has murdered many men, and yet he is not destitute of mercy, and finds no gratification in deeds of blood. He has tried to imitate the traditions of Claude Duval, whose fictitious adventures Frank has read until he can repeat them like the written narrative.

Jesse James is a strongly made man, standing five feet ten inches in height, and will weigh one hundred and sixty-five pounds. He has brown eyes, dark hair and is of a nervous temperament. Jesse's peculiarity is in his eyes which are never at rest. In his youth Jesse was troubled with granulated eyelids from which he has never fully recovered, which is seen in the constant batting of his eyes and a slight irritation of the lids; besides this marked peculiarity, the first joint of the forefinger on his left hand is missing. He usually wears full whiskers of apparently one month's growth. His education is very limited, barely enabling him to read and write. He is revengeful in his nature, always sanguine, impetuous, almost heedless. It is due to Frank James' strategy and Jesse's desperate bravery that the latter has not long since been punished for his crimes. In deeds of violence Jesse finds especial delight, and in his entire nature there is not a trace of mercy.

It is asserted, by those who know them best, that Jesse and Frank are only half-brothers, having the same mother, but that Jesse's father is a physician in Clay county. What truth there is in this report the writer does not assume the responsibility of confirming, giving it only as the assertion of many prominent men of Clay county.

On one occasion, so George Shepherd relates, while Jesse and Frank were dining with their mother, with Shepherd as their guest, a dispute arose over a trivial matter, in which the brothers became very angry and drew their pistols. Mrs. Samuels made no effort to interfere, and the difficulty terminated without a fight. In the row Frank told Jesse that he knew they were not brothers, to which assertion neither Jesse nor Mrs. Samuels made any reply.

It is well known among the confederates of the James Boys, and it has been so declared by Shepherd, the Younger boys and Cummings, that there was no love between Frank and Jesse, and Shepherd told the writer that instead of Frank avenging the attack on Jesse at Short Creek he would applaud it. Going still farther. Shepherd said that at his last meeting with Frank, two years ago, the latter declared he would kill Jesse if he ever met him again; that Jess, as he called him, had tried to have him (Frank) ambushed and captured in Texas, and that that was not the first time Jess had played the stake to have him murdered.

The fact of Jim Cummings' association with Frank James in the robbery of the Mammoth Cave stage coaches gives color of truth to Shepherd's declaration that he killed Jesse James near Galena, or to Cummings' statement that Shepherd's shot, while not killing Jesse, had paralyzed his brain and destroyed his mind.

Frank James was married to Miss Annie Ralston, of Jackson county, in September, 1875. The marriage was one of those romantic episodes which brought great sorrow to Mr. Ralston, an industrious farmer living eight miles from Kansas City. Miss Annie was but a school girl whose reading of dime novels had so far impaired her judgment as to make her long for the association of a hero. Her meeting with Frank James was accidental, but she had read of his exploits and he was her ideal. Annie left her home clandestinely and met Frank James many miles from the old homestead; a Baptist minister performed the ceremony and the outlaw and his now ostracized wife went into the shadows of cave and forest, severing the bonds which bound them to society and civilization.

When Mr. Ralston learned of the desperate step taken by his daughter he was almost crazed with grief. He went direct to Kansas City and, with eyes suffused with tears, begged Judge Mumford, of the Times, to prepare for him and publish an article which would relieve him of the stigma which might attach to him by the error of his daughter. Mr. Ralston was anxious the public should know that he never had any association with the outlaw and that, though Annie had been a child who had filled his heart with love, yet her alliance with a highwayman had banished the very memory of her from the fond heart which would know her no more. Such an article did appear in the Times, and if Mr. Ralston ever became reconciled to his bandit son-in-law his neighbors never learned the fact.

Jesse James was married to his cousin, Miss Zerelda Mimms, in the Autumn of 1874, at the home of his mother in Clay county. Miss Mimms was an orphan, who had lived with a married sister in Kansas City. Being of age there was no one to criticise her act, and she stepped across the threshold of prescribed citizenship to share the perils of an outlaw's life.

The peculiar profession followed by Jesse and Frank James has prevented them from having any permanent residence, and their wives have been compelled, in a measure, to lead a life of seclusion, traveling from place to place, concealing their identity and experiencing few pleasures because of the constant anxiety to which they are subjected. It is understood that Frank is the father of two children, and Jesse finds consolation in two little boys and a baby girl. The outlaw brothers make affectionate husbands and loving and indulgent fathers.

- THE UNION PACIFIC EXPRESS ROBBERY -

The following account of the Union Pacific train robbery is not published in chronological order with other robberies, because it is not certainly known that the James Boys had any connection with it, and in this history of these noted desperadoes we have endeavored to give only such facts as are, sustained by indisputable evidence. It is generally believed, however, that the two noted brothers led the party, and, with their usual shrewdness, succeeded in escaping southward with a large amount of booty. The following letter, written by Jesse James to a former comrade, in March previous to the robbery, is strong presumptive evidence that he and Frank were the planners and executors of the scheme, and that they had it in contemplation even before the raid in- to Minnesota :

Fort Worth, March l0th, '77.

Dear ----,

The boys will soon be ready. As soon as the roads dries up, and the streams runs down, we will drive. We expect to take in a good bunch of cattle. You may look out. There will be lots of bellering after the drive. Remember it's business. The rainge is good, I learn, between Sidney and Dedwood. We may go to pasture somewheres in that region. You will hear of it. Tell Sam to come to Honey Grove, Texas, before the drive seson comes. There's money in the stock. As ever,

Jesse J.

There is a mystery connected with the Union Pacific Railroad robbery which, for more than three years, has remained impenetrable and will, doubtless, continue so to the end of time. The particulars of this daring outrage, gathered principally from newspaper reports at the time, are as follows :

On the l0th day of September, 1877, a party of nine men, well armed and mounted, rode to a point on the Union Pacific R. R. near Ogallala, the capital of Keith county, in the extreme western part of Nebraska. They made no special effort to deceive the people of the town, as the purpose of their visit was never mentioned. On the day following the encampment, one of the party, afterwards known to be Jim Berry, a former resident of the State, went into Ogallala and purchased four large red handkerchiefs and a gallon of whiskey. That night the camp presented a hilarious scene and the wild orgies were continued such an unusually long time that the citizens began to make remarks respecting the character of the nine strange men. Three days afterward the camp was abandoned, none of the citizens knowing which direction the party had taken, so that suspicion was directed against the object of the singular visitors.

On the 1 8th following, the mysterious nine suddenly appeared at a small station called Big Springs, fifteen miles west of Ogallala, where the engines of the Union Pacific railroad almost invariably stop for water. The express train was due from the west at eight o'clock, p. m., and the party disposed themselves, directly after dark, in favorable positions for the work in hand. Promptly upon time the train came thundering up to the station and the engine stopped under the water tank. As the fireman was about to mount the tender for the purpose of directing the water spout, two men wearing red handkerchiefs for masks rushed up toward the engine. For some reason the engineer had a presentiment that some trouble was brewing, so seizing his pistol he stepped to the side of the cab and peered into the darkness. It was too late; the fire through the open furnace door reflected his actions distinctly and in a moment the engineer realized that he was looking down into the fatal depths of four navy revolvers and he and the fireman were forced to surrender and keep quiet.

At the same time the two robbers took possession of the engine, two others, with the same mask of red handkerchiefs, boarded the express car, while the other five commenced discharging their pistols in order to intimidate the passengers. The express messenger made an effort at resistance, but he was struck a desperate blow on the head with a pistol and then forced to deliver up the keys to the Wells Fargo & Co.'s safe. The contents of the safe in gold, silver and currency amounted to; $60,000, besides 300,000 ounces of silver in bars, the latter consigned to the Treasury at Washington. The robbers could not handle the heavy silver bars, so they were compelled to be satisfied with the other contents of the safe and about $2,000 which they took from the passengers. They then permitted the train to go on its way, and having divided their plunder they loaded the coin on three pack-mules and made off with it.

The men had been carelessly masked and a passenger had recognized one of them as a fellow named Joel Collins, who had been passing, for a stock man about that section. From this the railroad detectives obtained information on which to act, and though the pursuit which was organized failed to overtake the outlaws, there was still a hope of recovering some of the treasure. Part of the gang had gone directly south into Kansas, and word was sent along the Kansas Pacific to be on the lookout for them. On the 25th of September, Sheriff Bardsley and ten soldiers were patrolling a section of the road near Buffalo station. They had a description of one of the parties who were expected to strike about that point, and sure enough two men were seen coming down from the north with a pack animal. The soldiers kept out of sight in a ravine near by, and when the men reached the station and were watering their horses the sheriff talked with them long enough to be satisfied that they were the men he was expecting. They only stopped a few minutes, then pushed on south. The sheriff immediately brought out his squad and demanded a halt, calling Collins by name. The men even then did not seem to apprehend that they were known as the train robbers, but on being told to surrender they drew their pistols. This brought a volly from the cavalrymen which killed them both. In the pack was found $20,000 of the gold. Collins' companion's name was Bass, and he is generally supposed to have been the Texas desperado, Sam Bass. The point at which this treasure was first recovered was only 300 miles south of where the robbery occurred. Subsequently the detectives succeeded in tracing several others of the band and making them give up some of the money, but the greater part of it was lost. It was claimed at the time that Jesse and Frank James were along with this band and that they made enough out of the haul to reimburse themselves very well for what they lost on the Northfield trip.

After the fight at Buffalo the remaining bandits separated for the purpose of dividing the trail which was being followed closely, and the hope was indulged for some time that all the robbers would certainly be apprehended. But after the bandits divided the chase was unavailing and the pursuing parties returned to their homes.

Nearly three weeks after the robbery, Jim Berry returned to Mexico, Missouri, with a large sum of money, principally in gold. He had been a resident of the neighborhood but had left for the Black Hills — so he claimed — some months before. He had never borne a good character and was known to be an acquaintance, at least, of the James and Younger Boys and other noted outlaws. Further than this he was seen in Nebraska, near the place of the robbery, by parties who knew him. The exhibition of so much suddenly acquired wealth, together with the circumstances of the express robbery fresh in the memory of every one, created a suspicion on the part of the sheriff of Audrain county that Berry was one of the robbers. He kept his own counsel, however, and waited further developments. They came soon enough. Berry sold several thousand dollars in gold to the Southern Bank at Mexico; exhibited several fine gold watches which he offered to sell at surprisingly low prices, and besides this he exchanged his ordinary habit for the finest clothes he could have made. Another very suspicious circumstance was in the conduct of Berry; he kept himself in secret places and appeared apprehensive of some effort to catch him. The sheriff, Mr. Glascock, now felt certain that his suspicions were founded upon facts. In the middle of October a young fellow by the name of Bozeman Kazey came into Mexico with an order from Berry for a suit of clothes then being made by a tailor of the place. The sheriff learned of this and he at once arrested Kazey, after which a posse consisting of Robert Steele, John Carter, John Coons and Sam Moore was deputized by the sheriff to assist in the capture of Berry. Kazey was compelled to act as guide, and on the 14th of October the official party set out for the haunts of Berry near Kazey's house. They reached the latter's home before daylight on Sunday morning, and leaving their prisoner in the custody of Steele the remainder of the party surrounded the house for the purpose of catching Berry when he should come to obtain the clothes he expected Kazey to bring.

Shortly after daylight sheriff Glascock made a little tour out in the woods, and after skirting a bridle path for some distance he saw Berry hitching his horse preparatory to walking to Kazey's house. The sheriff crept cautiously towards Berry and was within forty feet of him before the latter discovered the officer. Berry then started to run, heedless of the sheriff's cry to halt, and never paused until the second discharge of buckshot from the sheriff's gun tore through his leg and felled him to the ground. Prostrate as he was the bandit tried to draw his pistol, but the sheriff was upon him too quickly. Berry was disarmed and then carried to Kazey's house and surgical aid speedily summoned. On his person was found nearly $1,000 in money, and a fine gold watch and chain.

After the surgeon arrived, Moore, Coons and Steele were left in charge of the wounded man and Kazey, while the sheriff and John Carter rode over to Berry's house to see if new discoveries might not be made.

When they entered the house the sheriff addressed Mrs. Berry and said:

"Mrs. Berry, where is your husband?"

"I am sure I have no idea," she responded; "he has not been at home for several days."

"Then let me inform you," said the sheriff, "that we have just captured him, but in so doing he was badly wounded. You had better go over and see him, at Kazey's house."

Mrs. Berry manifested the greatest grief, and the wailings of the wife and little children quite unnerved the sheriff and his deputy for some time, but they had to do their duty, and, before leaving, the house was thoroughly searched for money and valuables, but nothing was discovered.

On the same afternoon Berry was taken to Mexico in an ambulance and given quarters in the Ringo hotel, where he was attended by the best surgeons in the town. The wound was much more severe than at first supposed. Seven buckshot had penetrated the leg, cutting the arteries and fracturing the tibia bone. His sufferings were excruciating until Monday night when mortification began, and on the following day he died.

At all times Berry positively refused to give the names of his associates in the express robbery, nor did he ever admit his own participation.

The mystery connected with the robbery is found in the impenetrable veil which masks the identity of the robber band. The three who were killed gave no clue as to who were their comrades. In the absence of any proof, judgment being laid entirely upon circumstances and conjecture, it is popularly supposed that the four whose personnel has never been discovered were Sam Bass, Jack Davis and the two James Boys.

- AN INTERVIEW WITH THE YOUNGER BROTHERS -

In the early part of September, 1880, Col. George Gaston, of Kansas City, while spending a summer vacation at Minnetonka and the Minnesota lakes, went to Stillwater for the purpose of seeing the Younger Boys, whom he had known before the war. He was accorded an interview with the imprisoned bandits, the result of which was published in the Kansas City Times of September 6th, from which the following is taken.

This interview is of special value, considering the obscurity which surrounds the shooting of Jesse James by George Shepherd, and the identity of the James Boys in the Northfield robbery.

After describing his introduction to the prison authorities and entrance into the penitentiary, Mr. Gaston proceeds as follows :

" There was a man at the top of the steps to receive us, another official with the conventional bunch of keys. ;Come this way,' said he, and we followed him into a square room with walls and ceilings of stone. There were chairs and we sat down. A door at one side opened and three men walked in. They were Cole, Jim and Bob Younger. They took chairs opposite and directly facing us. They wore the prison garb, and their faces were shaven and their hair cropped close. They looked so genteel, despite their striped clothing, that my nervousness disappeared at once. I told them who I was and whence I came, and introduced my wife. They were very courteous, and bowed, and said they were glad to see me. Jim hitched back in his chair, and addressing my wife, said, laughingly: 'It is so long since we have been permitted to converse with anybody that I don't know as we can talk.' Then followed a desultory conversation. Cole said his health was poor; he complained of suffering from the effects of the wound in his head, received at the time of his capture. The rifle ball entered near the right ear and lodged under the left ear and has never been removed. Jim was shot in the mouth, but there are now no signs of a wound. Bob had his jaw broken, but he too has entirely recovered, and is the handsomest one in the trio. He is the youngest. I remember him as a boy. He has developed into a robust, fine-looking young man. The escape from death these men had at the time of their capture was a miracle. Sixty guns were discharged at once. Cole and Jim lay on the ground— the one with a bullet through the head and the other with a frightful wound in his mouth; Bob's jaw had been broken but he did not fall — he threw up his arms and cried, ' Don't fire again, gentlemen, they're all dead.' And so they were to all appearance. The pursuers picked them up and carried them back. Slowly they began to mend and ultimately they recovered. By pleading guilty to the crime charged they escaped the death penalty and were sentenced to life imprisonment."

"It was really very touching," pursued Col. Gaston, " to hear them talk of the past and of the present. Cole told of his army life — how at the age of nineteen he had been promoted to a captaincy in the Confederate army. He spoke of the murder of his father and of his career since the close of the war.

'My exploits in the army were exaggerated,' said he, ' just as my exploits as an outlaw have been exaggerated. In one instance I have been too highly praised, and in the other grossly wronged.'

"I learned from their own lips the story of their prison life. Cole Younger is a changed man. I found him positively entertaining. He converses with a correctness, fluency and grace that are charming. None of the brothers are compelled to do very much work; they spend a great deal of their time reading in their cells. Jim is reading law books and Bob is studying medicine; Cole seems to have developed a theological turn of mind. These three men are great favorites in the prison — they are looked up to by their companions as sort of demi-gods, creatures immeasurably above the ordinary inmates of the penitentiary."

"The most dreadful feature of their life," said Col. Gaston, "is the fact that though they occupy adjoining cells, they are not permitted to converse with each other. It is only once a month that they can meet and talk to one another, and then only for a few moments. They told me that they prayed earnestly every night that the month might pass quickly. It was touching beyond expression to hear Cole speak of his early days. His misspent life he charges to the faults of his early training. He says he was taught to be ruled by his passions and his passions alone. And as he talked in this vein the tears came into his eyes and I felt that he was indeed a penitent man. He inquired after his old army friends, and I told him what I knew of them and their whereabouts. In the course of our conversation the James Boys were mentioned. 'Do you believe Jesse is dead?' I asked. Cole straightened up, glanced quick as a lightning flash at his brothers on either side of him, and replied, 'He is, if George Shepherd says he is.' I asked him what he meant, and he answered: 'There are sometimes two things alike in the world, and Jesse James and George Shepherd were as near alike as they could be, in character, I mean. Both are quick, nervous and brave. Jesse was so nervous that some- times he did things rashly.' As Cole said this he leveled out his right arm as if he were aiming a pistol. Instantaneously it struck me that he sought to convey the impression that it was Jesse James who perpetrated the Northfield bank murder in a moment of nervous rashness. But the subject was pursued no further. As we left them I felt that we were leaving the most wretched and hopeless of men."

Col. Gaston said that upon his return from his interview with the Youngers, Inspector Reed told him the following, which has never before been made public: "A short time before the Northfield robbery," said the inspector, " I was on my way home to St. Paul from a point in Iowa. I endeavored to secure a Pullman car berth, but found that I had been preceded by two men who had engaged eight berths — the only ones remaining in the car. Later, however, I was informed that I could have one of the berths, as one of the party had failed to put in an appearance. As I sat in that car that evening a man wearing a slouch hat sat directly behind me; in the seat opposite him was a man whom I subsequently discovered was Cole Younger. While thus seated, a big, boisterous countryman, accompanied by his young lady, entered the car and demanded my seat. ' We've been to a dance and are tired ' — that was his apology. I told him that his lady could sit beside me, but I didn't propose to yield my seat to a man. As we were arguing, the man in the slouch hat came over and said to me quietly, 'Why don't you throw the d — d yahoo out of the window?' I made no reply, whereupon he turned to my persecutor and said, 'Here, you d — d loafer, if you don't go about your business I'll throw you off the train. You have been dancing and enjoying yourself and I guess you can stand up awhile. This gentleman has a long way to travel, he has paid for his seat, and by G — d, he shall keep it.' This was quite enough. The big man moved off. The next day, when I was in my bank, in walked the two strange men who had secured the berths on the car. They asked for a bank almanac of last year. I told them we had none to spare ; that the almanacs were issued to banks alone and were really invaluable. Then they asked if they could borrow an almanac of the previous year, and I said yes, if they would be sure to return it. As I passed it over the counter the man in the slouch hat pushed a ten dollar bill toward me. 'Take this,' said he, 'so you will be compensated if we should fail to return the book.' I reminded him he had promised to return the book — that it was part of a file and could not be spared. He insisted, however, that I should retain the money, because something might occur preventing the return of the almanac. Well, the book never came back. Three days later the Northfield Bank was robbed, and shortly afterward I identified Cole Younger as one of the two men who had taken the almanac from me. From the descriptions I have read and the pictures I have seen of the men, I am satisfied that the other man, the man with the slouched hat, the one who came to my rescue on the train, was the notorious outlaw, Jesse James."

- ANECDOTES OF JESSE AND FRANK JAMES -

Sometimes incidents, in themselves trivial, serve to reveal the character of persons connected with them better than those actions which are esteemed as more important. The James Boys are robbers, but nevertheless they are still capable of generous actions. It may be that the remembrance of former days

THE BORDER BANDITS

sometimes disposes their minds to the contemplation of the true, the beautiful and the good in humanity. Jesse James was once baptized, and became a member of a Baptist church in Clay county, Missouri, and it is said that for a considerable time before the war, his conduct was exemplary in the highest degree. But he has since sadly fallen from grace.

Some years ago a tenant on the Samuels farm had a difficulty with the mother of Jesse and Frank. In the heat of passion he denounced the old lady as a liar. Jesse heard of the affair, and, as he always exhibited the warmest affection for his mother, those who knew of the circumstance fully expected that the tenant would be called to account in the usual way by Jesse James. One day the offending tenant was engaged in some domestic labor near his home and adjacent to a corn-field, when suddenly there was a rustling of the dry corn-blades and the next instant the dreaded outlaw leaped his horse over the fence and dashed up to the affrighted citizen with a heavy revolver ready cocked in his hand." I have come to kill you!" he said, at the same time making an ominous motion with the pistol. "Did you not know better than to call my mother a liar? Now, if you want to make your peace with God, you had better be at it." The poor man dropped upon his knees and began to pray. As he proceeded, he became more and more fervent. He asked God to pardon his transgressions and have mercy upon him. Then he commended his loved ones to the protecting care of that Beneficent Being to whom alone they could look, now that he was so soon to be taken away from them. The prayer had become pathetic in its earnestness. As the man proceeded, the hard lines in Jesse James' features relaxed, a shade of sadness stole over his countenance, the muzzle of the pistol was unconsciously lowered, and when the poor frightened farmer had finished, the look of stern resolve was all gone, and the outlaw's pistol had been sheathed. "I cannot kill you thus," he said, "but you must leave the country," and Jesse James wheeled his horse and disappeared as he had come.

What tender reminiscences may have come to Jesse James then? Who can tell? The farmer settled up his affairs and departed from the country soon afterward. His prayer had prevailed with Jesse, and he was spared to his loved ones.

The following anecdote illustrates a trait prominently developed in the character of the outlaws, that is, their willingness to make personal sacrifices to serve anyone whom they regard in a friendly light.

It was during the war. Col. J. H. R. Cundiff, now editor of the St. Louis Times, had been in North Missouri on recruiting service for the Confederate army. The whole country was overrun by Federal soldiers, and the situation of the recruiting officers in that region was perilous. One night Col. Cundiff and several officers visited the house of Mr. Bivens, in Clay county, to obtain food and secure a trusty guide to pilot them out of that region. They learned that a man who resided some miles away was thoroughly acquainted with the by-ways of the country, and could be relied upon in such an emergency. Among all the men present not one knew the way to the house of the person whose services were sought. Miss Bivens, a beautiful and accomplished young lady, at length offered to venture through the darkness and find the guide. Frank James was there, and spoke up, "Oh, no, that is not necessary. Just get on my horse behind me, and I will take you there." The lady, who was at that time very fond of the society of the guerrilla, trusted herself with him, and mounting on the horse behind him they rode away into the night, she indicating to him the route to be taken. Though the roads were guarded by Federals, the gauntlet of pickets was successfully run, and the guide was secured. In those days Frank and Jesse James were esteemed as chivalrous gentlemen, and fit guardians of female honor. Col. Cundiff and his fellow officers were enabled to effect a change of base in comparative security, by the chivalrous services rendered by Frank James.

A story is told of Jesse, which shows that he is not impervious to the appeals of the suffering. One day he was riding in a sparsely settled region in western Texas. Passing through a belt of timber along a stream, he came to the camping place of an emigrant family. There a most distressing spectacle presented itself. The "movers" were people in indigent circumstances, evidently. The old blind horse and poor mule which had drawn the rickety wagon seemed as if their days of toil were about numbered. The man who had driven them had died there under a tree two days before ; the woman was extended on the earth, almost in the agonies of death, and three children, the eldest not more than nine years of age, were crouched around, wailing piteously for something to stay the ravages of hunger.

Jesse saw the miserable condition of the unfortunate emigrant family. He at once dismounted, examined the poor sick woman, administered to her necessities as best he could, and also save the children something to eat from his own small store of supplies. He then bid the woman be of good cheer, promised to come again before night, mounted his horse and galloped away in search of assistance. Ten miles from the camp he found a physician, and two miles further he found a coffin-maker. The first he sent to the lonely camp by the stream, the other he set to work to make a coffin. Then he found a man with a spring wagon and engaged his services. With a supply of things of present necessity, he turned once more toward the camp. Arrived there he prepared the food and made the coffee himself for the unfortunate family. The physician came and prescribed for the sick lady. The undertaker brought the coffin, and the owner of the spring wagon came to remove the bereaved woman and her little ones to a place of shelter. The stranger was buried — where ? — in an untimely tomb.

"No human hands with pious reverence rear'd, But the charmed eddies of autumnal winds, Built o'er his mouldering bones a pyramid Of mouldering leaves in the waste wilderness."

The bereaved one and her orphaned children were carried to the house of a pioneer some miles away, and every want was bountifully provided for, and in a pleasant farm-house she and her children call their own home, she blesses the outlaw, and prays that he may be kept from harm, and that he may be led aright at last.

They tell a story of Frank James which illustrates one peculiar trait of the outlaw's character — that is, his gallantry and knightly devotion to the honor of the fair sex. It happened in Kentucky. There was a young lady resident in a neighborhood where Frank James was a visitor, who had become the victim of the persecutions of a certain fellow whose addresses she had refused. On every possible occasion this low-bred person sought to mortify and insult the young lady, who was unfortunate in not having any near male relatives to champion her cause. One evening, at a social entertainment, the neighborhood coxcomb and instinctive ruffian approached the young lady in a very rude and offensive manner, just at the time when she was engaged in conversation with Frank James, who had been only a few minutes before presented to her. Without apparently noticing the insolence of the person, Frank suggested a promenade, and the young lady took his arm, and they walked away. In no long time they met the rude fellow again, and he took special pains to mortify the young lady, and threw out a gratuitous insult to her escort. Very politely Frank begged the lady to release him for a moment, and he followed the coxcomb. Coming up with him, he quietly requested him to step aside for a moment. The fellow treated the request with contempt, and added insult to injury. 'Without the least show of passion, Frank rejoined the lady and conducted her to her friends. He then calmly awaited his opportunity. It came that same evening. Some persons present knew the desperate character of Frank James, and had told the fellow he was in danger. The fellow attempted quietly to withdraw from the company, but he could not effect his purpose. Frank James had his attention fixed upon the ill-mannered man. When he had gone away from the house some distance, Frank arrested his progress. He had a pistol drawn, which he presented. "You deserve to die," said Frank James in a low, quiet tone, "but on one condition I will spare you, under the circumstances. Will you comply ?" "Name your conditions!" responded the other, now thoroughly frightened "These:" said Frank James, "You must write a note to the lady, abjectly apologizing for your conduct. It must be done before ten o'clock to-morrow, and you must leave the country within five days, and never return. If the letter does not reach the lady by noon to-morrow, I will hunt you until I find you, and then as sure as there is a God in heaven I will kill you. If after five days you are found in this country, I will shoot you. Remember what I say! " The man promised compliance, and Frank James returned to the merry-makers, and no one who saw him suspected that the quiet gentleman had thoughts of bloodshed in his mind. The letter came, and in three days the neighborhood fop had disappeared.

- BASSHAM'S CONFESSION OF THE GLENDALE ROBBERY -

The robbery of the Chicago and Alton train at Glendale, Missouri, as already described, has been surrounded with considerable mystery, concerning the identity of all those engaged in the outrage. The large rewards offered for the apprehension of the robber-band, — amounting to $75,000 — caused a very active search, which resulted, at last, in the capture of Daniel (better known as Tucker) Bassham, under circumstances already related on an earlier page. The writer visited Bassham at the county jail in Kansas City, in October, 1880, for the purpose of interviewing him, with the hope of obtaining some interesting facts concerning the robbery, but though he had made a written confession, he refused to talk on the subject, saying that he had already told too much for his own good.

On the 6th day of November, Bassham was brought into court for trial, having entered a plea of "not guilty," despite his confession, but this plea was soon changed to that of "guilty," and he then threw himself upon the mercy of the court. The following summary of his confession appeared in the Kansas City Journal of November 7th :

"On Monday night preceding the robbery,' said Bass-ham in his confession, "two neighbors of mine came to me and said they had put up a job to rob a train, and wanted me to go in with them. I told them I didn't want nothin' to do with robbin' no train, and wouldn't have nothin' to do with it nohow; but they kept on persuadin' and finally went away, sayin*" they would come back in the morning and that I must go with them. They said a very rich train was coming down on the C. & A., and that we could make a big haul, perhaps $100,000. Wa'al, that kind o' half persuaded me, but still I didn't like to go. They finally told me that Jesse James was arrangin' the thing and that it was sure to be a success.

"Wa'al, then they left, My wife kept pesterin' me to know what was goin' on an' what they wanted, but I didn't like ter let on. I kept thinking about it all night. Of course I'd heerd often of Jesse James and kinder had confidence in him, then I was pretty poor, there wasn't much crops on my place and winter comin' on, and I tell you it looked pretty nice to get a little money just then, no matter whar it kum from. 'Sides I thought to myself, ef I don'l go it'll be done jest the same anyhow, they'll be down on me and ten to one I'll be more likely to git arrested if I ain't thar as if I am.

"Wa'al, I kep' kinder thinkin' it over an' in the morning they came to the house early and eat breakfast, and then went out and loafed around the timber and in the cornfield all day so nobody wouldn't see 'em. In the evenin' they all cum in and we eat supper and then they giv' me a pistol, an' we all got on our horses an' rode off together. We soon met another man on the road, an' when we got to Seaver's school-house, 'bout a mile and a half away from my house, they giv a kind of a whistle for a signal, and two men came out of the timber an' rode up. I was introduced to one of them as Jesse James. This was the first time I had ever seen Jesse James in my life."

"And who was the other?" demanded the prosecutor.

"The other was Ed. Miller, of Clay county."

Bassham said that Jesse James then gave him a shot-gun and furnished each man with a mask, and that they all then rode on in silence toward Glendale. No instructions were given to any one man. When they arrived at Glendale they noticed the light in the store, and Bassham was ordered by Jesse James to go in, capture the inmates and bring them over to the station. On looking in the windows he found the usual crowd of loiterers had left the store and lounged over to the depot to wait for the train to come in. He then went on over to the depot and found the crowd in the waiting-room guarded by one of the men. Jesse James then told him to walk up and down the platform, as the train approached, and fire off his shot-gun in the air as fast as he could. The telegraph operator was forced, at the point of the pistol, to lower the green light and thus signal the train to stop. Jesse James then asked him if there were any loose ties there that they could lay across the track, and he said he "didn't know of any. The men then went and got logs and laid them across the track to obstruct the train if it should take the alarm and not stop for the green light. Meanwhile the train approached; Bassham walked up and down the platform firing off his gun; Jesse James and one of the men jumped into the express car, and Miller jumped on the engine in the manner already described and with which all are familiar. The train was not stopped more than five or six minutes.

As soon as it was over, Jesse James fired off his pistol, which was the signal for all to leave, and they jumped on their horses and rode rapidly for about half a mile, till they came to a deserted log-cabin. Here they alighted and entered. Somebody produced a small pocket-lantern and somebody else struck a match. Jesse James threw the booty down on a rude table in the middle of the compartment, divided it out, and shoved each man a pile as they stood round the table. Bassham's share was between $800 and $900. Jesse then said : "Now, each one of you fellows go home and stay there. Go to work in the morning, and keep your mouths shut, and nobody will ever be the wiser. This country will be full of men in the morning hunting for me and you."

It will be observed that in the confession, as reported, only the names of Jesse James and Ed. Miller appear, when it is now positively known that the gang comprised not less than six persons. The confession implicated two of the most respectable farmers in Jackson county, Kit Rose and Dick Tally, one a brother-in-law and the other a cousin of the Younger brothers, both of whom were arrested, but soon afterward released, as not a scintilla of evidence could be discovered corroborating Bassham's disjointed statements. The other party, who Bassham swears was connected with the robbery (and in this he certainly guessed rightly), was Jim Cummings, who shot George Shepherd in the affair at Short Creek.

In November last (1880), Bassham was brought into court with a plea of "not guilty," notwithstanding his confession, but he had so completely convicted himself that the plea was withdrawn, and he threw himself upon the mercy of the court. He was then sentenced to the penitentiary for a period of ten years. Since his confinement at Jefferson City, there has been a considerable change of opinion respecting his guilt, and there is no doubt but that now a large majority of persons believe Bassham innocent of any complicity with the train robbery, and that his so-called confession was the result of influences which the writer does not wish to assume the responsibility of naming.

The James Boys Heard From Again.

THE TRAIN ROBBERY AT WINSTON, MO., JULY 15, 1881.

FIFTY THOUSAND DOLLARS REWARD OFFERED FOR THE ARREST OF THE GUILTY PARTIES.

The Border Outlaws, those whose crimes began with the hot and infectious breath of war and left a bloody trail around Jackson, Clay and Harrison counties, Missouri, still survive to wreak a desperate vengeance, and live by tributes levied upon corporations and individuals. Many of the old band, it is true, have been palsied by death, dying, belted and armed, by a fate anticipated, but like the excision of a cancer, the germs have remained from which a new growth has constantly developed to harass the State and disorder society.

The James boys, aside from their reckless courage, are possessed of extraordinary capabilities, cunning resource, domineering resolution, woods-craft and dash. As if by a thorough consideration of the beneficial result to be secured thereby, they first terrorized the people of Western Missouri, and then heroized themselves in the eyes of those whose political sympathies were in consonance with their own. Thus upon the one side the people were afraid to attempt any punishment of the outlaws or give information of their rendezvous ; while upon the other they were protected and encouraged without concealment. It is for these reasons that the James boys and their confreres have eluded every pursuit and been able to give free license to their impious passions.

There are peculiar features, however, connected with every outrage perpetrated by the James gang which readily manifest them in the deed. Among these several distinguishing features are : their appearance in the vicinity where the robbery occurs some days before its accomplishment; the thorough maturity of their plans ; the wearing of long linen dusters; unhesitating disposition to commit murder; a splendid mount; the invariable sack carried in which to deposit the plunder; the line of retreat always southward when the robbery has been committed north of Clay county, and vice versa ; masks of red handkerchiefs, and the ease with which pursuit is eluded. In addition to these unmistakable peculiarities, another fact is particularly noticeable, viz: within twenty-four hours after the James boys commit a robbery, Mrs. Samuels, their mother, never fails to make her appearance in Kansas City, the purpose of these visits being undoubtedly to discover what means are employed looking to the apprehension of the gang, and gather up any and all such information as might prove serviceable in aiding the escape of her sons.

Considering well all these points of evidence, any shrewd analyzer of human nature can readily determine whether or not either of the James boys was connected with any robbery reported.

On the night of July 15th, 1881, an outward going passenger train from Kansas City over the Chicago, Rock Island & Pacific Railroad was robbed at Winston Station, Daviess County, Missouri, under the following circumstances: The train left Kansas City at 6:30 p. m., in charge of William Westfall, the conductor; Wolcott, the engineer, and Charlie Murray, express messenger. The train consisted of six coaches and a sleeper, all of which were well filled with passengers. Reaching Cameron, a stop was made for supper, and when the train started off two men were observed to jump on, each of whom wore a large red bandana handkerchief around his neck, partly concealing his features. Nothing indicative of the robbers' intentions, however, transpired until the train reached Winston, at 9:30 p. m., at which station four men took passage, each having his face covered with a handkerchief identical with those worn by the two that got on at Cameron, and all wearing long, linen dusters. Getting under headway again, the train had proceeded nearly one mile from Winstoit when suddenly, as Conductor Westfall appeared in the second car to collect tickets, the passengers were startled by the largest of the robbers rising from his seat and shouting out in a loud voice, "A11 aboard !" which was the signal for action. The large man, heavily masked with a red handkerchief, as were all the others, seven in number, thrust out a large pistol, and saying to Westfall, " You are the man I want," fired. The ball struck Westfall in the arm, producing only a flesh wound, but as the wounded man turned to run out of the car two more shots were fired by the same robber without effect. This bad shooting seemed to exasperate another one of the outlaws, who gave an exhibition of his skill by shooting Westfall in the brain, killing him instantly, the body falling off the platform onto the ground.

While this unprovoked murder was being perpetrated three others of the outlaw gang rushed through the cars toward the engine. Wild confusion followed, and a stone mason named J. McCulloch, from Iowa, who had been working near Winston, attempted to get out of the baggage car as the robbers entered it. Suspecting that he was either the engineer or intent upon raising an alarm, one of the outlaws shot him dead and pushed his body off the train, which had now come to a stop.

The robbers then went about their business of robbing, two mounting the engine, three were left to guard the passengers, while the remaining two made for the express car. Mr. Murray, the express agent, hearing firing and suspecting the real cause, made a hasty attempt to close and lock the doors of his car, which had been left open, owing to the oppressively warm weather, but while he was thus engaged one of the robbers jumped through the partly closed door and grabbing Murray, struck him a violent blow on the head with his pistol, at the same time saying, "Open up, d — n you, or I'll kill you!" Looking into the muzzles of two large pistols, Murray was forced to comply, and delivered up the safe keys. The treasure box was quickly opened and its contents extracted, consisting of coin and currency to the amount of $8,000 or $10,000, which was thrown into a sack the outlaws carried for the purpose. The train was then started up by one of the robbers, but after proceeding a few hundred yards stopped again and the bold free-booters jumped off, running for their horses which were tied in a clump of trees less than one hundred yards from the track. They did not take the time to untie their horses, but cut the reins, and mounting, rode in a half circuit around Cameron, then took a course almost due south. They crossed the Missouri river near Sibley's Landing, in couples, having divided up immediately after the robbery was consummated.

On the morning following the robbery, an examination of the immediate vicinity about where the train was stopped, resulted in finding where the robbers had tied their horses, and there, lying on the ground, was found the following letter :

Kansas City, July 12.

Charlie — I got your letter to-day, and was glad to hear that you had got everything ready in time for the 15th. We will be on hand at that time. Bill will be with us. We will be on the train; don't fear. We will be in the smoker at Winston. Have the horses and boys in good fix for fast work. We will make this point again on the night of the i6th. All is right here. Frank will meet us at Cameron. Look sharp and be well fixed. Have the horses well gaunted, for we may have some running to do. Don't get excited, but keep cool till right time.

THE BORDER BANDITS

Wilcox or Wolcott will be on the engine. I think best to send this to Kidder. Yours time and through death.

Slick.

After receiving the first particulars of the robbery by telegraph, I went to Kansas City, and from thence to various points in the vicinity, for the purpose of prosecuting an investigation with the view of discovering, if possible, who the outlaws were, where they came from, whither they went, and how the authorities prosecuted the pursuit. From these efforts I am prepared to state, with circumstantial positiveness, that Frank James and Jim Cummings were the parties who planned, and with the aid of their confreres, executed the robbery at Winston, and that the proof may not be wanting, the following several facts are recited :

A few weeks ago I received a letter from Frank James, acknowledging the receipt of a copy of "Border Outlaws," which I sent to him by a relative. Shortly after its receipt, this same relative, who is known to be in communication with Frank James, visited St. Louis and confidentially conferred with my publisher upon the advantages which we might mutually reap by a sudden stimulation in the sale of "Border Outlaws," for which he was then acting as agent. His proposition embraced a statement that Frank James and Jim Cummings were at that time in Missouri planning a campaign; that a large robbery would soon be consummated, attended with some startling results. All these facts he agreed to furnish us the very moment the robbery should be completed, comprising the names of those engaged, how they had organized, where assembled, cause for their acts, etc., provided my publisher would give him a certain sum of money. The incentive on our part to comply with his proposition was in securing this reliable information, which might be added as an appendix to a new edition of "Border Outlaws," and issued contemporaneously with the first newspaper reports, thereby creating a largely increased demand for the book. Of course there appeared so much doubt involved in this singular proffer, and the proposition within itself being of such questionable character, that it was rejected with little consideration of the probability of a robbery such as was declared about to take place. At this time, however, the assertions then made assume an interest which throws much light upon the problem, " Who committed the robbery?"

But this is not all the evidence I am in possession of respecting this latest adventure of the old gang. In pursuing my investigations I visited Olathe, Kas., twenty miles south of Kansas City, and there found a gentleman well known in that town, who had met Frank James walking on the south side of Olathe's public square, well-armed, on the 10th inst., or only five days before the robbery occurred. It was not a mistaken identity, for the gentleman in question was raised within four miles of the present residence of the James boys' parents, and was for years upon terms of the greatest social intimacy with them, attending the same school, participating in the same sports, and in later years meeting with them as old acquaintances. Being well acquainted myself in Olathe, I can positively state that this information regarding the presence of Frank James in the town referred to is true beyond all doubt. But what his business was" or when he left, I could not ascertain.

Within eighteen hours after the robbery, Mrs. Samuels appeared in Kansas City, evidently for the purpose of collecting such information as might be useful to Frank James and his confederates. She talked freely of the robbery, but protested, with repeated declarations, that both Frank and Jesse were dead, going so far in her assertions as to say that Frank died three years ago of consumption, in Texas. What she hoped to gain by a claim so easily disproved it is difficult to conjecture.

From the best evidence attainable, the gang who robbed the Rock Island and Pacific train, among whom were Frank James, Ed. Miller, Jim Cummings and Dick Little, after leaving the train, mounted their horses and rode south westwardly until they reached the outskirts of Cameron, when they turned and took to the brush again, making directly for the Missouri river, which they crossed near Sibley's landing, and on the following evening, the 16th, they certainly passed through Sni-a-bar township of Jackson county, and, taking a southwestwardly course, continued on to the Indian Territory. The party, however, did not remain intact, but divided up into couples, so as to destroy the trail which so large a number as seven riders would have made conspicuous. They were at no time so far apart, though, but that a prearranged signal would have concentrated the outlaws.

It is a singular fact that with all the atrocious crimes credited to the James boys and their confederates, there was not so much as one dollar of reward offered at the time of the Winston robbery, although at one time the rewards offered by the State and railroad and express companies aggregated $75,000. During Gov. Hardin's administration nearly all the rewards offered by the State were withdrawn, then the private corporations that had suffered so seriously at the hands of the bold knights of the road withdrew the incentives they had advertised, after which Gov. Phelps wiped out the few figures remaining.

On the 26th of July, eleven days after the train robbery at Winston, Governor Crittenden visited St. Louis and called a meeting of leading railroad officials in the gentlemen's parlor of the Southern Hotel. The call was responded to by representatives from nearly all the principal roads running into Kansas City and St. Louis, and upon assembling plans were thoroughly discussed for the apprehension of the notorious outlaws who have wrought such injury to Missouri's reputation. The session lasted for nearly four hours, though there was the greatest unanimity of feeling and disposition, and at its conclusion the Governor expressed much gratification at the results. The power of the Executive is limited by law, so that he could not offer a State reward sufficiently large to accomplish the arrest of such notorious desperadoes as the James boys and their gang are known to be, so he conceived the excellent idea of calling upon the interested railroad corporations for needful assistance. The result of this conference was the immediate issuance of a proclamation by Governor Crittenden, in which an aggregate reward of fifty-five thousand dollars ($55,000) was offered for the capture of the seven train robbers, or five thousand dollars for the arrest and conviction of each one of the robber gang. This proclamation was supplemented by the offer of an additional reward of five thousand dollars each for the arrest of Jesse and Frank James, and delivery of their bodies to the sheriff of Daviess County, and a further reward of five thousand dollars each for their conviction.

The public which, generally speaking, believe that Jesse James was never shot by Geo. Shepherd, credit the assertion made by many that both Frank and Jesse were engaged in the Winston robbery, but whatever the impression, this belief is undoubtedly without foundation. The most intimate acquaintances of Jesse James, those who have seen him many times during the past year, are ready to make oath that he is a paralytic from the effect of Geo. Shepherd's shot; in fact, in a demented, helpless condition.

At one time arrangements were about perfected, through the outlaws' cousin, by which I was to have a personal interview with Frank James, each of us to be accompanied by a friend, but owing to some engagement, which was never explained to me, that meeting never occurred. Frank, after receiving a copy of "Border Outlaws," expressed a desire to make a statement, with the understanding that I would embody it in all subsequent editions of the book; this I agreed to do, but I am now convinced that the intended interview was not granted because of the engagement which was kept at Winston.

JAMES BOYS

DEEDS OF DARING

A COMPLETE RECORD OF THEIR LIVES AND DEATHS
NARRATING MANY OF THEIR STIRRING ADVENTURES,
WHICH HAVE ONLY RECENTLY COME TO LIGHT, AND
WHICH HAVE NEVER APPEARED IN PRINT BEFORE

BY

JAMES EDGAR

PREFACE

Stories of the life of the highwayman, bandit and train robber, with the romance of deadly adventure entwined about his life, hare ever fascinated the novelist and reader alike, and the tales of his daring have ever proven of absorbing interest to both young and old, despite the fact that his deeds were criminal, and on the principal of 'the mills of the gods grind slowly, but they grind exceedingly fine' his punishment by imprisonment or death surely awaits him at the end of his career.

Robin Hood and his merry band of robbers of Nottingham Forest have been the theme of song and story for a century or mere. Dick Turpin and Jack Sheppard, the dashing highwaymen, have furnished material for many tales of romance and daring. Captain Kidd and Blackboard, the pirates, have furnished material for volumes of thrilling reading, and so through all times and ages the desperado has alike horrified and fascinated, in many instances combining some good with bad in the roving, dangerous life he led.

Among all the annals of soul-stirring adventure and desperate achievements in the history of the highwaymen of the world the James Brothers Jesse and Frank undoubtedly stand at the head. They committed more daring robberies than all the other outlaws of the world combined, and while they lived, a perfect reign of terror prevailed those whom circumstances placed them at their mercy.

But the last of the bad men of the West have passed away. Nevermore will the equal of the James Boys be heard of again. This latest and perhaps last book of their lives will recount in new form many of their famous accomplishments as robbers of high degree, and will perpetuate some of their deeds which have come to light of recent years and which have not appeared in print before. It will appear in the form of a galaxy of short stories now so popular with magazine readers each a complete narrative in itself; an act from the drama of real life, which is stranger than fiction.

James Edgar
The Author

JAMES BOYS DEEDS OF DARING

THE JAMES BOYS' EARLY HISTORY

BIRTHPLACE OF THE FAMOUS OUTLAWS AND THE HISTORY OF THEIR EARLY CHILDHOOD AND GROWTH TO MANHOOD

THEY WERE A PREACHER'S SONS

HOW THEY BECAME OUTLAWS IN THE WEST.

Strange as it may seem the James Boys Frank and Jesse the most desperate and murderous of all bandits, were the sons of a minister of the gospel, whose early training of them was of the best and whose home influences were in no manner such as would have set them on a bad career.

Frank was the oldest of the two and was born in Scott County, Kentucky, in 1845. His folks later moved to Clay County, Missouri, where Jesse was born in 1849. Before he was a year old his father became enthused with the gold fever, and, bidding his little family good-bye, went west to seek his fortune. He never returned, but died on the Pacific Coast. His name was the Rev. Robert James and he was a regularly ordained minister of the Baptist faith.

But though he was responsible for these inhuman plunderers of their fellow-men being brought into existence, he was in no way responsible for their education in the school of crime, or the shaping of their desperate characters.

It were idle to discuss what might have been the career of Frank and Jesse James had not death deprived them of a father's care and admonition in early infancy. From what little is known of the life and character of that father it is safe to conclude that it would have made but little if any difference to the boys; for the mother was the ruling spirit in that household, and in any event would have exerted the dominant influence in shaping the characters of her sons.

An old proverb says, "Like father, like son," but history establishes the fact that most of the remarkable men that the world has produced received their characters from their mother. Frank and Jesse James were no exception to the rule.

In many respects Mrs. Zerelda Cole James was a remarkable woman, and it is probably as natural that she should have given birth to Frank and Jesse James as that Cornelia, the famous Roman matron, should have been the mother of the Gracchi.

Mrs. James has been represented by certain self-styled "compilers" of the lives and exploits of the James boys as being little short of a brutal, uncivilized Amazon. Such misrepresentation is uncalled for as it is untrue. No one who knows anything about the personal life and character of the noted bandits' mother would make any such outrageous, because unfounded, assertion.

Mrs. James belonged to a respectable and well-to-do family, and though by no means a model of meekness, she could not truthfully be called a termagant.

While she could not be considered of a refined and gentle disposition, she had the reputation among her neighbors of being a kind and helpful friend and an affectionate and only too indulgent mother.

If, like the famous Roman matron, her character was cast in an iron mold, and her temper and bearing were stern and imperious, so too, like the Roman mother, she idolized her sons and in her heart said of them, "These are my jewels." Indeed, so wrapped up in her boys was she that she believed that, like a king, they could do no wrong.

This rare but misplaced confidence which their mother had in them was fully reciprocated by them, for although no matter how bad they became, they always respected and loved her whom was responsible for their being. This was their one virtue, linked as it was with a thousand crimes.

Being left by the death of her husband with a family of four children, two boys and two girls, to provide for single handed, Mrs. James had to struggle pretty hard for a number of years. She sent the children to school, and did the best she knew how to train them up in the way they should go. But as she lacked tenderness and feeling herself, she failed to inspire it in her children, the boys especially.

Then came the outbreaks among the mountaineers, who formed themselves into factions, and between which factions feuds ensued. The seeds of the war were brewing and the hearts of the young James boys became imbued with the spirit of war.

Everybody in the border counties sided with one or the other party of marauders. The excitement was intense. The mother of the James Boys was distinctly Southern in her sentiments, and her boys were with her "tooth and toenail" at the outbreak of the war, and Frank and Jesse James were among the first to join the guerrillas.

At the beginning of hostilities, in 1861, the border warfare increased in virulency, and the sympathizers were forced into extreme measures. The "Border Ruffians" were now termed guerrillas, among the most noted of whose leaders was Charles William Quantrell.

Quantrell is said to have been the most heartless, blood-thirsty marauder that ever lived in any country.

As Frank and Jesse James were introduced to guerrilla life and started on their career of crime by this celebrated guerrilla chieftain, it may be of interest to the reader to know something of his history and the causes which made him the inhuman dare-devil ruffian he was.

Charles William Quantrell was born in Hagerstown, Maryland, July 20, 1836. While Charles was yet a boy in his teens his father died, and shortly afterward the family moved to Cleveland, Ohio, where Charles and a brother several years older attended school. Shortly after they arrived in Cleveland the mother died; the older brother moved to Kansas, but Charles continued to attend school in the Ohio city. For several years he paid his way in Cleveland by doing odd jobs out of school hours, and was progressing finely in his studies. His habits were good and he was respected by all who knew him. In 1856 his brother wrote him from Kansas that he was about to start on a trip to California to seek his fortune in the new Eldorado of the Pacific coast, and he would like to have Charles accompany him. Although much attached to his friends in Cleveland, and anxious to complete his education in the splendid schools of that city, Charles had such affection and confidence in his brother that he could not resist the latter's appeal. So, bidding his friends and schoolmates good-bye, young Quantrell joined his older brother in Kansas.

The exciting accounts of the dare-devil doings of Quantrell and his chosen band of guerrillas, which the papers published with glaring headlines at the commencement of the war, sent a thrill of feverish excitement through the nation, and many a youth in Missouri burned to be enrolled under the folds of the black flag of Quantrell's guerrillas.

Jesse James was among them. His brother Frank was already with Quantrell. Jesse made repeated and persistent efforts to join the band, but was rejected by Quantrell on account of his youth, he being then but little over fourteen years of age.

The sympathies of his mother and step-father, Dr. Samuels, whom she had recently married, were all with the South. Mrs. Samuels, especially, was loyal to the Confederacy. By various means she managed to learn of the movements of the Union troops, and whenever the information was important she would mount Jesse upon a fleet horse and send him to Quantrell. So open and obnoxious was Mrs. Samuels in her demonstrations to Southern love that the Federal militiamen began to notice it. From mere notice suspicion was aroused.

Her house was watched and it became known that several secret midnight conclaves had been held there.

The part played by Jesse and the open and decided expressions frequently made by Dr. Samuels and his decidedly demonstrative wife greatly excited the Federal soldiers, and it was determined to make an example of the family. Accordingly, in June, 1862, a company of Missouri militia approached the Samuels homestead, which is near Kearney, in Gay county, and, first meeting Dr. Samuels, they addressed him in language that could leave no doubt in his mind that they meant to carry affairs to the bitter end. It was in vain he pleaded that he was leading a peaceful farmer's life, and didn't desire to be mixed up in the strife of the time. They told him what he knew much better than they did that he and his whole family were in secret alliance with Quantrell and his followers. Frank was at the camp, Susie was away from home, Jesse was plowing in the fields. Mrs. Samuels was nowhere to be seen. But she saw all that was going on, just the same.

They had not come unprepared for their work. A strong rope was produced, with which he was securely pinioned, and then led away from the house a distance of about one hundred yards. Here the rope was fastened in a noose around his neck, while the other end was thrown over the limb of a tree, and several men hastily drew him up and left him suspended to choke to death. Mrs. Samuels, however, had followed stealthily, and the moment the militia had departed she rushed to the rescue of her husband, whom she hastily cut down, and by patient nursing brought him back to life. The James Boys made good their escape before the invaders could capture them, but determined on revenge, and to get it was ever afterward their constant thought.

When Quantrell organized his band of Border Ruffians to avenge the murder of his brother he never dreamed that he would ever have to fight the soldiers of the United States in addition to the murderous Jayhawkers. But when the Civil War began the Jayhawkers, being Abolitionists, were all ranged on the side of the Union, while the "Ruffians," being pro slavery, sided with the South, and Quantrell and his band found themselves more often pitted against the boys in blue than against the Jayhawkers.

The guerrilla chieftain accepted the situation, however, without faltering in the least, and entered the service of the Confederacy with greatest enthusiasm. Up to the time when young Jesse James was accepted as a member of the band the guerrillas had been engaged in but few skirmishes, their services consisting chiefly in small foraging expeditions, making themselves thoroughly acquainted with the topography of the country, preparatory to engaging in more effective measures.

The town of Richfield, on the northern bank of the Missouri River, was occupied by a squad of thirty Federal soldiers, under the command of Captain Sessions. Quantrell determined to attack this garrison, and detailed a small company of his most intrepid guerrillas to make a dashing raid on the town.

Frank and Jesse James were among the number, Frank James leading the attack.

The garrison was taken by surprise and a desperate conflict ensued.

Ten of the Federals were killed, including Captain Sessions, and the remainder taken prisoners.

When the attacking party returned to their company Jesse James was sent out with orders from Quantrell to scour the counties adjoining Clay and locate the militia.

After passing through Clinton County he paid a short visit to his mother, who received him with many manifestations of pleasure, and then began to unload herself of the valuable information she had gathered for the benefit of the guerrillas. She told him that the attack on Richfield had resulted in massing the militia for a determined stroke, and that the troops were concentrating near that point; that Plattsburg had been almost entirely relieved of its garrison and would fall an easy prey to the guerrillas if they chose to profit by the opportunity.

Jesse lost no time in communicating the situation to Quantrell, and, accordingly, three days after the capture of the squad of militiamen at Richfield Captain Scott took fifteen men and silently stole upon Plattsburg, which he found defended by less than a score of Federals.

Shortly after the scheme materialized to sack the town of Lawrence, Kansas. Quantrell consulted with his chief lieutenants, the James boys, and they heartily backed him up in the scheme, Quantrell did not neglect to inform his followers of the danger such an undertaking involved; that their road would be infested with militia, the forces of which would be daily augmented when the first intimation of the purposes of the guerrillas should be made known; that it would be ceaseless fighting and countless hardships, and many would be left upon the prairies to fester in the sun. He then called his command to arms and acquainted every man with the decision in the following speech:

> "Fellow-soldiers, a consultation just held with several of my comrades has resulted in a decision that we break camp tomorrow and take up a line of march for Lawrence, Kansas; that we attack that town, and. if pressed too hard, lay it in ashes. This undertaking, let me assure yon, is hazardous in the extreme. The territory through which we must pass is full of enemies, and the entire way will be beset by well-armed men, through whom it will be necessary for us to carve our way. I know full well that there is not a man in my command who fears a foe; that no braver force ever existed than it is my honor to lead; but you have never encountered danger so great as we will have to meet on our way to Lawrence; therefore, let me say to you, without doubting in the least your heroism, if there are any in my command who would prefer not to stake their lives in such a dangerous attempt, let them step outside the ranks."

At the conclusion of Quantrell's remarks a shout went up from every man, "On to Lawrence!" Not a face blanched, but, on the other hand, there was but one desire, to lay waste the city on the Kaw.

On the following day the order was given to "mount," and with that dreadful black flag streaming over their heads the command, two hundred strong, turned their faces to the west. As they crossed the Kansas line at the small town of Aubrey, in Johnson county, Quantrell compelled three men, whom he found sitting in front of a small store kept by John Beeson, to accompany him as guides.

The command passed through Johnson county midway between Olathe and Spring Hill, and through the northern part of Franklin County. When they reached Cole creek, eight miles from Lawrence, the three guides were taken into a clump of thick woods and shot by Jesse and Frank James.

One of the party, an elderly man, begged piteously to be spared, reminding his executioners that he had never done them any wrong, but his prayers for mercy ended in the death rattle as a bullet went crashing through his neck.

Quantrell had been agreeably mistaken concerning the resistance he expected to encounter. Not a foe had yet appeared, but he never permitted a person to pass him alive. No less than twenty-five persons whom he met in the highway after getting into Kansas had been shot, and yet he avoided the public roads as much as possible.

Early in the morning of August 21 Quantrell and his band came in sight of the fated town. The sun was just straggling above the undulations of the prairie and the people of the place were beginning to resume the duties of a newly-born day.

With a cry which froze the blood of everyone in the town who heard it, Quantrell and his two hundred followers descended upon the place with pistol, sword and firebrand. Their work of devastation soon completed, they moved on other scenes of war and bloodshed.

Quantrell was the most heartless of all. What cared he for the glory won to his name by the sacking of the unprotected and defenseless city? It would bring him not fame, but infamy. And, indeed, because of that inhuman act he has ever since been known as "Butcher Quantrell."

Disgusted with the extent of their own hellish propensities, Quantrell and his band of murderers hastily retraced their steps, but they were terribly harassed during the entire return march by the Kansas militia and federal troops that hurriedly concentrated and went in pursuit of them.

Just how many men engaged in this pursuit of the retreating guerrillas is not definitely known, but the force has been reliably estimated at fully seven thousand, and nothing but hard marching, determined fighting and an endurance that has never been equaled saved the guerrillas from total destruction. At Black Jack, about fifteen miles from Lawrence, a stand was made, and some brisk fighting occurred. The guerrillas took to cover in a large barn which stood at the edge of an orchard.

Several assaults were made to dislodge them, but in vain. The horses of the guerrillas were suffering severely, however, and realizing that without horses they would be unable to get out of Kansas, the guerrillas made a desperate charge, in which thirty-two of the militia were killed, and a panic was the result. But the guerrillas did not care to follow up the victory, as every moment was precious. The militia were swarming and closing in upon them rapidly, and it was only by the rarest stroke of fortune that Quantrell and his men ever escaped from Kansas. When once more safely across the border on their old stamping ground in Missouri, the guerrillas disbanded and once more mingled among their friends and sympathizers in Jackson and Clay counties. When the Civil War had ended, and the restoration of peace had forced the guerrillas out of existence, the monotony of a peaceful life began to pall on the James boys, and they quite naturally took up the wild existence which subsequently made them the most feared desperadoes of America.

JAMES BOYS DEEDS OF DARING

THE JAMES BOYS' FIRST LESSON IN CRIME

AS SMALL BOYS THEY WERE FOND OF TAKING ANIMAL LIFE AND CAUSING DUMB BEASTS TO SUFFER
THEIR CAREER OF CRIME BEGAN WITH PETTY LARCENY AND THEIVING

"As the twig is bent so the tree inclines."

The boyhood of the James brothers was not in accord with the usual ethics of happy childhood. They delighted not in the innocent sports and pastimes usually sought by boys of their tender ages. They associated with but few boys of the neighborhood where they were raised, and even these few they seemed to shun at times. They were ardent in woodcraft, and spent much of their time in the forest hunting squirrels and birds and such. They seemed early in life to take an inhuman delight in bringing about death and suffering. They would not even wring the neck of a wounded bird to bring an end to its sufferings, but would watch its agonized struggles with glee and let it die slowly, that their cruel delight might be prolonged. When they were scarcely big enough to handle a firearm, they each owned a shotgun and knew how to use it

Later they purchased revolvers, which they constantly carried. They robbed when their money ran short for arms or ammunition. Poultry, eggs, livestock or anything else they could lay hands on became their legitimate prey - or at least they considered it so. When anything disappeared the people used to say right away, "The James boys again." Thus they grew up to manhood in an atmosphere of lawlessness and crime, with little distinction between right and wrong, good or bad. They were wild over firearms, and became the dead shots they were by reason of constant practice in the woods. When they were fourteen years old they could cut the top off a parlor match with a rifle ball almost as far away as they could see it. Their skill with the revolver was remarkable, and they were famed the country round as the boy dead shots.

Thus all through their youth they led wild, aimless lives, spending much of their time in the woods and seeking nothing in the line of work by which to earn a livelihood. They hunted, fished, stole whatever they could lay hands on easily, and spent their time generally in idleness and mischief. Much of their idle time was spent in card playing, and they became amateur gamblers in a sort of a small way. Much of their time was spent with men of unsavory reputations much older than themselves, and from whom they soon learned what deviltry they had not already educated themselves in. They read all the trashy novels they could get their hands on, and gloried in the old stories of lawlessness and vandalism. Their ideal was the road agent or highwayman, and it is little wonder they grew up to follow the course of crime they adopted. Many acts of vandalism are attributed to them, and the poisoning of neighbors' live stock, the mutilation of their crops and live stock and other misdemeanors of similar character were charged against them in many instances. They were arrested several times in their boyhood days, but on account of their youth and promises to do better in future they were released. They had not the slightest regard for their word, and as soon as released went right back to their waywardness. They were young men when the war broke out, and just as naturally as ducks take to water did they fall in with the guerrillas, which were on land just about what the pirates were on the high seas. While ostensibly an arm of the Confederate Army, they were a lot of freebooters and cut-throats, who respected the property of no one and used the gray uniform as a cloak to mask their villainy and crime. In their youthful days they associated much with the Younger brothers, with whom they quite naturally formed an alliance later, making up a quartette of the worse desperadoes the country ever knew.

JAMES BOYS DEEDS OF DARING

THE JAMES BOYS AS BANK ROBBERS

THEY FREQUENTLY VARIED THE MONOTONY OF LOOTING TRAINS IN ORDER TO CARCK A RICH BANK NOW AND THEN

Life at best is monotonous and causes desperadoes engaged in lawlessness to seek other pastimes where gold is in sight. Bank robbing offers a most alluring diversion, for which reason, perhaps, the James Boys frequently flitted from the prairie to the cities and small towns, where they put in their time robbing a few banks. This they did to recuperate their frenzied finances and to keep them in practice, perhaps. The notion of these bank robberies took them all of a sudden as a rule, and they were usually committed on the spur of the moment, little preparation being made for the raid and but small planning having been done in advance.

One of their most successful robberies was that of the Bank of Gallatin, Mo., in 1869. It was a dark and gloomy day in December, when the bank was flush with funds, the farmers having nearly all deposited the proceeds of their big grain crops and having drawn little or no money out for spring planting and other expenses. Without a moment's warning a gang of mounted men rode wildly down the main street of the little town, firing revolvers and driving everybody into the houses on pain of instant death. Several men who dared their fire dropped dead in the street and others staggered to places of safety badly wounded.

Stopping in front of the bank, the marauders dismounted and, with their revolvers in their hands, dashed inside, leaving two heavily-armed members of the gang to mind the horses. The cashier was held up at the point of a revolver, and when he made a move to slam the vault doors, but was shot dead in his tracks. The paying teller was wounded and the other clerks and attaches driven into a room and held prisoners while the others looted the bank. They secured only about $7,000, owing to their hurry and the fact that they overlooked several hundred thousand dollar bills, which were in a secret compartment of the vault, which they did not know of. Cursing their luck at getting so little, they fled outside, and, mounting their horses, rode away, still firing at everyone they saw out of sheer malice.

Before they left they openly announced themselves as the James robbers and threatened to return some other time, when the bank was more well burdened with cash, and clean it out again.

Perhaps more by reason of the cold murders and audacity of the affair than the rather small proceeds of the robbery the people demanded that the James

Boys and their gang of villains be rounded up, and while the Governor was at first tardy to act, public opinion at last became so strong that orders were at last issued that they must be run down.

Amongst those who believed most thoroughly in the guilt of the James brothers was Capt. John Thomason, of Clay County, Missouri. He thought that it was no use in the world to deal in half measures with these miscreants. He was persuaded that there would be no peace, no security for life or property, as long as they were at large, hence he put himself at the head of a band of men who were resolved at all hazards and at any cost to arrest Frank and Jesse James and bring them to justice. Captain Thomason had served during the war on the Confederate side; he had also sustained the office of Sheriff of Clay County to the great admiration of the county at large. He carried with him great moral influence as a man who was the outspoken friend of law and order. No man in Clay County could command a larger following for any good purpose. The James brothers were made acquainted with the purpose of Captain Thomason; they knew the man they had to deal with, but they were not in the least dismayed. They went out to meet him and his band. The meeting is said to have taken place near the home of the Samuels. Captain Thomason demanded their immediate unconditional surrender.

Of course, as may be well supposed, they laughed the demand to scorn, and seemed disposed to treat the whole affair as a huge farce. When the thing assumed a move serious aspect and Captain Thomason hinted at force, then there was nothing for it but to meet fire with fire. And the guerrilla boys proved themselves ready for the encounter. A shot from Jesse's pistol brought down Captain Thomason's horse dead under him. The fray lasted only a few minutes.

The pursuing party felt that to proceed would only be to endanger life, with little prospect of capturing their prey, so they returned, and Frank and Jesse rode back home scathless and triumphant.

A whole year or more had passed since the last bank raid, and the public mind began to rest in a sense of security. Besides which, the managers of banks, as may well be expected, looked more diligently to the means and methods of security and defense. But while there is no insurmountable difficulty in guarding against ordinary dangers, the special and unexpected and hidden dangers are not so easily foreseen.

Columbia is a pleasant little village in the County of Adair, in Kentucky. A quiet, sleepy little place that knew nothing to disturb the even tenor of its way, save when the holding of the Courts of Session stirred the dull monotony of the place.

On the afternoon of April 29th, 1872, all was in status quo. It was about 2 o'clock in the afternoon.

The bank was still open. The president of the Bank of Deposit was chatting with Mr. R. A. C. Martin, the respected cashier of the bank, and Mr. Garnett, an old citizen of Columbia. All in a moment the conversation was interrupted by a most unusual occurrence. Five well-armed horsemen dashed into the street. Promiscuous firing of pistols, oaths and threatenings; every human being was driven into the house on peril of instant death. Those who lingered got a bullet dangerously near their heads, which put them into instant movement for safety. The cashier of the bank, who had just closed and locked the safe, was ordered to open it, and did so, with a revolver pushed alongside his head, accompanied by the threat of having his brains blown out if he didn't. The bank president came out of his office with a revolver in his hand, and was shot through the head the next instant.

Gathering what money they could get their hands on, the robbers put it into bags, and, after a few parting shots, fled. This time they secured even less than on the occasion of the former robbery, for they had neglected to inform themselves that that very day the bank had met some heavy obligations and had little funds on hand. As before, the fact of their small booty seemed to enrage the robbers, and they shot at everybody they saw. After they had left town, the usual indignation meeting was held and the authorities aroused to action, but none seemed particularly desirous to pursuing the gang, and, after a lot of bluff and bluster, the matter was again dropped.

The third robbery of the series occurred some time later at Corydon, Iowa, which was about the same as the other two which preceded it. It was on the 28th of June, 1873, at about 10 o'clock in the morning. The bank was just opening for business, when seven desperadoes charged furiously into the center of the town, firing right and left and swearing to shoot dead everybody who remained in the streets. Their commands were obeyed. The streets were cleared. None of the inhabitants thought of offering any resistance. Three of the robbers dismounted and, with cocked pistols, entered the bank, swearing to blow the heads off any who dared to interfere with them. The six heavy dragoon pistols served to terrify those who were in the bank, and they yielded at discretion. The safe was opened and the contents thrown into a sack. It is said that the robbers made by this one haul a sum nearly approaching $40,000. The people in the bank were charged to order and silence, and one of the robbers' brood boasted that he could fetch a button off the coat of any of them with his pistol; so they had best have a care.

Of course, after the consternation had given place to quieter moments, the inhabitants instituted a vigorous pursuit. The common result followed. Not one of the robbers were caught

JAMES BOYS DEEDS OF DARING

THE JAMES BOYS' FIRST TRAIN ROBBERY
AFTER BANK ROBBING BECAME MONOTONOUS THEY TACKLED HOLDING UP EXPRESS TRAINS, AND WERE SO SUCCESSFUL THEY KEPT AT IT FOR SEVERAL YEARS

Ever since the world began man has grown tired of the same old thing over and over. It would hardly be credited that such an exciting, perilous vocation as bank robbing could become monotonous, but if the James boys and their close associates, the Younger brothers, are to be believed, even bank robbing palls on one's nerves after awhile and something more exciting must be hunted up.

Naturally, train robbery offered the greatest allurements in the excitement line, and therefore it was to it that this quartette of bad men turned after they had decided to shelve bank robbery for awhile and try a new line of thieving.

The idea of a change to a more daring and reckless species of robbery is supposed to have originated with Frank James and Jim Younger.

These two desperate bandits had been absent from the band for several months, and it is probable that they were on a tour of observation. They made a trip westward by rail as far as Cheyenne, and evidently learned a great deal regarding the running of trains, shipment of money by express from the Pacific Coast and other important information necessary to be possessed in the successfully carrying on of their new business enterprise of wrecking and robbing railroad trains.

The result of their confab was a determination to inaugurate a new order of "knights of the road." The "road agents" of the Far West were to be completely thrown into the shade. Holding up and robbing mere stage coaches on lonely roads in England had made the names of Claud Duval and Dick Turpin world renowned. What would the world say of this daring scheme to tackle the great railway trains, the giant stagecoaches of this latter part of the nineteenth century?

This thought fired the vaulting ambition of the James boys to the intensest degree, and the terrible crime it involved of the indiscriminate slaughter of helpless women and children did not cause them a moment's hesitation.

It was on the night of July 21st, 1873, in pursuance with the plan agreed upon at their meeting in their Jackson county cave, the gang of eight bandits met at a point near Council Bluffs, Iowa, where they were to hold up their first train. At this point there is a sharp curve in the road, which is also in a deep cut, and it was decided that these existing conditions would greatly add to the success of the plot and render the train crew and passengers more easy victims than if it took place elsewhere.

James Boys Robbing the Missouri Pacific Express,

Their conjectures in this line proved right, for the train fell an easy victim to their wiles and the desperate attack that followed the stopping of the train.

The train consisted of seven coaches, including two sleepers, and was in charge of Engineer Martin Kelly, who was looking sharply along the glistening rails, when he saw the ties piled across the track.

He instantly threw the reversing lever, applied the air brakes, but too late. The robbers had also loosened a rail.

The engineer saw the movement and uttered a cry of despair.

The screaming engine struck the loosened rail and plunged sideways into, the bank, while the cars telescoped and piled up in terrible confusion. Engineer Rafferty was instantly killed and a dozen passengers seriously injured. Regardless of all this, however, the robbers quickly boarded the wreck, two of them entering the express car, while the others forced the excited and demoralized passengers to deliver up all their money and valuables.

DEEDS OF DARING

The express messenger was made to open the safe and give the bandits what money he had in charge, but the amount was small, consisting of about three thousand dollars. From the passengers nearly as much more was obtained. This was a bitter disappointment to the outlaws, for they confidently expected to find not less than fifty thousand dollars in gold, as reported. Fortunately, the bandits were twelve hours too soon, as on the following day the express carried over the same road seventy-five thousand dollars in gold.

After securing all the booty possible, the seven daring wreckers waved their hats and shouted farewell to their victims, and, gaining their horses, they rode away to the south.

The excitement created over this dreadful outrage was very great, and hundreds volunteered to assist in apprehending the desperadoes.

The trail led straight through Missouri and to the Missouri River, where there was unmistakable evidence that the outlaws swam the stream with their horses. Following the track on the other side, the band was followed into Jackson County, where, as usual, every trace disappeared. A party of detectives went down to Monegaw Springs in search of the outlaws, and found Jesse James and two of the Younger boys, but they made no effort to bring them away, and were glad to escape, themselves alive.

JAMES BOYS DEEDS OF DARING

THE FAMOUS LIBERTY BANK ROBBERY

ONE OF THE MOST DARING AND SENSATIONAL OF THE JAMES BOYS' LONG LIST OF BANK ROBBERIES

HOW THEY LANDED $20,000 IN A VERY SHORT TIME

It was ever the game of the James boys to make their operations a complete surprise. They found by experience that when they could surprise a town or a bank absolutely they had things pretty much all their own way. The very suddenness of the attack seemed to daze the victims, and they did not even think of resistance, in most instances.

The war had made the guerrillas expert in massacring repugnant citizens, and in appropriating the property of their victims. Many of the old crowd were banded together by the sinews of the "black oath," and scarcely had the smoke of battle been lifted up and assimilated with the refreshing dew clouds of heaven before plans were matured for the robbing of country banks.

On the 20th of January, 1866, the sheriff of Harrison County attempted to execute a capais for the arrest of Bill Reynolds, in Pleasant Hill, who was under indictment for crimes committed during the war.

Geo. Maddox and N. P. Hayes were in town at the time, and as the three were members of the same organization, resistance to the officer was made. It became necessary for the sheriff to summon a posse of citizens to his assistance. A fight in the open street then ensued, ending in the death of Reynolds and Hayes and the capture of Maddox. Threats of an attack on the town by guerrillas were rumored, and for several days nearly every male citizen was bearing arms in anticipation of an attempt being made to liberate Maddox.

The excitement was unabated in Pleasant Hill until the 14th of February, when the robbery of the Clay County Savings Association at Liberty, Missouri, was reported. The reason why rumors were so persistently circulated of an intended attempt to deliver Maddox was now clearly understood to be for the purpose of making the surprise on Liberty more complete.

Early in the morning of St. Valentine's Day a squad of the old guerrillas, numbering an even dozen, rode into Liberty from different directions and, meeting in the public square, they disposed themselves as follows: Three of the robbers were stationed some distance from the bank at eligible positions, which would most readily detect any centralizing attack or suspicious movement of the citizens; the other nine rode directly up to the front of the bank, where two of the number dismounted and entered with drawn revolvers.

The hour being early, luckily for the bandits there was no one in the bank except the cashier, Mr. Bird, and his son.

A pistol was presented at the head of each, and under threats of instant death, in case of refusal, Mr. Bird opened the bank vault, from which the sum of seventy-two thousand dollars was taken and crammed into a pair of saddle bags carried for the purpose. As the robbers were regaining their horses for flight, Mr. Bird thrust his head out of a window and called to a little boy by the name of Wymore, whom he saw passing, telling him that a robbery had been committed and to raise the alarm. As the little fellow, not more than twelve years of age, raised the cry of "Robbers! Help!" he was fired on by the bandits, and fell dead with five fatal bullets in his body. The robbers then began firing indiscriminately and yelling with savage fury, so that for some time after the bandits had departed the citizens were too badly intimidated to think of pursuit. A posse, under the leadership of the sheriff, was organized about one hour afterward, however, and started out on a spirited chase. The trail led to Mount Gilead Church, where the evidence of bank paper showed that the robbers had tarried a few moments to divide the spoils. It was also evident that the band had separated and taken various directions so as to elude pursuit, which they accomplished so effectively that not one of the bandits was apprehended.

JAMES BOYS DEEDS OF DARING

ROBBING THE OVERLAND STAGE COACHES

THOSE VERSATILE BANDITS AND THEIR EXPLOITS AS ROAD AGENTS IN SEVERAL SENSATIONAL HOLD-UPS OF THE OLD TIME STAGE COACHES

Although they favored train robberies as being more prolific of profit, the James boys did not hesitate now and then to engage in a little road agent business on the side, when things were dull and opportunities were good, and they made a number of pretty big hauls in that manner. The hold-ups were all tragic and sensational, and in several of them rather sharp battle preceded the robberies. One of the first stage robberies perpetrated was that of the regular coach which ran between Malvern and Hot Springs. These coaches were more in the nature of ambulances for the sick who went to Hot Springs for treatment, but as these patients were of the rich rather than the poor, the James boys decided to take a chance, and, as they expected, the chance panned out well. At a little place called Sulphur Vale the stage halted for change of horses, and it was there the bandits decided to attack it. It had proceeded about a mile from the relay station when the driver of the coach was suddenly accosted:

"Stop! Stop! Or I'll blow your head off!"

With this unceremonious challenge five men, dressed in Federal uniform, sprang from their ambush, each with cocked revolvers in their hands, threatening the lives of every passenger who dared to resist them. Of course, the passengers were struck dumb with consternation and terror. Presence of mind is an uncommonly good thing, but by no means common under such circumstances.

"Come, d--n you! Tumble out quick; we have no time to spare!" was the order of the foremost robber.

"Oh, certainly!" said a Mr. Charles Morse. "We can do nothing else."

"I am paralyzed in my legs and cannot walk," cried a poor old victim of rheumatism within the stage, as the other passengers came tumbling out.

"Never mind! Stay where you are," was the reply.

The stage was emptied, save of the one lame old gentleman. The rest of the passengers were ordered, with oaths and threats, and with pointed revolvers to confirm the threats, to form in a circle and hold up their hands, which they did without delay.

The brigands then began to search, examine and rob every passenger. Not one escaped, and not one seemed equal to offering the least resistance or making the slightest remonstrance. The net result in money and valuables approximated the sum of $4,000.

The Overland Stage Robbery.

The next stage robbery was that of the Concord stage. It came rumbling along with eight passengers, seven men and a woman. The coach had scarcely entered the shadow of a deep woods, when the driver noted two horsemen some distance ahead in the woods. Suspecting nothing, he drove on until he came up with them, when he wheeled suddenly across the road, and, pointing rifles at his head, ordered him to halt. There was nothing to do but obey and he did so with alacrity. He saw at once he had stage robbers to deal with and accepted his fate. He recognized them as the James Boys and begged his passengers if they valued their lives to offer no resistance.

"You see, they'll have your money, anyhow, and if you bother 'em they'll have your life as well as your money."

"Come out the stage, please," said the rider who had first commanded the halt.

The order took the shape of the most polite request.

The passengers looked through the open windows and saw the muzzles of two pair of revolvers, commanding the whole line of the stage. The passengers needed no further argument. Mr. R. S. Rountree, of the Milwaukee Evening Wisconsin, was wide awake to the importance of the hour, and managed to slip his gold watch and pocketbook under the cushion as he rose to leave the stage. Miss Rountree, daughter of the Hon. R. Rountree, of Lebanon, Ky., the only lady on board, was permitted to retain her seat. After the passengers were out and stood in single file, Frank James tossed his rein to his companion, who covered the whole line with his pistols, and then proceeded to search their pockets, while they were charged to hold up their hands and keep them up. There seems not to have been the first thought of resistance.

When they were through with their examination and robbery, they generously returned the railway passes and tickets that were no manner of use in the world to them. Then, with the utmost nonchalance, they proceeded to explain that they were not robbers! Oh! Dear, no, nothing so vulgar! They were only moonshiners who, unduly pressed by an unreasonable government, were compelled to leave the country, and, of course, they could not go without money.

And, therefore, though much against their principles, they were compelled to levy toll after this fashion.

They were extremely sorry if they had given any undue annoyance. It might be some consolation to know that they had taken toll from the outgoing coach that very afternoon, and Mr. George Grogham, one of the owners of the celebrated cave, had contributed the handsome sum of $700.

Turning to Mr. Craig, of Georgia, Frank said he hated worse than anything to take his money, for in the late war he had fought in a Georgia regiment himself, but then he had no option.

"You know, my dear sir," said Frank, with a smile, "needs must when the devil drives."

Turning to the only lady of the party, the impertinent robber inquired her name.

"Miss Rountree, of Lebanon," said the lady, scarcely able to hide her disgust.

"Indeed!" said Frank, his face quite lighting up with a smile. "Why, then, you'll probably know some friends of mine. I have some very dear friends in Lebanon. Do you happen to know the Misses Smithers who live there?"

"Yes, sir, I. do," replied Miss Rountree.

"Dear me," added Frank, "what a coincidence! Nice."

After sarcastically bidding the party good bye, and asking Miss Rountree to remember him to the Smithers girls of Lebanon, when she saw them again, the robbers rode off, headed by Frank James, while the coach and its terror-stricken passengers got under way once more and proceeded on its trip.

JAMES BOYS DEEDS OF DARING

ROBBING THE RUSSELLVILLE BANK

ANOTHER DARING ACHIEVEMENT OF THE JAMES BOYS BY WHICH THEY SECURED NEARLY $75,000, WHICH, AS USUAL, THEY SOON SQUANDERED

The robbery of the Russellville (Mo.) National Bank was another of those daring deeds of lawlessness, which very daring proved beyond doubt it was the work of the James gang and left its "earmarks," the indisputable evidence of their clever work. Whenever those desperadoes planned they planned well and whatever they attempted they came pretty near making a success. This was particularly true of their bank exploits. They never failed to land the treasure in a single instance.

Russellville is a pleasant little town of about five thousand inhabitants, saving and thrifty, and highly proud of their bank and its contents that is, they were proud of its contents prior to the James boys' visit. There wasn't much contents to be proud of after they went away. It was in the center of a very thriving agricultural district, and its bank was well filled with farmers' money.

It was a beautiful spring morning in 1873. The stores were open and the store dealers were beginning their business for the day. Now and then a rumbling wagon, corn laden, creaked along the quiet street. The bank was just about to open its doors, when suddenly a clatter of hoofs was heard. Sharp, quick and terrible as the crash of doom, a dozen horsemen, each armed with two pairs of revolvers, dashed down the street, to the terror and amazement of the villagers. With the most fearful oaths and threatenings these armed brigands commanded the people to go into their houses and keep quiet on pain of instant death, and to confirm their purpose they fired in all directions. Two of the men of whom Jesse James was one and Cole Younger the other dismounted at the bank and entered. The cashier had opened the safe and the books were out on the counters, and a quantity of gold was spread out before the cashier, which he was then in the act of counting. The sudden entrance of these armed men astonished him for a moment. He turned at once to the safe and was in the act of swinging back the door, when Jesse James said:

"Leave that alone and keep quiet, or I'll blow your brains out"

What could the cashier do with such a threat in his ears, supported as it was by the loaded revolvers, too close to said brains to be pleasant? The cashier, setting a higher value on his life than all the gold in the safe, kept quiet, and the safe was rifled. The loose gold on the counter was swept off by Cole Younger.

Everything of value was taken away except a few revenue and postage stamps. These the robbers thought hardly worth the trouble of taking, and so Jesse, to whom a joke was never untimely, tossed back the stamps, remarking to the affrighted cashier that he "might want to mail letters later in the day!"

The booty secured, the robbers departed as they came, cursing and threatening instant death to any who dared to follow. No one blamed the cashier of the bank. He was thoroughly helpless.

Robbing the Russellville Bank,

As with their other robberies, the James Boys were so quick in this instance that the robbery was over and the robbers gone almost before anyone realized it had happened. It was the very boldness of it that carried it through successfully and the very audacity that appalled every one who was about when it occurred.

The usual appeal to the authorities was made, and the customary posse was organized to run down the robbers, but in a little while the sensation died out; the robbers were reported hundreds of miles away, and the matter came to an end.

JAMES BOYS DEEDS OF DARING

A $50,000 EXPRESS CAR ROBBERY

HOW THE JAMES BOYS CLEANED UP A WELLS-FARGO EXPRESS CAR AND GOT AWAY WITH A BIG SUM OF BANKNOTES AND BULLION

Muncie, Kansas, is a little hamlet, about eight miles west of Kansas City, on the line of the Kansas Pacific Railroad. It is usually as tranquil and quiet as sleepy country stations are reputed to be, and seldom, if ever did anything occur, to awaken it out of its normal terpidity. For years it had slumbered by the side of the railroad tracks just about on the map and that was all. But on December 12th, 1874, there came its awakening, and after a reign of the wildest excitement, it became known the country over, by reason of the sensational doings that took place there.

It was on the afternoon of the day above mentioned that five horsemen, heavily armed, rode into town, led by a man wearing a heavy black beard and carrying two heavy Colt revolvers. They were all masked with black dominoes, and as they entered the town limits attracted the attention of a few straggling villagers, who saw them riding slowly down the main street. In front of Purdee's store, on the main street, they dismounted and went inside, leaving one of their number outside with the horses. Almost instantly they held up Purdee with their revolvers and robbed his till of the few dollars it contained.

Then they compelled the store-keeper to accompany them to the railroad water-tank near the station building and point out a quantity of old cross-ties. These they piled on the track, effectually blocking the line.

They also set out the flag at the station as a signal for the next train to stop.

During this time a horseman, a wagonload of women and children, and several villagers happened along. These the robbers immediately herded together altogether twenty-five persons and put under guard of one of their number.

The 4.45 passenger express from the West was the next train due. As it neared the station the engineer, Robert Murphy, saw the signal and the pile of cross-ties on the track and pulled up his train within a hundred feet of the cross-ties.

The next minute he was gazing into the cold steel barrels of a quartette of revolvers, while his cringing fireman was also in a similar predicament, both being threatened with instant death if they moved a muscle.

Meanwhile others of the gang were at work in the passenger coaches robbing the affrighted passengers and trainmen. They next tackled the express car.

In the meantime the robbers on the locomotive had forced the engineer to uncouple the express car and run it up the track several hundred yards, to where the pile of cross-ties on the track prevented any further progress. The express messenger had not time to lock the doors of the car before he was covered by a couple of guns and forced, under pain of instant death, to open the safe.

He did so reluctantly, and almost in less time than, it takes to tell it, the robbers had tumbled out some $55,000 and stowed it away in a mail sack, the contents of which they dumped out for the purpose.

The robbers left the car, carrying the treasure, after warning the express agent they would fill him full of lead if he even dared look out of the rifled car.

At a signal from the leader, the gang collected around him; they held a momentary consultation, and then mounting their hordes, rode back to where the white-faced passengers were peering out of the car windows and bade them, "Give our regards to the folks in Kansas City." Before riding away they returned several watches they had taken from women passengers, saying they might need them later on.

Wheeling their horses, the robbers dashed off at top speed, going in the direction of Kansas City and carrying with them nearly sixty thousand dollars in booty.

With the arrival of the train in Kansas City, posses were sent out in pursuit of the robbers. The chase was futile, for the gang had crossed the State line into Jackson County, Missouri where their trail was lost in the mountains.

The methods of the robbers and the descriptions of the black-bearded leader convinced the authorities that the gang was headed by Jesse James, who, although scarcely thirty years old, was already known as a desperado, with a score of robberies and murders in Missouri to his credit. Associated with him were his brother Frank, three years older than he; Bill McDaniells, Clell Miller, Arthur McCoy, and several others.

The only one of the gang captured was Bill McDaniells, who was arrested while on a spree with some of the jewelry taken from the Muncie train in his possession. Two months later McDaniells escaped, but was discovered and shot by an officer who attempted to capture him.

JAMES BOYS DEEDS OF DARING

A COUPLE OF DARING BANK ROBBERIES

JESSE JAMES AND THE YOUNGER BROTHERS PLAY A FOUR-HANDED GAME AT BANK-ROBBERY AND CLEAN UP TWO MONEY DEPOSITORIES FOR GOOD ROUND SUMS

From the standpoint of a criminal critic, the James Boys and Younger Brothers did their best work in the line of bank robbing, when they undertook a job together. They were adepts at planning such events and went into such details that they seldom failed to make a complete coup when they started in to get away with the treasure. The rapidity with which they worked precluded all possibility of the assembling of a posse and subsequent capture or death.

As a usual thing the bank was robbed and the robbers and booty gone before the people of the village fully realized what was happening. From this it must not be inferred that they always chose night for their operations, as they more often worked in mid-day, for the reason that at that hour the vaults were unlocked and open and the money easier to get at. For instance, the robbery of the Bank of Lexington, Mo., occurred at high noon, October 30, 1866. At that hour, four determined men rode down the main street and leisurely hitched their horses in an alley near the banking house of Alexander Mitchell & Co. Two of the men walked into the bank, meeting the cashier, Mr. J. L. Thomas, in the doorway, who went behind the counter to attend the wants of the strangers. One of the men handed a $50 7-30 bond to the cashier with the request to have it changed. As Mr. Thomas opened the cash drawer two more of the robbers appeared at the door with drawn revolvers, the fifth man being left in charge of the horses. It was quick work now, for, looking into the muzzles of four deadly pistols, the cashier was compelled to hand over all the money in the bank, $2,000, which being placed in a sack, the robbers coolly walked out of the bank with a parting admonition to Mr. Thomas that if he raised any outcry they would kill him. Mounting their horses, the robbers rode swiftly away, and it was more than an hour after the robbery before the pursuing party was organized. Twelve well-armed citizens started after the bandits, and spent two days in a fruitless search for the despoilers. People began to consider the insecurity of country banks and the means of apprehending the daring outlaws; meetings were held and various plans discussed, but in two weeks' time the outrage was almost forgotten.

For six long months nothing startling was heard from the James and Younger brothers, and they were supposed to be far away from their old stamping ground. But, like the proverbial bad penny, they always turned up unexpected.

Savannah is the capital seat of Andrew County, a thrifty little village of twelve or fifteen hundred inhabitants, that has suffered but little from the blight of war. The place contained a small banking institution, under the proprietorship of Judge McLain, with small capital.

On the 2nd of March, 1867, five ex-guerrillas, J. F. Edmunson, Jim White,, Bill Chiles, Bud McDaniels, and a fellow named Pope, rode into Savannah in such a manner as indicated they were on important business. It was nearly high noon, and no one was in the bank except the Judge and his son. The bandits rode up and four of them dismounted, leaving their horses in charge of the fifth man. As the four entered the bank with drawn pistols, the Judge looked earnestly over his spectacles, and at once comprehended the character of his customers. He slammed the door of the safe shut, and, seizing a revolver which lay on the bank counter, he met the bandits halfway, but the shots proved ineffectual, while a big navy pistol ball went tearing through his breast, which made him sink to the floor as one death-stricken. Young McLain ran into the street and gave the alarm, which brought many citizens to the rescue. The robber left in charge of the horses shouted for the return of his companions, who, finding their position becoming very serious, mounted the ready horses and fled.

A posse of twenty-five citizens went in pursuit of the bandits a few minutes after their hasty departure and trailed them for a few miles, after which they lost all trace of them and the chase was abandoned, Judge McLain's wound was desperate, but he eventually recovered.

The next robbery and raid occurred a few months later at Richmond, Mo., where the James and Younger boys, with a gang of ten other desperadoes, terrorized and looted the town, robbing the private bank of Hughes & Mason of some $5,000.

The robbers next began an attack upon the jail, which at that time held a number of prisoners whose arrest, it was claimed, was due to the expression of secession sentiment. The jailer, B. G. Griffin, and his son, fifteen years of age, were at the jail, and they received their assailants with remarkable bravery. The boy stationed himself behind a tree, and was emptying a revolver in the face of the outlaws when he was surrounded and shot to death. Mr.Griffin, seeing the fate of his brave boy, rushed up, and, standing over the lifeless body, fought like the frenzied man he was until, pierced by seven bullets, he fell dead across the bleeding and lifeless body of his son. By this time the citizens recovered their lost nerves, and from a score of windows there poured the rifle and pistol flame, yet throughout the Combat not a single robber was harmed.

JAMES BOYS DEEDS OF DARING

ROBBING THE 'DAVENPORT LIMITED'

HOW THE JAMES BOYS' GANG HELD UP A WELL-FILLED TRAIN AND MURDERED AND ROBBED THE PASSENGERS

One of the most notorious as well as brutal robberies committed by the James Boys gang was that of the Davenport Limited, from Kansas City for Davenport, Iowa, on the Chicago, Rock Island and Pacific Railroad. July 15th, 1881, it left Kansas City at 6.30 P.M., and was due at Davenport the following morning, running over the southwestern division of the road. The make-up of the train was a combination baggage and express car, a smoker, two day coaches and a sleeper. There was a fair number of passengers on board and everything was going along nicely, when the train stopped at Cameron, a small station, some sixty-four miles from the starting point, where several rough looking men got aboard and seated themselves in the smoker. Although the lights were dim, there was sufficient light to see these men four in number were deeply engrossed in discussing some plans or scheme they had on hand.

Finally the train rolled into Winston. The stop was a short one, but during the few seconds that the cars lay beside the platform several things happened.

One of the four men in the smoker carelessly placed his white handkerchief against the window-pane, and held it there for a moment. Outside it was very dark and quiet, only the monotonous chugging of the engine disturbing the silence.

Waiting until the trainmen were on board again, two men slipped across the platform and mounted the front end of the baggage car next to the tender. Several other dark figures flitted toward the train, and two more men swung on the platform between the baggage car and the smoker.

Then, without the slightest warning, the tragedy began.

As the two men climbed to the platform between the smoker and the baggage car the conductor swung his lantern from the front platform of the smoker as a signal for the engineer to go ahead. Turning, he entered the car, the two men behind him following with a rush. At the same instant the four men inside the smoker sprang forward with drawn revolvers.

There was a yell of "Throw up your hands!" and a revolver exploded, the flame shooting toward the ceiling of the car.

The conductor dropped his lantern and made a movement of resistance. The next instant a pistol shot rang out, and he fell dead on the platform.

The other men stood near the doorway, close beside the tall brigand, who was now recognized as Jesse James, holding their revolvers so as to cover the passengers in the seats. Just then the sleeping car conductor entered the car from the other end and was promptly shot the whole length of the car.

In the smoker the rapid discharge of revolvers formed a dense, white smoke in the forward end of the car. The passengers, seeing an opportunity to flee, were the more desirous to escape, as one of the desperadoes now proposed to "go through the gang."

Robbing the Davenport Limited.

Several men sprang up, among them a Mason named John McCullough, who had a heavy stone trowel in his hand. As he jumped into the aisle, still clinging to his trowel, he unconsciously swung it near the head of one of the outlaws. The brigand immediately shot McCullough through the head.

Fatally wounded though he was, the stone mason managed to stagger to the rear door, where he fell off the platform and, like Conductor Westphal, was afterward found dead in the ditch.

This third murder completed the panic of the passengers. Yelling with fear, and pursued by the jeers of the murderers, they fled to the rear of the train, fighting with each other to get ahead. When the car was empty the two young girls, who had shown the greatest courage throughout the whole scene, left their seats and followed the others,

The utmost confusion now reigned in the train.

DEEDS OF DARING

On the rear platform of the first day-coach, when the mob of passengers came tearing through the train, was C. F. Chase, of the Topeka Police Department. With him was Harry Thomas, the rear brakeman. After the crowd had passed him, Chase looked forward through the cars. Three or four terrified passengers were crawling under the seats of the day coach. Chase drew his hair-trigger revolver.

"For God's sake, put that up!" Thomas cried.

"They've got the train. We've got to stop the engineer."

Chase still stood with his pistol in his hand, watching the men in the smoker, and Thomas swung out from the platform, waving his lantern frantically to the engineer, knowing that every rod they went from the station meant a rod farther from help.

The train continued to run on. Either the engineer did not see the signal or there was trouble on the locomotive.

"I'm going to stop him!" Thomas cried. He sprang into the car and pulled down the cord that controlled the automatic air-brakes, setting the brakes on every car on the train and stopping it with a jolt. He swung out again from the platform, shouting, "Robbers!"

But the desperadoes on the train knew their business. They were prepared for just such an emergency, and they acted promptly. As soon as the airbrakes stopped the train, the gang in which there were at least twelve men - separated, some running to the engine, the others making for the express car. As the first two ruffians jumped into the cab, revolvers in hand, the fireman jumped from the other side. Running back to the rear platform of the smoker he concealed himself in the darkness on the lower steps.

The engineer was trying to release the train from the grip of the automatic brakes. One of the boarding party clapped a revolver to the engineer head.

"What in --- are you stopping for? Pull ahead!" the man shouted.

"I can't," the engineer said. "Someone's put on the automatic."

A robber's pistol flashed in the darkness and a bullet whistled by his head the next instant the engineer had tossed the cab lantern out of the window and was out on the running board of the engine from which he reached the pilot and lay down across it, to be safe from the robber's fire. The James gang then began ransacking the train and went from car to car, shooting right and left those who offered the slightest resistance. The car floors were covered with blood, and the cars perforated with bullets. No less than nine men were killed, and their bodies lay in the car aisles they robbed everybody, battering in the doors of the express and mail cars and robbing the safes of both. The express and mail clerks were among those killed for trying to protect their safes.

The James gang got over $40,000 out of this robbery, which was divided among them, as was their usual custom, for despite their being such murderous robbers, they were fair to each other.

JAMES BOYS DEEDS OF DARING

A BOLD DAYLIGHT ROBBERY

HOW AN EXPRESS CAR WAS ROBBED OF $70,000 IN BROAD DAYLIGHT BY THE JAMES BOYS AND THEIR GANG

The task of holding up a long train and robbing the express car of over $70,000, in broad daylight, is not an easy one that would be essayed by the average train robber, but that is just what the James gang did to the car containing that amount in Calumet and Heckla miners' pay envelopes.

This was back in 1880 and in the days when the name of the James boys was the synonym of deadly daring and expert highwaymanism. One of the robbers held up the engineer at the point of a rifle, another chased the fireman down the track, while the rest of the gang broke into the express car, killed the messenger and got the money.

The engineer and fireman were joking in the cab about the trip and the joy pay day always brought to the miners. The conductor paid no attention to the passengers except to collect their fares and chat a bit with a few whom he knew. It was 9.50 when the train wheezed up to a little shanty in the woods, dignified with the name of Stanley. Several persons alighted and the conductor gave the signal to go ahead when the outbreak occurred.

With the suddenness of a lightning flash, a tall fellow with a black mask over the upper part of his face, arose from between the engine and tender with a big revolver in each hand and advised the engineer and fireman to throw up their hands quick. They instantly obeyed.

There was seventy thousand dollars aboard that train, and he was the engineer in charge, on whom its safety depended. But then there was that gun, on which his life depended, and it yawned in an ugly way. Discretion was much better than valor under such circumstances.

Back in the express car things were moving at a swift pace also. At the moment the shot was fired from the tender two more men, masked and enveloped in linen dusters, like the first, sprang up, also apparently from nowhere, and forced themselves into the car.

It was only the work of an instant for the robbers to enter the express car and cover the messenger with their pistols. Then they clearly and concisely stated that they were after about seventy thousand dollars of Calumet and Heckla money and proposed to have it even if they had to kill off all the express messengers in Christendom. The messenger did just as the others had done and threw up his hands. When directed to open the safe and pass out the two big sacks containing the money, he did so without a word.

No sooner was the swag in a bag than the big fellow fired a single shot. It was not for the messenger, however, but a signal to let their pals know they had the money and were ready to escape. An answering shot came from the front of the train.

With that the men jumped off the train and made for the woods, but not before bidding the engineer to "keep her going for a hundred miles or so."

There was a great hurrah when the train reached Heckla and the news of the robbery spread. A whole army of detectives were put to work on the case, and many of them followed false trails, but the Pinkerton men, who were also at work, sized it up right away as another of the James Boys' jobs.

JAMES BOYS DEEDS OF DARING

SOME HIGHLY VERSATILE DEPREDATIONS

A VARIETY OF DARING ROBBERIES OF A FAIR GROUNDS, A RAILROAD TRAIN, A BANK, A STORE AND OTHER PLACES – SHOWING THE WIDE DIVERSITY OF THE JAMES BOYS' OPERATIONS

As has been said before in this volume, the James Boys were not at all particular as to the character of the robberies they committed so long as they yielded golden profits, and the whole gamut of crime was run in their thieving operations during their wild career of crime and desperadoism.

It was a great day of the fair, the "big day" of the Kansas City Exposition. From early morning there had been a din of drum and trumpet and gong. Thousands upon thousands had poured in from all quarters. Leavenworth and Sedalia, St. Joseph and Moberly, Lawrence and Clinton and regions further removed had sent in their crowded trains. All went merry as a marriage bell.

There were twenty thousand people on the fair ground that September afternoon, and thirty thousand more were crowding and surging up and down the streets of Kansas City.

One of the special features of that afternoon's entertainment was the races. Ethan Allen was to trot against a running mate at five o'clock. The people were crowding into the fair grounds between four and five in masses. The ticket sellers and the gatemen were doing a roaring trade. Mr. Hall, the secretary and treasurer of the association, had counted up the receipts of the day and found the same reached nearly $10,000 in hard cash. Arrangements had been made to bank this money at the First National Bank, though it was considerably after banking hours.

Mr. Hall called one of his trusty assistants and gave him a tin box containing the money, and sent him to deposit it in the bank according to arrangement. The idea of this box being stolen in a street crowded with tens of thousands of people was never dreamed of. It would have been regarded as quite preposterous to think anyone would have the daring to attempt so wild an exploit. The young man who had charge of this box started off, carrying the treasure in his right band.

Just at this moment the general attention of the crowd was attracted by the clatter of hoofs. Seven heavily armed horsemen rode along, the leaders being recognized as Jesse and Frank James. Their dress and manner was such as to mislead many spectators into the belief that they were a part of the show contingent of the fair. They realized their mistake when the horsemen were seen to surround the man with the money box, and as one of then felled him with a blow from the butt of a big revolver, the others grabbed the treasure and all rode away like the wind. So quickly was it accomplished that although there were thousands of people all about, they were all too surprised to even start in pursuit of the robbers and they escaped with ease.

The robbery of the Craig store at Bentonville, Ark., was another instance of sleek action on the part of the James gang. The firm did a large business on a strictly cash basis and therefore always had considerable money in the store. Mr. Craig and his son were alone in the store when the two James brothers entered as though to make a purchase. "What can I do for you, gentlemen?" asked the elder Craig affably, as he approached from the rear of the store.

"You can keep quiet," was the blunt answer of the foremost of the men as he presented a revolver in each hand and continued: "If either of you speak a word or stir an inch, I'll blow your brains out, so if you value your d---d lives, why be quiet!"

Looking round the Craigs saw two other men keeping guard at the door. Resistance was utterly impossible. The safe door was open; it was the work of a moment to rifle it of its contents. But the robbers were disappointed. They expected to make a big haul, but the Craigs had banked all their cash on hand at four o'clock, and the safe only contained about $150. This greatly disgusted the rogues, so they swept up about $200 worth of valuable silks and went as quickly as they came, leaving strict charge

Robbing the Craig Store, Bentonville, Ark.

that if they attempted to raise an alarm before they had time to leave the town, they would shoot them dead at sight.

Another bank robbery of note which was successfully accomplished by the James Boys, was that of the Savings Bank of St. Genevieve, an old Catholic town of Missouri. The town is more than a century old - the home of the French aristocracy. The residents were among the most thrifty of the State, and nearly all of their money went into the bank, instead of being invested in the many wildcat schemes of the day. The vaults of the old bank often contained as much as $100,000 at a time, and it was regarded as one of the most prosperous financial institutions of Missouri. Its fame reached the ears of the James Boys and quite naturally its looting followed.

It was a beautiful spring morning, the 27th of May, 1873. St. Genevieve was looking its very loveliest. Mr. O. D. Harris, the cashier of the bank, accompanied by F.A. Rozier, a son of the Hon. Forman A. Rozier, the president of the bank, had left his garden home all bright and cheerful, little dreaming what an episode was at hand. The cashier and his young companion arrived at the bank, the door swung open, and suddenly Mr. Harris and young Rozier were confronted by four armed men and accosted thus: "We have come to help you to open the bank. Open the safe instantly, d--n you; we have no time to lose"

"I am helpless and cannot resist you," replied the overpowered Mr. Harris.

Meantime another of the robbers pointed a pistol at the head of young Rozier, and called out:

"You keep still, d---d little rat, if you don't want to have your brains blown out in an instant!"

"I? What for?" asked the young clerk, who had shown signs of desiring to create an alarm.

"Not another word, young devil," said his stern-faced foe; "that's enough! A blabbing tongue can be stopped d---d easy."

Taking advantage of the moment, and desiring that these strange visitors should have all his room and none of his company, he made a bold leap and sprang down the steps of the bank into the street. As he fled the fellow fired at him and cried: "Halt! halt! you wretched young cuss!"

Several shots were fired after him, one grazing his shoulder, but he managed to dodge the bullets and got away, giving the alarm. Noting the townsmen were arming themselves, the robbers hastily completed their task of looting the bank of some $70,000 and mounting their horses rode swiftly away.

The next event on their criminal calendar was the robbery of a train in Nebraska. A regular meeting of the gang was held at which a number of projects were discussed.

Comanche, Tony a desperate Texas Ranger, was added to the plundering brotherhood. The gang comprising the James Boys, the Youngers, Bob Hoore, and this Texas Tony, met each, of course, coming different ways at a point about fourteen miles east of the city of Council Bluffs, on the Chicago, Rock Island and Pacific Railway.

The train was due to pass their point of ambush about three o'clock in the morning. All night they waited and watched, scarcely exchanging a word with each other, and when they did, not above a whisper.

Three or four rails were loosened and torn from their places. Several cross-ties were placed in position to be used the moment they were required. They worked and watched and waited in silence. They had chosen a most suitable spot. It was fourteen miles from Council Bluffs, six miles from Adair, and about the same distance from Des Moines. There was not a single human habitation for miles around.

The rumbling of the train was heard in the distance. The gang set to work with dogged determination, resorting to the old game of piling railroad ties on the track to derail the engine. It succeeded well.

The train came bowling along at a good rate of speed, struck the ties and not only derailed the engine, but upset it as well, killing the brave engineer in the wreck. Then this band of desperadoes broke loose like the demons of hell, firing their pistols in the windows of the coaches at the panic stricken passengers. When they were sufficiently cowed, they were systematically robbed of everything of value they possessed.

The express car was broken into and the messenger in charge had his arm broken and was forced to unlock the safe. The robbers secured some $6,000, and the poor guardian of the mails had his watch taken and ten dollars, the only money he possessed. After this every passenger was searched and robbed of money and jewelry. The spoils were put in a sack and the masked robbers sought their horses, and as the light broadened that peaceful summer morning they took their way southward, $25,000 richer for their dreadful exploit.

A reward of $50,000 was offered for their arrest. But it was offered in vain.

JAMES BOYS DEEDS OF DARING

ROBBERY OF THE CHICAGO AND ALTON EXPRESS

THE JAMES BOYS' FAMOUS HOLD-UP NEAR GLENDALE, MISSOURI, AND WHAT CAME OF IT, WITH DESPERATE PURSUIT AND CAPTURE OF SOME OF THE GANG

Early on the morning of September 7th, 1881, ten or a dozen roughly clad men drifted into a farm house a mile or so west of Glendale, Missouri, in the very heart of the hold-up district. They ranged in age from youth to half a century and looked like farmers from the adjacent wheat fields. That is their attire denoted peaceful farmers, but their heavy revolvers and repeating rifles did not. They were several hours assembling, and when the last men who, by the way, were the James Boys, had arrived a conference was held in a carefully guarded room.

As soon as the last arrival had taken his place at a large table, one of the company, a tall, determined looking fellow with a sneering, treacherous face, formally addressed the meeting, tapping with the muzzle of his revolver upon a small railroad map spread out before him.

"There isn't any talk necessary, boys," he said.

"I sent for you to come ready to take the train, under my direction."

A chorus of voices announced the willingness of the men to follow their chief.

The tall man ran his eye over the crowd, and then looked at the map.

"It's dead easy," he said. "We're going to do it tonight, and we'll make a whole lot of money. The C. and A. passenger goes through this cut here between Glendale and Independence, about nine o'clock tonight. We'll do it there."

"She always carries a lot of United States Express money, and those big excursion parties are always going through besides if we need them."

The men crowded around the chief as he proceeded with the details of the robbery, agreeing to all of his proposals. None of the band paid any attention to a dark-faced, middle-aged woman who brought some liquor to the table, and who listened eagerly to every word of the conversation, occasionally casting spiteful glances at the chief and at a short man whom the former addressed as "Dick Little," and who seemed to be second in command. .

After their conference of half hour or so, the robbers disappeared, after agreeing to meet near .the railroad tracks that night. Jesse James mounted his horse and rode away, his followers scattering in every direction, while a sinister-looking woman, who seemed in charge of the house, gathered up a few articles of clothing and left the house also.

At the cut selected by the chief of the gang, the Missouri Pacific crossed the line of the Chicago and Alton.

It was considered a dangerous point for numerous reasons. Glendale, only three miles away, had been the scene of several railroad robberies with- in the past few years.

Finding a Dead Outlaw After the Train Robbery

Aside from the bad reputation of the district, the crossing in the cut, with its steep sides and thickly wooded summits, was a constant menace to passing trains. Knowing this, it was the custom for engineers, especially on night trains, to slow up a little just before entering the ravine.

It was due to this fact, and to the quick eye of Engineer Foote, that the Chicago and Alton passenger train, west-bound, to Kansas City, owed its escape from derailment on the night of September 7.

It was nearly nine o'clock when train Number Forty-Eight entered the east end of the cut. Luckily, it was a fairly clear night, for just before the locomotive reached the deepest part of the cut Engineer Foote saw a light as of a small torch flare up and wave across the track. He saw something else, too, that made him jam down his brakes with every ounce of pressure, not a moment too soon.

The gleam of the headlight showed Foote a pile of rocks heaped up five feet high between the rails and surmounted by a small stick with a red flag tied to the end flapping in the wind. The engine ran right up to the obstruction, the pile thrusting itself in among the stones as the train stopped.

Just beyond the pile of rocks stood a tall masked man, holding a revolver in each hand. In the glare of the headlight, Engineer Foote could see the whites of the fellow's eyes as he stared into the cab.

Foote knew then that the train was held up by road-agents, but there was no time for him to back away. The masked man waved his revolver toward the bank and shouted:

"Now, men, to your work! Fire away!"

A rolling discharge of firearms came in response to his order.

After thoroughly cowing the train crew and passengers, the robbers went though the train and "cleaned up" everybody. They even took the porter's tips and his dollar watch. "They went through the bunch with a fine-toothed comb," as a drummer, whose samples were even taken, expressed it.

As the looters went through the cars, each person was compiled under threat of death to empty the contents of his or her pockets into the huge sack, where everything money, watches, and articles of jewelry was jumbled together indiscriminately.

Neither women nor children were spared.

There were a number of emigrants aboard, who begged to be allowed to retain at least a small part of their money all that they had in the world. They were left nothing of value.

Women were compelled to sit on the floor of the cars while the robbers stripped them of their jewelry.

Valuables that had been hidden in the car seats and elsewhere were hunted up and tumbled into the sack: Every car was swept clean.

On the train was an excursion party of forty persons from Penn Yan, New York, going West in charge of the regular traveling agent of the Fort Scott road for the purpose of buying land. From this party alone the robbers took over six thousand dollars in money and valuables.

While this part of the robbery was in progress an emigrant from one of the forward cars came running after the robbers, half-crazed with grief and fear, crying to them to give him some of his money for his wife and children. As the man passed the platform from one car to another he was fired upon, but was dragged back uninjured by his friends.

Meanwhile the passengers in the Pullman cars in the rear of the train were trying to conceal their valuables with frantic haste. Several of the ladies in the car managed to secrete their valuables about their clothing, but even this would not have saved them from search, and the surrender of them, but for the fact of an unexpected interruption.

It occurred in this manner. The conductor had been rounded up with the rest of the crew, after he had been fired on twice.

While the robbers were going through the coaches it suddenly occurred to him that a freight train was following his train West and must be about due at the cut, where the passenger train had now been lying about fifteen or twenty minutes.

Hazelbacher knew that Frank Burton, the rear brakeman, ought to be on the rear platform of the sleeper, and he shouted to him. Burton was at his station. He heard the call from the conductor, and knew what it meant. At the same time he heard the robbers entering the other end of the sleeper and heard them call out to the Pullman passengers that they were "coming in and going through the car."

In spite of the proximity of the bandits, and of the guard with rifles on top of the bank, Burton determined to risk getting back up the track to flag the freight train. Holding two Pullman lamps in front of him, he started back over the line.

At that moment he heard the train approaching, and he knew there was no time for explanations. He started off top speed.

Before he had gone a car length the men on the bluff opened up on him with their rifles. The bullets came pinging all around him, striking the rails and stones as he ran for his life, hugging the Pullman lamps in his arms. Twenty-five or thirty shots were fired at him, two of them going through his coat.

Then he heard Engineer Foote, of the passenger train, call out:

"For God's sake, don't shoot the boy; he's trying to save the lives of all these people!"

In the meantime the brakeman had managed to signal the approaching freight train with his lanterns and it came to a stop within twenty feet of the rear Pullman. The robbers by this time realized that the freight crew would reinforce the men of the passenger train, hurriedly packed the last of their booty in small bags and made their escape over the hills as fast as their horses could carry them.

Great excitement followed this robbery, and the authorities made strenuous efforts to capture the gang. At first it was not suspected the James Boys had a hand in it, but later on certain circumstances cropped up, which put the blame fully on them.

The theory of the officers concerning the composition of the band was quickly confirmed, though in an unexpected manner.

A dark, middle-aged woman called, at the headquarters of the Chicago and Alton road in Chicago and gave information which convinced the authorities that they had to deal with a dangerous league.

The woman, who sought revenge for personal wrongs, revealed the whole plot. She gave names, and described in derail the proceedings of the plotters.

The woman's information was confirmed. Investigations by the railroad officials showed that the robbery had been planned by the James Boys.

To the east and west for one hundred miles picket lines were thrown out to pen in the robbers. All the members of the road-agent league were said to have their homes within thirty miles of Glendale, but it was thought probable that they might scatter for a time, to throw the officers off the scent.

Bodies of picked men were sent in from the cordon to rake the guarded district, and on September 8, the day following the robbery, the advance guard of captives came in. The sheriff of Saline County, with his posse, rounded up Creed Chapman and Sam Chapman the latter a mere boy and John Ziegler, all taken with weapons in their hands.

A fourth robber, John Wilkinson, alias Nolen, was arrested the same day, after he had taken a train to Kansas City, where he was endeavoring to gather information about the movements of the officers, for his comrades now realized that they were caught in a trap.

Once landed in jail, young Chapman weakened, giving the names of the other members of the band, in the hope of saving himself.

With their usual good luck, the James Boys escaped capture and pursuit of them was temporarily abandoned. The others were sent to prison for long terms.

JAMES BOYS DEEDS OF DARING

SOME OF THE JAMES BOYS' FAILURES

A NUMBER OF CLEVERLY PLANNED ROBBERIES THAT DID NOT SUCCEED, AND WHICH CAME NEAR RESULTING DISASTROUSLY FOR THE DARING BANDITS

To successfully get away with it is the most important part of the game of the train robber. Not only must the plans be perfectly laid, and the whole scheme worked out to the final end, but the get away at the finish must be perfectly arranged for, in order that the escape may be made before the sleuths of the law are on the trail or a volley of shots poured into the escaping party by the train crew and passengers. Although generally successful, the James Boys, were by no means infallible, and not a few of their cleverly laid plans went wrong and disaster followed, even resulting in the death of several of their gang, from which luckily for themselves, the bandit chief escaped. It is when the robber's back is turned, when the attention is diverted or when he is riding away from the scene of his crime, that a splendid opportunity is presented to a good marksman to kill with a Winchester or revolver. Here are several cases in point:

The Helena express, of the Northern Pacific Railroad, was just crossing the Little Green River on a moonlight night, when the engineer and firemen when suddenly aroused by a stern command, "Throw up your hands, both of you, quick!" They turned to find a man confronting them with a pair of big revolvers and up went their hands. Then the engineer was given orders to stop the train, which he did.

The conductor and the train crew had surmised the reason for the stopping of the train, and they did not venture to show themselves any nearer to the engine than the rear platform of the last car. They would have been fools if they had, for they did not know how many were in the attacking party, nor from what point along the track a shot might come.

At the point of the bandits' pistol the engineer uncoupled the express car from the passenger coaches behind it and from the baggage car in front.

Then he returned from the engine and hauled the baggage car out of the siding, coming back on the main track and closing up to the express car.

He got down from the engine to turn the switch at each end of the siding, and again to couple the express car to the engine, on each occasion escorted by the desperado, with the pistol cocked and ready.

During all this period the train crew and the passengers remained inside the car. Indeed, few of the passengers knew that any unusual occurrence had stopped the train.

Under the robbers' direction, the engineer took the express car up the line a couple of miles away from the rest of the train, where he brought it to a standstill. There was no other train due along the line for several hours, so that there was no immediate danger of a collision, and now the engineer and his captor approached the baggage car, where the latter called upon the express .messenger, Ike Perkins.

There being no response, the robber produced a stick of dynamite from his boot-leg and made Fischer blow the door open, the explosion tearing out one end of the car.

Approaching this aperture, forcing Fischer to walk before him as a shield, the desperado discovered Perkins, with cocked revolver, standing guard over the property committed to his care, and called upon him to throw his weapon out of the car and empty his pockets. The express messenger obeyed orders. He could not shoot at the robber without endangering the life of Fischer. On the other hand, Perkins afforded a fair mark for Young.

Once inside the express car the Big Swede, cool and masterful, produced another revolver and more dynamite and, covering both of the other men with his battery, he ordered them to blow open the safe, which he knew to contain many thousands of dollars in actual cash.

And now a surprising thing happened. As the safe fell apart at the sound of the explosion a mass of loose yellow coin rolled out on the floor seventeen thousand dollars in gold double eagles. The sight temporarily unbalanced the Big Swede's mind, and, with a roar of delight, he dropped both of his pistols and fell head forward into the golden flood, attempting to pick up an armful. In a fraction of a second Perkins seized a piece of the wreckage of the car and struck the desperado a terrible blow over the back of the head.

The bandit did not recover consciousness until noon the following day, when he found himself under guard in the hospital at Montana. He proved to be Bill Horn, one of the James gang, and is at present serving a term of fifty years in State prison, for the holdup men get long sentences in Montana.

Another instance of a prearranged robbery failed was on the Chicago, Burlington and Quincy Road, where several of the James gang, headed by a burly ruffian, known as Al. Redding, attempted a little holdup without the aid or council of their leaders.

In order to accomplish this robbery the bandits boarded the train at a way station and intended to spring the hold-up when it got far away from civilization. But it so happened that the conductor became suspicious of one of the men who was sitting in the smoker and kept an eye on him, and when that person followed him out to the platform, a quarter of an hour after leaving Billings, he was prepared for him. The result was that each drew a revolver and that Jackman got his out first and shot the other man through the heart.

Meantime, the confederate had reached the tender of the engine; but, before he had attempted to hold up the engineer, the conductor had pulled the communication cord as a signal to stop the train, upon the shooting of rascal No. 1. - Rascal No. 2 evidently surmised that the scheme to rob the express was not working smoothly, for the engineer saw him jump from the engine as the train began to slow down.

JAMES BOYS DEEDS OF DARING

THE DYNAMITE TRAIN ROBBERY

THE JAMES BOYS RESORTED TO THE USE OF HIGH EXPLOSIVES IN THEIR LATTER-DAY EXPRESS CAR ROBBERIES, WHERE STRONG SAFES WERE OFTEN ENCOUNTERED

The introduction of dynamite as a factor in train robbing came with the latter day operations of the James Boys and their gang, and it is said that although the leaders themselves were wary of the high explosive and not over fond of being in any way associated with it or its usages, they were compelled to adopt it as a means of opening express car safes of the later improved patterns, and, in order to safely and expeditiously accomplish the same, enlisted, a former blasting expert in their gang, and to him fell the exclusive task of blowing the captured safes, white the others guarded him while at his work and kept the train crew and officers at bay. The introduction of the dangerous and powerful explosive came at a time when a perfect beehive of criminal industry was buzzing over the west, and lent new terrors to those whose duty it was to pursue and try to capture the death-defying train robbers. The most notable of all dynamite train robberies occurred on the Missouri Pacific, not many hundred miles west of St. Louis, in August, 1886. It was one of the most important trains of the road. It carried, besides the usual through tourist and passenger coaches, the baggage and mail, and a through express car of the Wells, Fargo Express Company.

The express car, according to the usual custom of the company, carried two treasure boxes, one being a "way safe" for the convenience of the express messenger, the other a through safe, which was billed to San Francisco direct, locked and sealed.

The through safe, of the strongest modern construction, always carried the bulk of the money and valuables for the Pacific coast. After reaching San Antonio from the East, it was again made up and relocked. It was not supposed to be opened en route, or until it reached the company's office in San Francisco.

The night run was made without unusual incident.

The train reached Clayton (nearly half-way on its journey) at 2.30 in the morning. It was in this vicinity that a previous attempt had been made to rob the train. The next stop was at a siding, called, by courtesy, Samuels, located about twenty miles west of Clayton, and twelve miles from the Rio Grande.

To this point the run was made at low speed.

It was a bright, cold morning, with a starry sky, such as can only be seen in southwestern Texas, that made the surrounding prairie almost as light as day.

Just before reaching Samuels the fireman remarked to the engineer that he thought "a bunch of horses was riding the train over to the left."

"Probably some cows broke loose from a herd," Seiver answered him. They paid no more attention to the matter until the engineer pulled up at the siding.

Everything was still about them; the cars closed and dark, and the only sound was the faint puffing of the engine or an occasional remark by the enginemen.

The fireman again remarked that he thought there was "a bunch of something" near them, on the prairie. They had stopped a little short of the siding. The engineer reached for the throttle to pull ahead, when from somewhere either on or near the train came a voice:

"All hunk, boys."

From the prairie came a sudden pounding of hoofs and clattering of spurs and accoutrements as the horsemen dismounted, and six or seven men came running toward the engine and cars. There was no time for the trainmen to realize what had happened, much less make any resistance, before a dropping volley of rifle shots was fired in the direction of the baggage and express car, the bullets thudding against the woodwork.

For a moment the engineer mistook the attacking party for a band of larking cowboys, for the starlight showed them plainly, dressed in "chaps," or riding breeches, sombreros, and the usual cattle riders' outfit. But he quickly noted that all the men were masked and carried rifles.

Immediately on firing the volley two of the bandits sprang upon the locomotive, guarding the enginemen.

Four others made for the express car.

"Just watch and you'll see a new Wild West Show," one of the robbers on the engine remarked.

The remainder of the robbers' troop, if there were more, stayed back out of sight with the horses, "planted" for the usual get-away.

One of the men at the express car yelled to the messenger to open up or it would be worse for him.

As there was no response from Messenger Smith or the United States mail clerk, who was in the mail car, the robbers began shouting threats. It was plain, from their language and appearance that the robbers were all Americans, and not a mixed band of Mexicans and renegade raiders.

They paid no attention to the passenger coaches, except to fire once or twice when a sound came from the rear part of the train and to yell to some others in the background to be on the lookout.

Unsuccessful in getting any answer from the messenger, the robbers called something to the mail clerk (who was working like a beaver secreting his valuable packages in the car). His reply enraged them, for one of them cried out with a curse:

"We've monkey'd long enough. Tote that dynamite over here, Vell."

A man came from where the horses had been left, carrying a small parcel in his hands and coolly smoking a cigar or cigarette.

They quickly laid the cartridge and fuse. One explosion was sufficient to shatter the safe so that the robbers could gain entry. Here they secured the real express treasure, in various forms and amounts approximating twenty thousand dollars.

The final booty satisfied them. One of the party brought up a led horse. Across the saddle they tumbled two mail sacks containing the money and miscellaneous matter. The leader shouted to the others to get away, and the men on the engine climbed down, still watching the enginemen, with their rifles in their hands while waiting for the others to fetch the horses.

It was broad daylight by this time, nearly five o'clock in the morning. The robbers had delayed the train almost two hours. The other members of the band sat their horses, in plain sight an ominous crew of brigands in the pale light of that prairie morning when the leader sprang down from the car with a parting word to the express, messenger:

"Here's your money," he said. "We don't want that now. And here's the other Johnny's, too," referring to the mail clerk who had also been relieved of his personal possessions. He picked up his rifle and turned to go, with a laugh and a final remark:

"Don't look so downhearted, Sonny. You aint the last express man that's going to weaken in front of dynamite!"

With a rush and a pounding of hoofs, as they had come, the bandits departed. In a moment only a cloud of dust told of the successful get-away of the first successful railroad dynamiters.

DEEDS OF DARING

JAMES BOYS DEEDS OF DARING

THE JAMES BOYS IN MEXICO

A WILD VISIT TO THE LAND OF PRESIDENT DIAZ AND THE GREAT SENSATION THE BANDITS' VISIT TO THAT COUNTRY CREATED

After having "played the devil generally," so to speak, in the United States and being the object of pursuit not only of the State and Government troops, but of the police authorities of nearly every Western State, the Pinkertons and railroad police in general, Jesse and Frank James decided wisely perhaps that they would leave the dominion of Uncle Sam for awhile and sojourn neath the tropic sun of Mexico, believing rightly that in that genial clime, where police methods are lax and American wrongs adjusted very slowly, they would be safe from pursuit or capture until things blew over a bit. After a few days journey they reached the Mexican border and passed over into the domain which seemed to offer them security and rest, it might be added peace, but that condition of human affairs seems not to have been intended for them, so the white dove perched not long above them. Their first social event after reaching the land of the cactus was a fandango or dance, which was held near the little country town where they were stopping. Of course, they had not been invited, but that fact cut little figure with gentlemen of as extreme nerve of the James Boys, so they literally invited themselves and went. More than that they actually danced with the Mexican senoritas, and thereby occasioned much jealousy on the part of the native cavaliers.

The onlookers were first amused and then broke out into open ridicule, and laughed at Frank and Jesse and began to mimic, with exaggerated contortions, the awkward dancing of the brothers.

Now, the boys could stand a good deal, but you were not to laugh at them. They were not very fastidious or exacting in their demands, but they would not stand being laughed at! So, quick as thought, down went one of the boldest beneath the strong hand of Frank. In a moment a strongly built Mexican struck Frank a blow on the cheek which sent him spinning headlong into the ample laps of two Mexican maidens, much to their amazement and disgust. This was no time to waver, so Jesse improved the moment by sending a bullet through the brain of the Mexican who had struck his brother Frank. This stirred the Spanish blood, and, what lovers of the sanguinary would say, the fun began, and the fighting was beautiful. Frank and Jesse made for the door, but their way was blocked by the furious and vengeful hidalgoes. Stilettos gleamed and glistened. But stilettos are poor where revolvers come. A desperate fight followed in which revolvers were freely used on both sides, and many of the revelers were wounded.

Carmen, a town in the northern part of the State of Chihuahua, Mexico, next saw the brother desperadoes. This town is on the line of travel from the silver mines for merchants and seemed to offer exceptional advantages for a hold-up. Just by way of diversion the James boys determined on it, "in order to keep in practice," as they afterwards admitted.

Not long afterward two seemingly affable young Americans approached a pack train of twelve mules from the silver mines and, after making friends with the muleteers and guards, offered to travel along with them a way, in order to help protect them against any stray bandits that might be hiding in the hills.

James Boy's in Mexico

They played their game so well, the simple Mexicans suspected nothing and seemed glad of their company.

They represented themselves as being anxious to get back to the, States, but afraid to travel alone, owing to bandits and Indians. Frank and Jesse had three other friends who were really in the same box with themselves. The chief of the guard was interviewed with a request that he would allow these young men, who had been inspecting mines, to go under their escort for safety just across the perilous border, of course, agreeing that if danger came they would fight in the interests of the guard and their treasure.

The chief consented, and so there started out next day from Carmen the procession of mules and their treasures and guards, and these five pious - looking young gentlemen goody-goody looking enough to teach in Sunday-school or exhort at a mission. And yet Mexico had not five such desperadoes from the North Fork to the most southerly sweep of the Rio Grande!

DEEDS OF DARING

For two or three days they were watched, but soon all suspicion gave way to confidence. It was noon, about the fifth day out, when the cavalcade halted near a most refreshing fountain. The burdens were taken from the mules that they might graze at leisure in the valley. The muleteers, all save two who were reserved to stand sentinel over the bags of silver were enjoying their noon day siesta. The ingenious five were under a tree apart, holding a quiet converse. The guns of the whole party were stacked against a tree. The two guards on duty over the silver pouches were holding their guns in the most formal and careless manner over their shoulders.

The opportune moment had come!

"Let's go, boys!" was the brief signal from Jesse, accompanied by his low, shrill whistle.

Crack! went a couple of pistols, and the two armed guards sank quivering to the earth, shot dead! The arms staged against the tree were destroyed in less time than it takes to tell. The other guards were ordered to hold up their arms, and were at once disarmed. They then ordered the muleteers to put the bags of silver on the best mules. All the rest of the horses were shot.

Then Frank and Jesse and their confreres rode off with their stolen treasure, threatening instant death to anyone who dared to follow. The robbers bore their treasure into Texas, divided the spoils, and congratulated each other on the success of the enterprise.

But they did not linger long in Texas, and then when things began to grow hot again they decided upon returning to Mexico, where living was easy and they had no trouble in turning a trick when their cash ran low. They went to a town called Monclova, in Coahuila, and here to their surprise met one of their old companions of wartime days.

He had returned after the war to peaceful pursuits and, having become enamored with the bright eyes of a pretty half-breed, had settled down to a quiet rural life in the country.

The sight of the James boys and the sound of their voices woke up a thousand pleasant memories. They talked of the old times, and sang the old songs, and fought the old battles over again, till the Mexican bride was alarmed to think how desperate a man she had married.

Now, it seems the one essential proof of Mexican kindness is to honor your friend who visits you with a fandango. Frank and Jesse, nothing loth, on the promise that the grace and beauty of Monclova should adorn the scene, accepted the honor. The night came, and with the night the fandango.

The honored guests were summering in beauty's smiles, the host was charmed that all went so well, and the gentle hostess beamed and smiled complacently around. All went well for a time, till the quick eye of Jesse thought he discovered a furtive glance in the eyes of two of the guests. A young lieutenant of the Mexican Army and an American from Matehuela were among the guests.

Jesse became more and more convinced that trouble was brewing and informed his brother Frank of his suspicions. His surmises were correct, for both men knew there was a reward of $1,000 hanging over the James Boys' heads and had secretly determined to earn it. They managed to communicate the news of the James brothers' presence to the Mexican authorities, and at midnight the house was surrounded by a large detachment of soldiers. When the festivities were at their gayest the raid was made. The door was suddenly thrown open and a stately uniformed officer strode into the room, followed by a military guard.

A scene of indescribable confusion ensued. The men were astounded, the ladies were panic-stricken.

The only calm people at the fandango were the two most concerned.

The officer marched up to Frank and Jesse, and in the name of the Mexican Government demanded their surrender. The brothers laughed derisively in the faces of the officers.

"Will you surrender peacefully?" he asked.

"Never!" was Frank's calm reply.

With that the officer motioned to his guards to move up.

"Stop!" It was Jesse's voice of command. The officer waved to his guards to halt. .

"We have a proposition to submit. Will you hear it?"

"If it means surrender, yes," replied the officer.

"It is this," pursued Jesse; not appearing to notice the purport of the officer's reply, "to allow these ladies here to retire, and we will discuss the question with you."

To this the officer finally agreed, and they did so.

"Now will you surrender?" demanded the officer.

"No," yelled Jesse, and the next moment a pistol flashed and the officer lay dead at his feet.

Three more shots rang out in quick succession and three more Mexican soldiers fell dead to the floor.

The guard became demoralized and fled. The boys now rushed for the street. The soldiers guarding the house fired, but they fired aimlessly in their confusion, and Frank and Jesse only received a few scratches.

In a little while the whole town was mad with excitement, and the wildest stories got abroad. All the ladies of the fandango had been remorselessly butchered by hireling murderers, the soldiers were all shot, and the work of massacre was going on.

The wild stories grew and grew. The streets soon surged with a most excited crowd. The fire bells rang, the alarm drums beat at the barracks, the whole of the soldiery formed in line and marched to the scene of the disaster. Men, women and children made the night hideous with their screams.

The darkness was dense and favored the fugitives.

Frank and Jesse reached their horses, and while Monclova was hunting them about the region of the place of blood they were riding fast and furiously away.

After this desperate affair the James brothers lived quietly in a secluded spot in the mountains until the excitement had died out, and then, perhaps, tired of the bloodshed and excitement amid which they had lived so long, determined to seek rest in the simple pastoral life, and took up a sheep ranch, where they accumulated large and valuable flocks. They seemed doomed to warfare, however, and despite their really earnest efforts to live at peace with the world, even for a short time, they were soon again forced to take up the trail again. This came about by reason of the depredations of one Juan Palacio, a Mexican cattle thief, who had included sheep in his stealings. He robbed the sheepfolds right and left, driving away whole droves, which he afterwards sold. So long as he confined his stealings to the Mexican herds the James boys paid no attention, but when their sheep began to go they arose to anger and vengeance quickly. Although robbers themselves they quickly resented any attempt to rob them and started out after the greaser who stole their sheep, assisted by a murderer named Almonte, another outlaw.

Palacio proposed to carry away all the cattle, and if the cowboys on the various ranches objected well, cold lead and a short shrift. And the cold lead first. The stampede was complete.

Three of the "cowboys" were killed, but the herds were marched to the banks of the Rio Grande.

Two days afterwards Frank and Jesse heard of this from one of the sorely distressed herdsmen.

It so happened that Frank and Jesse had possessions in the valley, and their flocks had been carried off by the murdering Mexicans; and, of all men, they were not the men to sit down and be robbed in silence. Their plans were soon formed.

Prompt action was needed now. It was in October. Frank and Jesse soon got on Palacio's trail. They came to El Paso. All was silent, though the robbers had driven through the village. Palacio and Almonte came to camp in the mountains. They felt themselves quite secure, and so fell asleep in fancied safety. But they had but little sleeping time. They were suddenly aroused by the ports from the avenging pistols of the James boys. Shot after shot was fired, dealing death at every discharge. Roused from the midst of a fitful sleep, the robbers were dazed and bewildered, and thought they were surrounded by a huge company of avengers, and so they fled as fast as their weary legs could carry them, giving themselves no time, for they were in no mood to examine the state of things. Ten of these robbers lay dead, and the rest, terror-stricken, had hurried away in wild confusion to the shelter of the hills. The leaders, Palacio and Almonte, were not with the camp when Frank and Jesse made their murderous onslaught. When the tidings reached them they, of course, imagined what the rest of the thirty thought that there must be a company of avengers, or "Grino Diablas," as they called them, from the Pecos Vale. When they came to understand that this successful raid had been carried on by two men only they were furious, and swore by all their gods to be avenged. The whole troop of the twenty-five were on the trail of the brothers to recapture the cattle and strike death to the hearts of the graceless two who had wrought them such humiliation and decimated their band.

At last they came in sight of the great crowding herds of cattle, and there were only these two men to deal with. Who would give a pin's worth for the chances of the boys?

Arrived on the crest of the hill, he saw fifteen of these greasers coming up the hill. They were four hundred yards away, but Jesse's trusted long - range Winchester did splendid service. One after another of the Mexicans fell, till by the time Frank came up four of the leaders and one of their mustangs lay dead, and the rest of the company had beat a retreat. As Frank reached the brow of the hill, Jesse said:

"Well, I've prepared a feast for the vultures over yonder."

"How many are down?" asked Frank.

"Oh, only four men and one horse," he answered, with a grim sort of smile.

And the rest of the valiant Mexican host were galloping away for dear life.

JAMES BOYS DEEDS OF DARING

MORE CRUEL THAN NERO WERE THE JAMES BOYS

WHEN THOROUGHLY AROUSED OR WHEN THEIR HOME WAS ATTACKED BY RAIDERS, THEIR CRUELTY AND DESIRE FOR REVENGE KNEW NO BOUNDS AND NO UNDERTAKING WAS TOO BLOODTHIRSTY

There were two sides to the natures of the James Boys, and despite the fact that to their old mother they were all kindness and tenderness, and to women in general they were considerate and gallant, Nero was never more cruel in his worst moods than were these two outlaws when on the trail for revenge.

This vindictive spirit was particularly directed against the Pinkerton Detective Agency and its men, which had been remorselessly hunting them down for several years. Several times they had experienced very narrow escapes, and in more than one instance the Pinkerton man never returned to report what happened.

Governors Woodson, of Missouri, and Baxter, of Arkansas, offered large rewards for the apprehension of all or any of the bandits, as did likewise the American Express Company, who engaged Allen Pinkerton and his efficient force of detectives to hunt them down at all hazards and at any cost.

In a number of instances the pursuers became the pursued, and it was the bandits who chased the detectives instead of vice versa.

The following account of the meeting of Detectives Allen Wright and Daniels, of the Pinkerton force, I will give some idea of the character of these desperadoes:

"We were riding along the road from Roscoe to Chalk Level, in St. Clair County, which road leads past the house of one Theodore Snuffer. Daniels and myself were riding side by side, and our companion, Wright, was a short distance ahead of us. Some noise behind us attracted our attention, and, looking back, we saw two men on horseback coming toward us; one was armed with a double-barrel shotgun, the other with revolvers; don't know if the latter had a shotgun or not; the one that had the shotgun carried it cocked, both barrels, and ordered us to halt; Wright drew his pistol, but then put spurs to his horse and rode off; they ordered him to halt, and shot at him, and shot off his hat, but he kept on riding. Daniels and myself stopped, standing across the road on our horses; they rode up to us and ordered us to take off our pistols and drop them on the road, one of them covering me all the time with his gun. We dropped our pistols on the ground, and one of the men told the other to follow Wright and bring him back, but he refused to go, saying he would stay with him; one of the men then picked up the revolvers we had dropped, and, looking at them, remarked they were damned fine pistols, and that we must make them a present of them; one of them asked me where we came from, and I said, 'Osceola;' he then wanted to know what we were doing in this part of the country; I replied, 'Rambling around'. One of them said: 'You were up here one day before.' I replied that we were not. He then said we had been at the Springs. I replied that we had been at the Springs, but had not been inquiring for them; that we did not know them; they said detectives had been up there hunting for them all the time, and they were going to stop it. Daniels then said: 'I am no detective; I can show you who I am and where I belong' and one of them said he knew him, and then turned to me and said: 'What in hell are you riding around here with all them pistols on for?' and I said: 'Good God! is not every man wearing them that is traveling, and have I not as much right to wear them as anyone else?' Then the one that had the shotgun said: 'Hold on, young man, we don't want any of that' and then lowered the gun, cocked, in a threatening manner. Then Daniels had some talk with them, and one of them got off his horse and picked up the pistols; two of them were mine and one was Daniels'; the one mounted had the gun drawn on me, and I concluded that they intended to kill us. I reached my hand behind me and drew a No. 2 Smith & Wesson pistol and cocked and fired at the one on horseback; my horse became frightened at the report of the pistol and turned to run; then I heard two shots and my left arm fell; I had no control over my horse, and he jumped into the bushes before I could get hold of the rein with my right hand to bring him into the road; one of the men rode by and fired two shots at me, one of which took effect in my left side, and I lost all control of my horse again, and he turned into the brush, when a small tree struck me and knocked me out of the saddle. I then got up and staggered across the road and lay down until I was found. No one else was present."

Captain Allen was struck very hard in the left side, two inches above the hip; he was carried back to Roscoe, where he lingered for a period of six weeks, and then died, surrounded by his family, that had come to him from Chicago, directly after the shooting. His remains were enclosed in a metallic case and returned to Chicago, where they were buried with Masonic honors. Ed Daniels was laid away in the little churchyard at Osceola.

The torture and murder of Detective Wicher, also of the Pinkerton force, by the James Boys, was particularly brutal and aroused the entire country when its details became known.

Pinkerton received information that the James Boys and others of the band of robbers were in hiding near Kearney, in Clay County, Missouri, and he determined to send some brave, trusty man out there to definitely locate them, get into their confidence and prepare the way for an early capture of the whole gang. Pinkerton had come to the conclusion that open pursuit of the bandits would never result in their capture, for they had too many friends in the community where they operated to make it possible to apprehend them. They always had timely warning of the approach of an enemy, and ready shelter in the houses of their friends on a moment's notice.

The chief of detectives, therefore, resolved to capture the gang through strictly detective methods, and called upon his force for a man to do the delicate and dangerous work.

John W. Wicher, of Chicago, one of Pinkerton's most trusted men, volunteered for this delicate duty. Wicher was scarcely thirty years of age, but had seen much service as a detective, and was considered by Pinkerton to be one of his bravest, clearest-headed and most trusty men.

Young Wicher was fully informed of the dangers of such a mission, but his self-reliance and pride made him anxious to make the attempt which had already cost the lives of so many courageous officials.

The chief gave his consent, and Wicher set out at once for the Samuels residence. In the early part of March the detective arrived in Liberty, where he soon laid his schemes before the sheriff of Clay County, and asked for assistance when the time and circumstances were ripe for a strike. The Sheriff promised all needful aid, and gave Wicher all the information in his possession concerning the habits and rendezvous of the James and Younger Boys.

Determined to either capture the James Boys or forfeit his life in the attempt, Detective Wicher disguised himself as a tramp and started for the home of the bandits. He reached there in due time, and before he could even realize it had fallen into their clutches. Realizing that it was useless for him to try resistance at that time, he decided to resort to a ruse and solemnly averred that he was only a humble wayfarer. They accused him of being a Pinkerton man, which he indignantly denied.

"Well, gentlemen, I am nothing more than a poor man, without as much as a dollar in my pocket, and what I have told you as to my purpose is true. If you will be good enough to let me proceed, or furnish me with means by which I can secure work, I shall be thankful."

At this the bandits laughed scornfully, while Jesse James proceeded with the examination:

"I think you are from Chicago, and when you arrived at Liberty a few days ago you wore much better clothes than you now have on; besides, it seems that you and Moss (the sheriff) have some business together. Say, now, young fellow, haven't you set out to locate the James boys, whom you have found rather unexpectedly?"

Wicher saw that he was in the hands of his enemies, and his heart beat in excited pulsation as he thought of the young wife he had so recently wedded, and from whom an eternal separation appeared certain. Dropping his head as if resigning himself to cruel fate, Wicher hoped to deceive his captors, and in an unguarded moment be able to draw his pistol and fight for his life. Like a flash from a hazy cloud the detective thrust his hand into his bosom and succeeded in grasping his pistol, but ere he could use it the bandits sprang upon him, and in the grip of three strong men he was helpless. He was then disarmed and firmly bound by small cords which Frank James produced. Clell Miller went into the woods and soon returned, leading three horses, on the largest of which Wicher was placed and his feet tied under the horse's belly. A gag was placed tightly in his mouth, and Jesse James, mounting behind, the desperadoes rode into the deepening woods with their victim. They crossed the Missouri River at Independence Landing, and just before day they halted in the black shadows of a copse in Jackson County. Here they prepared for the torture and execution of their prisoner. Wicher was taken from his horse and bound fast to a tree; the gag was removed from his mouth, and then the bandits tried to extort from him information concerning the plans of Pinkerton and the number and names of the detectives he had engaged in the attempt to capture the outlaws.

Though they pricked him with their bowie knives and bent his head forward with their combined strength until the spinal column was almost broken, and practiced other atrocious torments, yet Wicher never spoke. He knew that death was his portion, and he denied the desperadoes and dared them to do their worst.

Finding all their endeavors fruitless, Jesse and Frank James murdered their victim, one of them shooting him through the heart and the other through the brain. The body was then carried to the nearest highway, where it was left to be found next day by a farmer who was driving into Independence.

JAMES BOYS DEEDS OF DARING

THE IRON MOUNTAIN TRAIN ROBBERY

Perhaps the most celebrated train robbery committed by the James brothers and their close accomplices, the Youngers, was that of the Iron Mountain express in Missouri, near a place called Wayne, which for daring and actual audacity certainly eclipses all their other achievements in this line. It was the big sensation of the entire country at the time, and is still recalled by Westerners as the most desperate affair of its kind that ever occurred in that country. The spot where the robbery occurred was ideal, inasmuch as it was inhabited by only a few people. The surrounding country was a perfect jungle, which made the escape of the bandits comparatively easy after the perpetration of their crime.

The Iron Mountain express was due at Wayne at 5.40 P. M., and a little before that hour a band of six men rode up on horseback, halting a short distance from the railroad station. They were all stalwart fellows, wearing gray felt hats and old blue army overcoats, and without close inspection might have been taken for a detachment of United States troopers, especially as they carried big revolvers in their belts and Winchester rifles in their hands. Dismounting, they fastened their horses to a clump of trees near by, and walked quietly up to the little railroad station. The few loiterers about the station were greatly surprised when the sextette drew their pistols and ordered them inside the station. But they stood not on the order of their going, and simply went without parley. They were all promptly locked inside, under threat of instant death if they attempted to escape.

Now in absolute control of the station, the brigands prepared to receive the Iron Mountain express. The switch leading into the side track was thrown open in order to prevent the engineer from running past the station in case his suspicions should be aroused, and a red signal flag was planted in the center of the track immediately in front of the station platform. Then the robbers lit cheroots and moved back into the shadow of the station house to await the arrival of the train.

The robbers had a definite purpose in holding up the Iron Mountain train. In the railroad robbery of the previous July they had missed $75,000 in gold by stopping the wrong train the one which preceded the treasure. Now they had learned that Treasurer Stanchfield, of the Clearwater Lumber Company, was to be on this train with $5,000, no mean sum in those days. Moreover, they counted on cleaning out the Adams Express car.

They had well timed the arrival of the train and had not long to wait, for in a very few minutes the faint trail of smoke from the locomotive was seen in the distant sky, and soon the puffing of the engine was heard as it came speeding across the prairie. Wayne was not a regular stop, trains stopping there on being signalled. This the robbers knew, and set the proper flag by the track for the train to halt. The engineer saw it and, suspecting nothing, brought his train to a stop beside the station platform.

For a moment there was no one to be seen. Then the leader of the gang made a dash for the engine cab and climbed into it with a drawn revolver.

"You fellows need some exercise," he remarked to the helpless engineer and firemen. "Climb down and take to the woods... No foolishness! You walk straight out, and don't come back until we whistle for you, unless you're tired of living."

The Iron Mountain Express Hold-Up

The conductor sprang down to see what the trouble was. He found himself looking into the muzzles of two revolvers, and was greeted with a command to throw up his hands or have his head blown off.

"Come along to the coop," the robber added cheerfully, through the black calico mask which he wore over his face.

A glance forward showed him that three other masked men were approaching with revolvers in their hands, and that he had no choice but to obey.

The work of going through the cars was done expeditiously to the accompaniment of a running fire of remarks. Then, after finishing with the passengers and warning them as they valued their lives to keep quiet, the bandits turned their attention to the express and mail car. They broke open the safe of the Adams Express Company, but in it they found only $1,080. One of them reported, from the door, the smallness of the sum to the leader, who was keeping a watchful eye upon the cars and the prisoners.

"Rip up Uncle Sam and see what he's got inside," he answered.

The United States mail bags were immediately cut open and rifled. In one letter the robbers found $2,000 in bills, and varying sums in a number of others. Coolly counting up the entire proceeds, the looters found that their booty was nearly $12,000, including $1,260 from the mail bags.

The robbers, "who were all six-footers and heavily armed, escaped on fine, blooded horses, going in a southerly direction."

This remarkable document wound up with the Statement: "This thing made a h--l of an excitement in this part of the country."

"Here's the last item" the leader said, when he handed the paper to one of the trainmen.

"We like to do things in style and save people all the trouble we can. All right, Al!" he shouted to the conductor, "You can travel on now."

Just as the engineer was pulling out, the robber who had thrown the switch discovered that he had left his overcoat on the track beside the switchboard. The engineer was again stopped while the fellow went forward and secured his coat, throwing back the switch at the same time.

As the passenger cars passed the robbers on the platform they waved their hands with sarcastic farewells.

"We'll see you some other day when we get short of funds," the leader cried.

A minute later they threw open the door of the station and released the prisoners. Then, mounting their "fine, blooded horses," the six ruffians rode leisurely away.

The robbery created a tremendous sensation, particularly as it was ascertained that the outrage was committed by the same men who had robbed the Hot Springs stage coach only two weeks before. Aside from the amount of the booty, which was a secondary consideration, the authorities, including the railroad, express and post office officials, realized that the audacity of the crime called for immediate action.

There was not the slightest doubt of the identity of the brigands. As an editorial writer remarked at the time: "No continent could produce two bends of such blithesome ruffians!" Besides, forty pairs of eyes had studied them, and there was plenty of material for identification,

Rewards amounting to a large sum were at once offered for the apprehension of the outlaws. After the Governor of Missouri had sent his indignant message to the Legislature, that body declined to allow him the use of the militia or to vote sufficient money for the organization of a secret police, but it did vote $10,000 to use as rewards.

The Governor immediately offered $2,000 apiece for the capture of the Iron Mountain desperadoes and subsequently the Governor of Arkansas offered $2,500 more. The Post Office Department also offered a reward of $5,000, making an aggregate of $17,500 from these sources alone for the apprehension of the robbers, "living or dead."

The Missouri Pacific Railroad and the Adams Express Company, besides offering any reasonable sum in rewards, also instituted vigorous measures to capture the gang. A number of St. Louis detectives were put on the case, and the Pinkerton Detective Agency sent out two of their best detectives.

Despite all these efforts to capture them, however, the James boys seemed to bear charmed lives, for they had seemingly vanished as though the earth had opened and swallowed them up.

DEEDS OF DARING

JAMES BOYS DEEDS OF DARING

THE GREAT MAMMOTH CAVE STAGE ROBBERY

DARING HOLD-UP OF THE COACH FILLED WITH SIGHT-SEERS AND THE EXCITING TIME THAT FOLLOWED THE ROBBERY

Generally, after a big train or bank robbery, the James Boys retired to their home with their booty and lived the easy and simple life until it was gone.

This period of inactivities, of course, varied in duration according to the magnitude of the haul and the laxness or activity of the law officers, who were in pursuit. If they lagged, and the bankroll was a big one, the desperadoes stayed home and took it easy for months. If not, they were on the warpath again in a week or two. As long as they kept away from the gambling table they had money, but very soon after they began bucking the tiger, they were invariably broke, for bold and successful robbers as they were, they lacked tact with the pasteboards, and were known to be very poor card sharps. It was while taking one of these periodical recuperative spells that they planned the robbery of the Mammoth Cave coach, the details of which are given below.

It occurred in September, 1880, at which season the great cave is visited by thousands of tourists from all parts of the country and world. One of the favorite routes to this natural wonder is by way of the Louisville and Nashville Railroad to Cave City, and thence by stage to the caves, about ten miles distant.

On the day of the robbery of the stage the passengers were the Right Rev. Bishop Gregg, of the Protestant Episcopal Diocese of Texas; Mr. Breckenridge, president of the First National Bank of San Antonio, and other ladies and gentlemen of good standing eleven in all. Merry, happy souls, who knew the brighter side of life, and knew no lack of earthly gear. The stage called at its usual halting place about six o'clock in order that man and beast might be refreshed.

Just after resuming their journey the driver descried ahead of him six mounted men, whom he took for rancheros; but as they drew nearer he became a little puzzled. They were mounted not on the rough mustang of the prairies, but on splendid American horses of the best breed. The driver became a little nervous.

It was about 6 P. M. that the stage was nearing Cave City on its return from the cave, that it was suddenly confronted by a number of masked horsemen, in a dark and deeply wooded ravine. In answer to a pistol shot, which whizzed close to his head, the driver reined up his horses, and the coach was at once surrounded by heavily armed horsemen.

The passengers, in terror, looked into the muzzles of what seemed to be a whole battery of revolver barrels and were ordered to alight. It was also explained by the highwaymen that the order applied to women as well as men.

"Come, tumble out!" was the brief command.

"Tumble out quick, if you don't want to die where you sit."

A scene of confusion ensued. The women of the party lost all presence of mind, and without the slightest regard for the proprieties, clambered over and clung to the gentlemen of the party for protection. Surely, never in the world, was a bishop hugged by a very ponderous maiden lady, of a very certain age, as she begged him for the love of God to protect her from "those wicked, horrid men."

But the bishop was more in danger than his stout clinging friend. Indeed, there was little danger to the women of the company, if they would but keep quiet. Jesse James did most of the talking on the occasion, though Younger occasionally put in a word.

The ladies were assured they had nothing to fear, if only the men behaved themselves.

"Behaving themselves on this occasion meant simply getting out of the stage and delivering all their possessions quietly.

"Come, tumble out or die" was Jesse's brief command.

And now came the plunder of personal possession.

"Gentlemen and ladies," said Jesse in a mock politeness, "it will be our painful duty now to trouble you for the money and jewelry you may chance to have about you."

"Do you mean to rob us?" asked the bishop in a tone of offended dignity, as he gazed on the scene.

"Oh! fie, fie," said the shocked young robber; "you shouldn't use such ugly language! Rob you! Oh! never, never! We would scorn the action! Do we look like robbers? No, gentlemen, we only wish to relieve you of a burden that's all; so out with your money and quick, we have no time to spare."

"Don't you call that robbery?" asked the bishop.

"Come, now, old coon! Dry up, or you'll not have an opportunity to ask any more nonsensical questions. Hand out your money."

The bishop reluctantly complied, handing out his pocketbook.

The eight gentlemen were all searched, but very little was obtained till they came to Mr. Breckenridge, of the Louisville bank. He proved to be a big bonanza. They obtained from him over $1,000. The ladies were ordered to yield up their treasures. One was evidently poor. They examined her pocketbook, and Jesse said:

"Madam, is that all you have?"

"Every cent in the world," she replied.

"And how far are you going?"

"To Louisville, sir."

"Well, then, take your money; we won't trouble you."

To her intense surprise, the affrighted old lady found, when she got home, that Jesse had slipped a twenty-dollar bill into her poorly furnished pocket book, and she was wont to say in after years:

"Well, well, the James Boys were bad enough, Heaven knows, but they might have been a good deal worse."

Being in need of fresh horses, the James Boys took the fine pair of leaders that belonged to the coach and rode away, leaving the coach and its passengers to proceed to Cave City with a single pair of horses, sadly and slowly, as may be imagined.

JAMES BOYS DEEDS OF DARING

QUICKEST EXPRESS CAR ROBBERY ON RECORD

ONE OF THE NEATEST AND MOST QUIET TRAIN HOLD-UPS IN THE HISTORY OF THE JAMES BOYS' DARING ESCAPADES

Alacrity was always one of the characteristics of the James Boys' robberies, but peace and quiet were not. They were usually accompanied by wild yells, pistol shots, etc., doubtless to terrify the victims into easy surrender. The robbery of an express car attached to a Missouri and Northern train, near Joplin, created one of the biggest sensations of the day by reason of the speed with which it was accomplished and the lack of bravado which characterized its success.

Four men assembled near the railroad station one dark night and boarded the west bound train when it stopped for a minute to take several passengers aboard.

Four men gathered about the depot a few minutes before the train was due and, after engaging the old crossing watchman in conversation, suddenly grabbed him, made him prisoner in his watch box and took away his signal lanterns. Warning him that they would shoot him if he made the least noise or outcry, they departed down the track, after locking him in. When the train had gotten a little way past the station the engineer noted signals ahead and brought his train to a stop. Instantly the engineer and fireman were confronted by an armed man in the engine cab, who drew a pair of pistols and warned them not to move. More armed men had held up the conductor and train crew, while several entered the express car and bade the express messenger open the safe on pain of instant death if he refused. Seeing no way out of it, he obeyed.

The United States safe contents were speedily transferred to a grain sack without examination. The messenger once more found himself in peril, because he had no key to the Adams through safe, but, as his explanation was reasonable, the robbers were convinced.

One of the robbers then ran out, got the fireman's hammer and began banging at the safe. He was unable to produce much impression, whereupon a herculean bandit caught the hammer, and with a few tremendous blows broke a hole in the side, into which he vainly attempted to force his hand. The first striker, however, remarked that he "wore a No 7 kid" and could do better.

In just two minutes the safe was plundered and the booty bagged. No attempt was made to rob the passengers. The train boy's box was broken open and peanuts and apples were gobbled up voraciously. Only one or two shots were fired from the train, the robbers keeping up a fusilade on both sides and moving from point to point, so that in the darkness it seemed as though the brush was full of men.

The train boy had a revolver, and early in the fracas he stepped out on the platform and blazed away at one of the robbers, who gave a loud, croaking laugh and called out: "Hear that little bark!" As soon as the safes had been emptied the robbers told the trainmen to remove the obstructions before and behind and pull out, which was done with alacrity. The train was stopped an hour and ten minutes, and the booty secured amounted to fifteen thousand dollars.

DEEDS OF DARING

JAMES BOYS DEEDS OF DARING

JESSE JAMES SHOT BY GEORGE SHEPHERD

AFTER THE GLENDALE ROBBERY SHEPHERD UNDERTOOK TO CAPTURE THE DARING ROBBER AND CAME NEAR KILLING HIM IN THE ATTEMPT

Perhaps the narrowest escape that Jesse James ever had from death was at the hands of George Shepherd, a daring law officer, who started out to bring him in dead or alive and came very near doing the former. For once in his life Jesse had met his equal with a revolver, and it did not take him long to find it out. After being severely wounded he managed to escape by the mere "skin of his teeth." It all came about in this way:

Living in Kansas City at the time of the robbery was George Shepherd, one of the most courageous men that ever faced danger. He was one of Quantrell's lieutenants, and fought in all the terrible and unmerciful encounters of that chief of the black banner. He was at Lawrence, and rode beside the James Boys in that dreadful cyclone of remorseless murder. He had run the gauntlet of a hundred rifles and fought against odds which it appeared impossible to escape. After the close of the war Jesse James accepted Colonel Shepherd as a leader and followed him into Texas, and would still be following his counsels had not circumstances separated them.

Major Leggitt evolved a scheme out of his hours of study toward the capture of Jesse James. He sent for Shepherd, who was working for Jesse Noland, a leading dry goods merchant of Kansas City, and to the ex-guerilla he proposed his scheme. It was this: Shepherd, being well known to have formerly been a comrade of Jesse James, it was to be reported that undoubted information had reached the authorities establishing Shepherd's connection with the Glendale robbery. A report of this was to be printed upon a slip of paper having printed matter upon the reverse side, so as to appear like a newspaper clipping. Shepherd was to take this printed slip, find Jesse James and propose to join him, saying that he was being hounded by detectives, and, although innocent, he felt that his only safety was in uniting his fortunes with Jesse and his fearless band. This being accomplished, Shepherd was to find opportunity for killing Jesse James, and the reward for him, dead or alive, was to be divided. In addition to this, Shepherd was to be provided with a horse and to receive $50 per month during the time of his service.

The conditions and terms were satisfactory to Shepherd, and the latter part of October, about two weeks after the Glendale robbery, he started out in quest of Jesse James.

The plan of Shepherd's operations and the manner in which he accomplished his hazardous undertaking is herewith detailed just as he related the story to the writer, but, while the relation is interesting, it is now proved to be untrue in part.

The Duel on Horseback

When Shepherd left Kansas City he was armed with several revolvers and a dagger. He rode direct to the home of Jesse James and, telling a concocted story, managed to arrange a meeting with the gang in the woods near by. He was duly installed as a member of the James gang, and his first assignment was reconnoitering a proposed bank robbery at Empire City, to which place he preceded the gang. Upon his arrival he found the bank lighted up and a dozen men inside armed with rifles and shotguns. Shepherd at once suspected that the news he had imparted to the authorities had been acted upon.

Finding everything in readiness to meet the intended attack, Shepherd went into a restaurant, and, while eating his supper, Tom Cleary, an old acquaintance, greeted him. After supper the two went to Geary's house and remained all night, and Shepherd told his friend the part he was acting in the effort to capture Jesse James. Ed Cleary, a brother of Tom, was also informed of the scheme, and Shepherd asked their assistance, or, at least, to follow him the next morning to the camp of the bandits. The understanding was at the time Shepherd left the outlaws that he should return to the camp by 9 o'clock Sunday morning, and, if his report was favorable, the raid on the bank would be made Sunday night.

Shepherd kept the appointment and returned to the place where the bandits had encamped, but found the camp deserted. He thought this strange, but soon found the old sign of a "turn out" had been made to let him know where they were. It is well known that the James Boys and their comrades frequently separated. They had a sign, however, by which it was not difficult for them to find one another, and he soon joined the gang just outside the town to find that they were already aware the bank was guarded. They asked him how about it, but he professed ignorance of who had tipped off the intended raid, and suggested they get out of the locality as soon as possible.

This was agreed upon, and they rode away.

When they reached a point twelve miles south of Galena, all parties maintaining their respective positions, Shepherd gave a smart jerk of the bridle rein, which caused his horse to stop, while Jesse rode on.

It was the work of an instant, for as Jesse's horse gained two steps forward Shepherd drew one of his large pistols and, without speaking a word, fired, the ball taking effect in Jesse's head one inch behind the left ear. Only the one shot was fired, for Shepherd saw the result of his show, and Jesse plunged headlong from his horse and lay motionless on the ground, as if death had been instantaneous. Shepherd says he viewed the body for nearly a minute before either of the outlaws made any demonstration. Ed Miller first started toward him in a walking pace, and then Cummings and the unknown drew their pistols and rode swiftly after him. Shepherd's horse was swift, and he put him to the greatest speed, soon distancing the unknown, but Cummings was mounted on a superior animal, and the chase for three miles was a hot one. Each of the two kept firing, but the rapid rate at which they were riding made the shots ineffectual. Seeing that he was pursued only by Cummings, who was gaining on him, Shepherd stopped and wheeled his horse, and at that moment a bullet struck him in the left leg just below the knee, producing, however, only a flesh wound. As Cummings dashed up Shepherd took deliberate aim and fired, and Cummings reeled in the saddle, turned his horse and retreated. Shepherd says he feels confident that he struck Cummings hard in the side and that he killed Jesse James. He rode back to Galena, where he remained two weeks under a surgeon's care, and after recovery returned to Kansas City.

As it afterward proved, the bullet only grazed Jesse James' skull and knocked him senseless from his horse. It did not even penetrate the skull, and he soon recovered from the injury.

JAMES BOYS DEEDS OF DARING

MYSTERIOUS ROCK ISLAND ROBBERY

HOW THE JAMES BOYS RIFLED AN EXPRESS CAR WITHOUT CREATING MUCH EXCITEMENT UNTIL IT WAS ALL OVER AND HOW THEY GOT AWAY WITH A LOT OF RICH PLUNDER

The James brothers and their gang were not alone noted for bold and desperate hold-ups and train robberies, but they have been credited, as well, with a number of robberies that were accomplished with remarkable stealth and quietude. Like the bold lion in some of their robberies, taking all sorts of chances of being shot or captured, they were like the treacherous leopard in others, took comparatively no chances, and had finished the job almost before anyone, even in the train, realized what had happened. They were brazenly bold or almost cowardly stealthy, it seems, as the occasion demanded or their fancy dictated.

The following story of the robbery on the Rock Island road will give an idea of how quietly and mysteriously some of their robberies were accomplished. One cold, snowy night in March, 1886, the Kansas express, running over the Rock Island road, started westward from Chicago. The train was heavier than usual that night.

Coupled on in front of the regular passenger coaches the train carried two express cars, the first one given over entirely to express, mostly through matter, and the other to express and baggage.

The first car was in charge of Messenger Kellogg Nichols, a man of middle age, who had spent twenty years in the service of the express company.

The combined baggage and express car was in charge of Baggageman Newton Watt, who previous to his trip had been head brakeman of the train and who had taken the place of the regular baggageman, who was ill. The rear brakeman, a young fellow named Henry Swartz, became front brakeman for the trip.

Both the express and combination car had doors on either end, besides the large sliding doors on the sides, but the front part of Messenger Nichols car was blocked with packages. The second car, besides carrying additional local express freight, also contained Messenger Nichols' safe, a small iron trunk with a peculiar lock, the key of which Nichols carried in his pocket attached to a chain, according to regulations.

The safe was known to contain a considerable sum of money. The messenger had referred to the fact in checking-out his run, remarking jokingly, as he deposited a bulky money package in it:

"If I had that I wouldn't work tonight. I'd take a day off."

The duties of the messenger required him to work in both cars, but the heaviest part of his work was in the front car, where he repaired to check up his run as soon as they pulled out of the Chicago depot, leaving Baggageman Watt to look after the combination car.

After passing Blue Island, the next regular stop was at Joliet, about forty miles from Chicago.

Here some express matter was put off, and shortly before 1 o'clock on that stormy March morning the train proceeded on toward Morris, a run of about forty-seven minutes.

Minooka was between Joliet and Morris, but it was not a stopping point for this train. The engine merely slowed up on a heavy grade outside the town, whistled for the station, and gathering speed again, thundered onward to Morris.

Thirty minutes later the snow-covered train rolled into the station. Conductor Wagner dropped off the train and came forward to get his orders with the engineer. Swartz, the head brakeman, also jumped down, and at the same time an apparition in the shape of Watt, the baggageman, disheveled, stammering, staring as if he had seen a ghost, burst upon the astonished conductor.

"Great God" he cried in terror, with his eyes almost bulging out of his head. "Look in there. The safe all gone and papers all over the car?" The man was almost insane with fright and surprise and could hardly talk, yet he managed to mutter something about Messenger Nichols and swung his lantern into the car, calling him by name and looking for him. By this time the conductor and others of the train crew came forward and, entering the car, began a search for the missing messenger. They found his dead body in the forward part of the car, under a great pile of disordered express matter. His head had been battered in as with an iron bar, his left arm was broken at the wrist, probably with the same bludgeon as he fought to ward off the blow that killed him, and a bullet hole was found in his shoulder.

Obviously it was the blows on the head, inflicted, apparently, with some blunt instrument, that had caused the death of the unfortunate messenger.

There was evidence of a terrible struggle. Up and down the car, on the floor and sides and over the express packages, blood was spattered right and left. Whomsoever the messenger had fought, the conflict must have been desperate in the extreme.

It seemed incomprehensible that this short, slender little man of forty, wounded and battered as he must have been, could have been so tenacious unless it was plain to him that he was fighting for his life. That there must have been more than one assailant was shown by the fact that in the clenched hands of the messenger were found locks of different colored hair, stained now with the messenger's blood.

The messenger's safe had been blown open and looted, all the money and valuables having been taken and the papers thrown all over the car. The loss was about $25,000. When the confusion of the first surprise had somewhat abated, the baggageman was asked to tell his story, and related the following remarkable experience, which goes to show the wonderful quickness and surprise with which the robbery was accomplished. The run was new to him and he had been unusually closely engrossed in his work for that reason.

In the noise of the train and storm he had heard nothing unusual until the engine whistled for Minooka. The moment after the barrel of a revolver was poked over his shoulder against the side of his head.

Glancing up with a start, he saw a man standing behind him, his face covered with a mask.

"If you move before this train gets to Morris" the man said, "you'll get your head blown off by that man up there."

Watt looked up at the ventilator in the roof of the car. A hand holding a big pistol was poked through the ventilator, the pistol pointing down at the baggageman. Then he realized that there was another robber on the roof of the car.

Sitting there under the threatening muzzle of the big gun, he heard the robber behind him unlock and empty the express safe.

"I couldn't give the alarm," Watt said. "They swore they would kill me if I moved. They must have gone to the front car and taken the safe key away from Nichols before they came back to me."

As a matter of fact, the murdered messenger's key with the snapped chain was in the safe-lock.

Watt sat still under the revolver until the train reached Morris. When the engine whistled for that station he noticed suddenly that the hand and gun had been withdrawn from the ventilator in the roof, and turning cautiously, he found himself alone in the car with the front door closed.

Then he immediately gave the alarm to Conductor Wagner, who was with Swartz, the head brakeman.

Of the fight in the express car and the murder of Nichols he had had no intimation until the train stopped.

It was one-thirty-five when the train reached Morris. By two o'clock the town was aroused, all the passengers were up, and the station was crowded with excited men, while telegrams and orders were flying back and forth between Morris and Chicago.

The local police, the railroad detectives and the Pinkerton men were quickly on the trail of the robbers but they failed to capture them even after the most strenuous efforts, although the evidence clearly proved it was another "trick" turned by the James Boys.

JAMES BOYS DEEDS OF DARING

THE JAMES BOYS AS GAMBLERS

DESPERATE POKER PLAYERS, WHO STAKED THEIR LAST DOLLAR EVERY TIME AND LOST THOUSANDS
THIS WAS WHERE MUCH OF THEIR STOLEN PLUNDER WENT
KNOWN TO HAVE LOST $25,000 IN A SINGLE NIGHT'S PLAYING

Like many more criminals, the James Boys were inveterate gamblers. They lost over gaming tables in all parts of the country, nearly all the money they accumulated, and never made a protest when the game was fair. They have been known to part with $25,000 in a night without a word, but on other occasions have turned the gambling rooms into a shambles when they suspected the cards had been stacked on them or other unfair advantage taken of them. They would bet on anything, and when no other opportunity for gambling offered have been known to place a lump of sugar on the table in front of each person and bet hundreds of dollars as to which one a fly would light on first. They always boasted this game was absolutely square, as there could be no collusion with the flies. It was one of their favorite diversions. Their uncle was owner and proprietor of the Paso Robel Hotel, at Hot Springs, Nev, and there they went to gamble and recuperate. They became friendly with everybody, and visitors from all over the country little suspected the two gentlemanly young men were the most desperate and notorious robbers the world had ever known. After a time their health greatly improved, and feeling they might wear their welcome out, or, in other words, that their real character might be discovered, they decided to go further west, with California as their ultimate destination.

Moreover, just at that time the newspapers of the Pacific Coast were filled with thrilling accounts of daring robberies by "road agents" who infested the mountain passes of California, Nevada and Colorado.

These accounts were read with avidity by Frank and Jesse James in their quiet retreat at their uncle's hotel.

The old desperado spirit was reawakened within them, and they began to look back upon their three months of indolent rest as just so much of their lives thrown away. The fever of unrest burned on in their veins until it drove them forth into the mountains in search of adventure. Burnishing up their old-time trusty friends their ever-faithful revolvers they buckled on their fighting paraphernalia and sallied forth into the mountain passes, prepared for any sort of adventure that might happen to turn up. When we remember that the mining camps of that region were filled with reckless adventurers, cut-throats and gamblers, it is not at all surprising that Frank and Jesse James did not have far to go before they found all the excitement and adventure they wanted.

One bright, sunshiny morning Frank and Jesse, with two of their old guerrilla comrades from Missouri, whom they chanced to fall in with, took a journey into the region of the Sonoma Mountains, where a small tributary of the Humbolt River cuts the foot hills of the range. There was a new encampment called "Battle Mountain." And, to use the emphatic language of these four Missouri boys, they thought they would break the monotony of life by going to Battle Mountain "just to shake up the encampment."

These camping towns spring up as if by magic, and very often just as readily pass from sight. So that now the traveler in these mountain regions comes often upon the relics of a deserted hamlet which has been simply left to rot, when the gold played out and the gang moved further on. Hard work by day and by night, women, whiskey and cards is the daily routine of these mushroom towns. One of these dugout villages was known as Battle Mountain, and it was well named, for battles with Colt revolvers were the nightly program, and gambling and every other form of dissipation were the favorite diversions. Into this town, if such it may, by courtesy, be called the James boys stumbled, and, of course, determined to "buck the tiger." They did not drink and were proud of their skill with cards. One fatal night they were playing in the "Golden Rule" gambling hall about the stiffest poker game they had ever engaged in. The table was laden with bags of gold and thousands of dollars were passing to and fro with the varying fortunes of the cards.

The gambler was about to remark something or other when his opponent cut him short by saying: "I discarded a king; when the cut for your deal was made the bottom card was exposed. It was a king. You got your third king from the bottom. You must not do that again."

"You lie!" retorted the gambler, with a gleam of murder in his eyes.

Immediately all was confusion in the room. An ominous calm prevailed for a moment, while all eyes were fixed upon the excited players. Then Jesse rose to the emergency. Cheating had been charged and the lie given direct. This meant death to one or the other of the parties concerned. Jesse's ready revolver decided that it should not be his friend. While the excited gambler was fumbling for his weapon Jesse's trusty pistol cracked twice, and the murder-plotting gambler fell dead on the floor. Lightning quick the partner of the slain gambler made a lunge at Jesse with a dirk, but with a quick movement Jesse avoided the knife, swung round his ready revolver, cracked away at the gambler, and literally blew the entire top of his head off.

Pandemonium reigned at once. With a wild yell the excited gamblers made a rush for Jesse and his companions.

"Back, you devils, back!" cried Jesse. The wild mob wavered for a moment, the lights went out, and Jesse and his comrade under the cover of darkness made a dash for the door.

Once outside they turned and fired a volley into the midst of the howling mob of pursuers. Two men dropped dead and three were mortally wounded.

Some one struck a light. The scene that the mob of demoralized gamblers gazed upon made the blood curdle in their veins. Three men lay dead upon the floor, and five others, fearfully wounded, were groaning and cursing by their side. Half drunken women, sobered by the ghastly sight, were screaming like beldams. For a while those of the gamblers who had escaped death or wounding at the hands of the Missourians were too utterly dazed by the sight of their dead and wounded comrades sweltering in pools of blood to take any action for revenge. Suddenly one of the gamblers shouted:

"Now, boys, for vengeance. Let's follow them to hell if necessary!" and with a yell of revenge ten stalwart gamblers put off in hot pursuit of the plucky Missourians.

The moon was shining brightly down upon the path of the fleeing ex-guerillas, and the maddened gamblers, made desperate by the death of their comrades, followed close and sure upon the heels of the fugitives.

About a mile away they overtook the four greenhorns from Missouri, as they considered the James Boys and their two friends to be, and with a wild yell of triumph dashed forward and demanded their surrender. "Surrender nothing!" cried Jesse, and, turning to his comrades, he said: "Let her go, boys!" and instantly four revolvers flashed in the moonlight and three more Battle Mountain gamblers joined the company of their departed comrades in the happy hunting grounds of disembodied shades. The seven remaining gamblers turned to retreat, but the ready revolvers of the Missourians flashed forth again, and two more of the Battle Mountain desperadoes fell to the earth wounded. The five others were glad to escape with their lives and whole skins. Jesse lost his hat in the encounter and one of the ex-guerillas had a finger shot off.

With these slight exceptions no damage was done to the brave quartet of Missourians, who had demonstrated their ability to do what they set out to do.

A man's life was as nothing when it stood in the way of Frank or Jesse James. The knowledge of this fact by the people constituted the James boys' most perfect safeguard.

But on their return trip from California the bandit brothers departed from their usual custom and traveled together. They had lived like gentlemen so long at their good old uncle's Hot Sulphur Springs Hotel that they became somewhat socialized and concluded not to abandon their new mode of life completely just yet awhile.

Frank and Jesse, you may imagine, traveled as first-class passengers. They had not exhausted their supply of greenbacks and gold obtained by them in their Russellville raid, and they proposed to experience something of the luxury of trans-continental travel. In this way they were thrown into the society of wealthy people traveling for the benefit of their health, and experienced no difficulty whatever in passing for well-bred gentlemen of the Pacific Coast.

They stopped over at Denver for a few days, and while there Frank was recognized by an ex-detective from Missouri named Ballintine. Ballintine was not inclined to let Frank James know that he understood who he was, but the latter stepped to the ex-detective on the street and, extending his hand, said: "Shake hands, my friend. Like myself, you seem to be having a 'lay-off' from your usual occupation. Can't you join Jesse and me in doing Denver for a day or two?" The result was that Ballentine, who was a little hard up just then, was treated to as jolly a three days' and nights' dissipation as he ever experienced in all his life. All the places of amusement, both reputable and disreputable, were visited by the trio, and, as the society reporter for a country newspaper sometimes says of a Sunday-school picnic, "A nice time was had."

It is said by some who pretend to know what they are talking about that Jesse even went so far in his good natured bantering as to make a visit to the detectives headquarters and ask for a job, but this seems hardly probable, for a chance recognition by any of the Pinkerton force would certainly have resulted in Jesse's arrest. Jesse, of course, knew this, and as he was no fool, it is not likely that he took any such reckless chances.

After enjoying themselves to their hearts' content in Chicago, the James Boys went to Missouri to visit their mother. Of course, their conduct in the neighborhood of their old crimes was not so open and above board as while on their travels, but they felt perfectly safe at home, where their faithful and affectionate mother was ever on the alert against surprise.

The James Boys were not altogether idle while at home, for they were thinking of new ways and means for replenishing their pretty well exhausted treasury.

After a few days rest they retired to their Jackson County cave, where with the advice and consent of a number of their old fellow-bandits, they speedily arranged a plan of campaign for another bank robbery.

JAMES BOYS DEEDS OF DARING

ONE OF THE FEW GOOD ACTS OF THEIR BLACK CAREERS

THEY BOLDLY ATTACK A BAND OF INDIANS, AND AT THE RISK OF THEIR OWN LIVES SAVE AN IMMIGRANT PARTY CROSING THE PLAINS

Black as was their career the James Boys are entitled to the credit for at least one good deed, on the theory that the devil is entitled to his due. This notable instance of the fact that, despite their badness, some good still existed in their make-up occurred in Colorado. They were trailing slowly along one day when news came that the Indians were on the warpath and they had best keep a sharp lookout. A few hours later they discovered traces of Indians ahead of them, which, together with the presence of wagon tracks, plainly showed them that the murderous redskins were trailing the immigrant party to murder them all and steal their outfit.

"Can we make it?" asked Frank.

"We've got to make it," replied Jesse, with more than usual feeling. "Think of them poor women and kids."

They dug their spurs into their horses and rode like demons. On the way they picked up several other plainsmen, who joined them. Ere long they came in sight of the distant band of pursuing Indians. It consisted of fourteen warriors, and they were slowly but surely closing in on the single wagon of the prairie schooner type. Rounding a point in the trail they saw the Indians preparing to attack the settlers.

Throwing themselves out of the saddles and grasping their revolvers, they started on a run with a yell as fearful as any red devil of them; they threw themselves among the yelling fiends. Panic-stricken and confused, as one after another bit the dust at the crack of the ready revolvers, the terrified savages scattered in all directions. A covered wagon stood in their way and the James boys could not see what was going on in the camp, but hearing a child scream out as if in its death agony, Jesse, with a six-shooter in either hand, sprang under the wagon and crawled out on the other side.

Two big Indians were doing deadly work. Jesse fired both revolvers in quick succession, emptying every chamber into the two Apache devils, and then rushed in to club the life out of them with the butts of his revolvers, if any yet remained in their infernal red skins.

Three minutes after the music began not a live Indian was in sight, and eight dead ones lay spread out on the ground.

After a breathing spell Frank and Jesse began to look about them. The little girl that screamed was only slightly hurt, having been dropped to the ground by the stalwart Indian when Jesse shot him full of holes. Two other little children escaped unhurt, as did also three women of the party. The three men were all seriously wounded. Frank and Jesse escaped without a scratch.

DEEDS OF DARING

Early in December the seven bandits returned to Missouri, thinking that, as had been usual, the excitement over their crimes had so far subsided as to permit them to visit their old homes and haunts.

Jesse James Saves Women from Indians.

Their appearance in Clay County, at least the James Boys, was noted on the 20th of January, 1875, and report of their return was at once made to Allen Pinkerton, who, after some correspondence with county officials and others, formed a plan for capturing the bandit.

JAMES BOYS DEEDS OF DARING

THE RAID AND TRAGEDY AT NORTHFIELD

THE JAMES AND YOUNGER BROTHERS FORM A FOUR HANDED ALLIANCE AND SACK THE BNK OF NORTHFIELD, MINN., WITH DISASTROUS RESULTS

After the long chain of train and bank robberies the James Boys formed an alliance with the Younger brothers Cole and James and arranged for a raid in the town of Northfield, Minn., which seemed to offer an easy mark for a bank robbery and which place they had long been considering as a place for some daring work in the bandit line. The town consisted of some 2,000 inhabitants and is located on the Milwaukee and St. Paul railroad. A small stream runs through the town, known as the Cannon River, over which is a neat iron bridge and beside which are the big Ames flour mills.

The town is chiefly noted for the location of Carlton College, one of the finest educational institutions in the State.

Just before noon, on the day of the raid, three of the bandits dined at Jeft's restaurant, on the west side of Cannon River. After eating they talked politics, and one of them offered to bet the restaurant man one hundred dollars that the State would go Democratic.

The bet was not taken, and they rode across the bridge into the business part of the town, hitching their horses nearly in front of the First National Bank.

They stood for some time talking leisurely near the corner. Suddenly there came like a whirlwind a rush of horsemen over the bridge. There were only three of them, but they made racket enough for a regiment. Riding into the square with whoops and oaths, they began firing revolvers and ordering everybody off the streets. Almost at the same moment two others rode down from the west, carrying out a similar program. It was a new experience for Northfield, and for a few minutes the slamming of front doors almost drowned the noise of the firing.

At the first sound of the onset the three men who first entered town Jesse James, Charley Pitts and Bob Younger had walked quickly into the bank and leaped nimbly over the counter. The cashier, J. L. Haywood, was at his place, and Frank Wilcox and A. E. Bunker, clerks, were at their desks. All were covered by the revolvers before they apprehended danger. The robbers stated that they intended to rob the bank. The cashier was commanded to open the safe, and bravely refused. The outer door of the vault was standing ajar, and the leader stepped in to try the inner door. As he did so Haywood jumped forward and tried to shut him in.

One of the others, afterwards found to be Charlie Pitts, promptly arrested the movement. At this moment Bunker thought he saw a chance, and so he broke for the back door. The third robber, Bob Younger, followed and fired two shots, one of which took effect in the fugitive's shoulder. The others then insisted that Haywood should open the safe, and, putting a knife to his throat, said, "Open up, d--n you, or we'll slit you from ear to ear!" A slight cut was made to enforce the demand. Haywood still refused.

Meantime the firing outside had commenced, and the men then began to cry out, "Hurry up! It's getting too hot here!" The three hastily ransacked the drawers, and finding only a lot of small change, jumped over the railing and ran out. Jesse James was the last to go, and as he was in the act of leaping from the counter he saw Haywood turn quickly to a drawer as if in the act of securing a weapon. Instantly the outlaw presented his pistol and shot the brave cashier dead.

The bullet penetrated the right temple and, ranging downward, lodged near the base of the brain. Haywood fell over without a groan, a quantity of his blood and brains staining the desk as he reeled in the death fall. The shot which struck Bunker entered his right shoulder at the point of the shoulder blade and passed through obliquely, producing only a flesh wound.

As the bandits rushed into the street they met a sight and reception quite unexpected. Recovering from their first surprise, the citizens began to exhibit their pluck, and were ready to meet the outlaws half way in a deadly fight. A search for firearms was the first important step, and Dr. Wheeler, J. B. Hyde, L. Stacey, Mr. Manning and Mr. Bates each succeeded in procuring a weapon, which they expeditiously put into service. Dr. Wheeler, from a corner room (No. 8) in the Dampier House, with a breech-loading carbine, took deliberate aim at one of the bandits as he was mounting and sent a big slug through the outlaw's body. The dying man fell outwards into the street. An unknown Norwegian who came along the street was ordered to get out quick, but failing to understand the order was shot dead in the street.

Frank James had a cloth around his arm and was holding one hand in the other, the blood dripping from his fingers, while his horse was led by a comrade. This, of course, explains how it happened that they got away no faster. Had they abandoned the worst wounded ones to their fate, there is little doubt but that the others would have gotten away easily enough. As it was, the story of the chase abounds in incidents almost too marvelous for belief.

Every point, including St. Paul and Minneapolis, was immediately notified of the robbery by telegraph, and police officers, detectives and sheriffs' posses were sent out after the fleeing bandits in such numbers that it was thought impossible for any of the outlaws to escape.

Very soon rewards were offered for the apprehension of the desperadoes, which stimulated the already active hunt. The State offered $1,000 for the arrest of the six bandits, which offer was changed to $1,000 for each of the gang, dead or alive; $700 was offered by the Northfield bank and $500 by the Winona and St. Peter Railroad.

A posse of fourteen men overtook the bandits on the night of the 11th in a ravine near Shieldsville, and fell back after a fight in which one of the robber's horses was killed. The dismounted rider was immediately taken up behind one of the others and the band took to the woods.

More than 400 men turned out to cut them off.

They got into a patch of timber at Lake Elysian and were run out of it the next day, and, though the scouting parties increased to a thousand, two days later the robbers had been completely lost.

The robbers got into a belt of timber, and, going through to the other side, saw a hunting party in a wagon, which they made a rush to capture. The men in the wagon instantly presented their shotguns, and the robbers, taking them for pursuers, went back into the brush. It so happened that the patch of timber they had struck was only about five acres in extent, and had bare, open ground all around it. Before they had discovered the disadvantage of their position the people began to flock in from all directions, in wagons, on foot, on horseback, equipped with shotguns and rifles. They soon established a cordon of one hundred and fifty men around the patch and began shooting into it to drive the game out. As the robbers paid no attention to this, Sheriff Glispen called for volunteers to go in and stir them up.

He quickly secured a posse of determined men, and the battle was on. They raided the patch of woods, and a desperate fight ensued. Several of the robber band fell badly wounded, and two of the sheriff's posse were also laid low. Frank James was shot in the shoulder and Cole Younger got a bullet through the leg. His horse was also killed. After several days' fighting, however, the posse drew off and the robbers once more escaped and made their way to their respective homes.

DEEDS OF DARING

JAMES BOYS DEEDS OF DARING

THE FAMOUS 'BLUE-CUT' TRAIN HOLD-UP
HOW THE JAMES BOYS COMMITTED A DARING ROBBERY AND GOT AWAY WITH A BIG BOODLE IN QUICK ORDER

One of the James boys most daring exploits which aroused the whole country and caused more newspaper publicity than any of their previous achievements was the famous "Blue Cut" train robbery on the Chicago & Alton Railroad.

The James Boys and their band of robbers had become utterly reckless of consequences, both to themselves and their victims, and seemed bent on deeds of desperation and outrage that would throw all former acts of highwaymen and bandits completely in the shade. The murder of Westfall and McMillan seemed to whet their appetites for new deeds of murder and outrage, and they lost no time in tackling another train, this time going through the passengers as well as plundering the express cars.

About four miles east of Independence, Mo., where the Missouri Pacific Railroad crosses over a deep cut of the Chicago and Alton, is a point known as Blue Cut. At this point, on the night of September 7, 1881, the James Boys and ten other bandits secreted themselves and waited for the night express of the Chicago and Alton road to loom in sight.

About 9 o'clock the express train from Chicago, in charge of conductor Hazelbaker, came tearing along.

Just before plunging into the; deepest part of the cut the engineer descried on the track just ahead of him a pile of stones some five or six feet high, and of course at once reversed his engine.

As soon as the engine slowed down Jesse James and four of his masked robbers confronted the engineer with drawn revolvers, and Jesse said: "Step down off that engine or I will kill you." The engineer lost no time in complying with the peremptory request, and was then commanded to get up again and get the coal pick, which he did, and was then, together with his fireman, marched off to the express car and ordered to break down the door. This request was also complied with under the persuasive influence of ready cocked revolvers.

The express messenger had climbed down out of his car at the first alarm and hid in the grass by the side of the road, but the bandits swore they would kill the engineer and fireman if the messenger failed to show up. The engineer called the express messenger to come forth, which he did, and entered the car with two of the robbers, who forced him to open the safe and pour the contents into a sack.

The robbers were disappointed in not getting more booty, and knocked the messenger down twice with the butt end of their revolvers, cutting his head in a fearful manner. They then marched the engineer and messenger to the coaches, where they kept them covered with revolvers while they robbed the passengers.

They began business on the coaches by firing off a volley of revolver shots into the roof and sides of the car and savagely shouting: "Hold up your hands, and be pretty damned quick about it; we're going through the entire outfit."

They held up every passenger and robbed men and women alike, including those in the sleepers, and decamped with a two-bushel sack full of money and valuables. Before leaving Jesse James stepped up to the engineer, handed him a ten dollar bill and told him to "buy himself a drink in the morning," at the same time telling him he was a good fellow, but advising him to change his job to some eastern road if he valued his life.

DEEDS OF DARING

JESSE JAMES

From a photograph taken in Platte City, Mo, 1864,
when Quantrell attacked the town.
Jesse James was then seventeen years old.

MRS. ZERELDA SAMUELS
Mother of the James boys.

JESSE JAMES
From a photograph taken in Nebraska City-, Neb. 1875.

JESSE JAMES MY FATHER

WRITTEN BY
JESSE JAMES JR

THE FIRST AND ONLY
True Story of His Adventures
EVER WRITTEN.

"It required, indeed, all the excesses of the civil war of 1881-5 to produce the genuine American guerrilla-more enterprising by far, more deadly, more capable of immense physical endurance, more fitted by nature for deeds of reckless hardihood, and given over to less of penitence or pleading when face to face with the final end, than any French or Spanish, Italian or Mexican guerrilla notorious in song or story. He simply lived the life that was in him, and took the worst or best as it came and as fate decreed it. Circumstances made him unsparing, and not any predisposition in race or rearing. Fought first with fire, he fought back with the torch; and branded as an outlaw first, in despite of all reason, he made of the infamous badge a birthright and boasted of it as a blood-red inheritance while flaunting it in the face of a civilization which denounced the criminals while condoning the crimes that made them such."

[From the book "Noted Guerrillas," by Major John N. Edwards.]

COPYRIGHT 1899, BY JESSE JAMES, JR.

Copyright 1906, by Arthur Westbrook.

PREFACE

Hundreds of different books have been written and published about Jesse James, and what is commonly known as "The James Band." Many of these books were false from cover to cover. A few had in them a grain or two of truth upon which were strung whole chapters of untruths. I have read them all, and there is not one of them that did not do cruel injustice to the memory of my father and to his family. In none of these books, and in none of the thousands of newspaper articles that have been written about him, have I seen him credited with having in his nature any of the human attributes of kindness, charity or honesty of purpose. In all of these writings his true character is entirely lost sight of and distorted into that of a veritable Frankenstein who slew mercilessly and robbed for the mere love of adventure.

This is because these writings were done by those who never knew my father. I defy the world to show that he ever slew a human being except in the protection of his own life, or as a soldier in honorable warfare. His only brother, whose name was linked with his in all the years of his life, is a free man to-day, acquitted of all crime.

There were lovable and noble traits in the character of my father, else why was it that for sixteen long years, when there was a price on his head that would have made his betrayer rich, not one could be found who would betray him. Did ever a man live who had such staunch friends, many of whom were persecuted and made to suffer because of the steadfastness of their loyalty to him? Is it possible that an ignoble character could win and hold such friendships? My object in writing this book is twofold.

Thousands have asked me why I did not write such a book, and promised to buy one if I did write it. If all of these keep that promise it will have been a good business venture for me. One of my objects, then, in writing this book, is in the hope that it will bring some money for the support of my mother.

My other object in writing it is to do something to correct the false impressions that the public have about the character of my father. Others may differ from me on this point, but I believe it my duty to the memory of my father that the truth about him be told.

I make no claim to literary merit in this book.

I have had little time in my life to go to school. In the years that boys usually spend in school I was at work earning wages for the support of my widowed mother and the education of my fatherless sister.

I have tried to make this book a straightforward account of the things I write about, as I see them.

JESSE JAMES, Jr.

Kansas City, Mo., June 1, 1899

CHAPTER ONE

THINGS I REMEMBER OF MY FATHER

I was born August 31, 1875, in Nashville, Tenn. I recall with vivid distinctness an incident that occurred in Nashville, when I was about five years old. At that time my father, Jesse James, was away from home. Dick Liddill was staying at our home during the absence of father.

It was the night of St. Valentine's Day. While mother and myself and sister and Dick Liddill were at home, there was a sound as if someone was throwing rocks against the front door. Dick started to open the door, but mother suspected that it was someone who had discovered who we were and were trying to entice Dick out to capture or kill him. She would not allow him to open the door. Dick then got my father's shot gun from a closet. Both of its barrels were loaded heavily with buckshot. Before my mother could interfere to prevent it, Dick aimed at the door and fired the charge of buckshot, tearing a great hole through the door panel and splintering it. Dick rushed to the door and threw it open and ran out on the porch. In the darkness he saw a man running around the corner. Dick fired the second barrel straight at him, barely missing him, the charge rattling against a lamp post on the street.

We lived in the suburbs, and a great crowd that had heard the shots gathered to see what was the matter. Dick told them simply that he had shot at a burglar.

We never knew positively who the mysterious one was that had frightened us so that night, but my father always thought it was a friend of his, who lived near us. Liddill had the reputation of being somewhat scary, and my father believed this friend threw the rocks at our house with the intention of playing a practical joke on Liddill, and to see how he would act. The theory seems all the more plausible because this friend came to our home very early the next morning and his face was unusually long and solemn. Whoever it was who threw the rocks, had a narrow escape from being killed.

This dramatic scene of the shot fired through our door so suddenly and unexpectedly that night, will never fade from my memory. It is one of the earliest recollections of my life.

The first remembrance I have of my father, was after we had moved from Nashville to Kansas City, a short time after this adventure of Dick Liddill's.

We lived in Kansas City, on East Ninth Street, between Michigan and Euclid; on Troost Avenue, between Tenth and Eleventh and on Woodland Avenue, between Twelfth and Thirteenth streets. I remember those different homes in an indistinct way, although I have often visited them since I grew up.

I remember very distinctly when we first came to Kansas City, we lived for a short time with Charles

McBride, who was married to my mother's sister. At that time there was a large reward for the capture of my father, and I suppose he thought it unsafe to leave us at McBride's on account of the well-known relationship, and that detectives might take a notion to look there for him. My father came one day, I remember, and moved us away. I asked him where we were going and he said, "To another town." We went to the Doggett House, at Sixth and Walnut, and engaged rooms. We had been there only two or three days, when, as I was playing on the street in front of the hotel, I saw my uncle, McBride, pass on horseback and I shouted to him.

"Hello, Uncle Charlie! How did you get to this town?" He spoke to me and rode on. When I went home and told my father about it, he at once paid his bill and took us away from there.

I have heard my folks tell since, that while we lived on Woodland Avenue, in Kansas City, there was a vacant lot behind our house, and the father of Con. Murphy, the County Marshall, lived on the other side of this lot. At that time Marshall Murphy was very anxious to capture my father and nearly every night a posse would gather at Murphy's house and start out for the country around Independence and in the "Cracker Neck" district in search of members of the James band. My father used to walk over to Murphy's house in the evening when the posse would be starting out, and talk to them about their plans, and wish them good luck on their trip.

I told Mr. Murphy recently about this and he laughed heartily at it.

I remember seeing my father walking with a cane and limping, while we lived in Kansas City. I have been told since, that he did this, not because he was lame, but to help disguise himself.

My strongest recollections of my father are of the times after we moved to St. Joseph, Mo. We went from Kansas City to St. Joseph in a covered wagon or "prairie schooner," drawn by two horses, and another horse, always saddled, leading behind.

Charlie Ford drove the team. I sat most of the time on the seat with him, and father stayed inside the wagon until we were well out of Kansas City. We crossed the network of railroad tracks in the West Bottoms of Kansas City and drove up through Leavenworth and Atchison, Kan. It was my father's intention, when we started, to stop in Atchison and rent a house. When we reached Atchison we drove through the town and unhitched the horses at the edge of the town. Father and Charlie Ford rode back through the town to see if they could find a house for rent. They came back very soon and said the people were watching them suspiciously, so they hitched up again and drove on toward St. Joseph.

This suspicion of my father's was probably unfounded.

He and Ford were undoubtedly stared at with the same degree of curiosity that any strangers on horseback would have been looked at. But at that time there was a big price on my father's head, and it would be strange if he was not suspicious. In St. Joseph we lived first in a house, the location of which I have forgotten. From there we went to the house on the hill where my father was killed.

It was while we lived in this house on the hill in St. Joseph that I best remember my father. I was then six years old. I remember my father as a tall, rather heavily built man, with a dark sandy beard.

He was very kind to mother and to sister and to me.

MY FATHER JESSE JAMES

I remember best his good humored pranks, his fun making and his playing with me. I did not then know his real name or my own. I did not know that he was concealing anything from the public or that he was in danger of capture. He was living then under the name of Thomas Howard. My name was Charlie Howard, but my father and mother always called me "Tim." Father never called me by any other name than "Tim." Charlie Ford, who was at the house a good deal of the time, went by the name of Charles Johnson. They claimed to be cousins.

In those days in St. Joseph, father always kept at least two horses in the stable back of the house.

Father was heavily armed at all times. In the house he kept a double barreled shot gun loaded with buckshot, a Winchester rifle, a 45-calibre Colt's revolver, a 45-calibre Schofield revolver, and three cartridge belts. He never left the house without both of the revolvers and the three cartridge belts loaded, and some cartridges in his pockets. That was the way he armed himself when he went down town. When he went away to be gone any length of time he carried in addition to this, a small valise full of cartridges. When on a trip he carried his Winchester strapped on the inside of a large umbrella.

After my father's death we sold a great many of these things at public auction. The little cartridge valise brought $15. We did not sell the revolvers or cartridge belts. T. T. Crittenden, Jr. has one of the revolvers now, which I gave him as a token of my friendship for him. My uncle, Frank James, has the other revolver. Two of the cartridge belts were stolen from the house by the people who crowded in after my father's death. The third cartridge belt I have now and I shall always keep it in remembrance of my father.

At this same auction sale, after my father's death, we sold a little cur dog for $15. I felt the loss of the dog very much. The dog was given to my father by his half-sister, Mrs. Nicholson, when my father last visited my grandmother's home a short time before his death, and father brought the dog to St. Joseph with him. He rode in his arms on horseback.

My father was a great deal of the time at home while we lived in St. Joseph. He often took me with him for rides on horseback when the weather was fair. I generally rode in front of him, sitting astride of the horse's shoulders, and clinging with both hands to the mane. Sometimes I would ride behind him and hold on to his coat. These horseback trips led away out into the country beyond sight or hearing of the town. I recall very distinctly that on one of these trips he sat me up on top of a rail fence, where I hung on by the stakes, and then he rode away and showed me how he used to charge the enemy when he was a soldier under Quantrell.

With the bridle rein in his teeth, and an unloaded revolver in each hand snapping the triggers rapidly, he charged toward me on the gallop, and I thought it was great fun.

One day the home of a preacher who lived in the suburbs of St. Joseph burned down, and the next day my father took me over on horseback to see the ruins. He talked quite awhile with the preacher and his wife. We found out after my father's death that this preacher used to live in Liberty, Mo., near the home of my people, and that both he and his wife recognized my father. But they kept the secret well. They could have earned the $20,000 by betraying my father, but they were loyal, as all friends of our family were in those days and in the trying times since then.

The spring my father was killed there was a great parade in St. Joseph in celebration of some public event. My father rode on horseback, with me in front of him, with the parade over its whole route. Leading the parade was a platoon of mounted police, and father rode right behind them.

One forenoon while my father was sitting at the window with me on his lap, he saw the chief of police of St. Joseph, and four men coming up the hill toward the house. Father got up hastily and sat me in a rocking chair, and told me to be very quiet. He ran out to the barn, and in a moment had his horse saddled. Then he came back into the house, and said a few words hurriedly to my mother while he put on his cartridge belts and revolvers, watching out of the window all of the time. He brought his Winchester rifle out of a closet and stood with it at the window, just far enough back so that the chief of police could not see him. The chief stopped in front of the house and put one foot and hand upon the fence as if to come in, and I saw my father take aim at him with the rifle. Then the chief evidently changed his mind and went away. In a moment more he would have been killed. My father thought of course that the chief had discovered who he was, and was coming after him. We learned after my father's death that the chief was simply showing some strangers over the city, and had brought them over the hill on which our house stood, because it overlooked the whole city.

My father used to hold me on his lap and talk a great deal to me about his adventures in the war. He used to talk to me about the James boys, and would read to me the accounts of their adventures that were published in the newspapers. He used to read to me from Major Edwards's book, stories about Quantrell's band of guerrillas, and show me the pictures.

I have only hazy recollections of these things, of course, but I remember that once he showed me a picture of one of the members of the guerrilla band who was living then, and said laughingly, that he had a good long neck to hang by.

In days that father was lounging around the house, he often took the cartridges from his revolvers and buckled one of them around me, and strapped one with a handkerchief around my sister's waist, and would say that I was Jesse James and that my sister was Sam Hildebrand. I remember well the name Sam Hildebrand, but I have never learned who he was, or if such a person ever lived.

My father was always heavily armed, and he told me that all the men went armed the same way. I thought that was true, because all the men I ever saw at our home were as heavily armed as he.

The morning my father was murdered we had just finished breakfast. I heard from the front room the loud roar of a shot. My mother rushed in and screamed. I ran in after her and saw my father dead upon the floor, and my mother was down upon her knees by his side and was crying bitterly. My father was killed instantly by the bullet that Ford shot into the back of his head. He never spoke or breathed after he fell.

Soon after the murder of my father a great crowd gathered outside the house. My childish mind imagined that these were responsible for the murder, and in great anger I lugged from its closet my father's shot gun and tried to aim it at the people outside, but my mother took it from me.

MY FATHER   JESSE JAMES

CHAPTER TWO

THE DEATH OF JESSE JAMES

The story of the murder of my father and the immediate events that led up to it I have learned since from my mother, my grandmother and others. Ten days before my father was killed, he and Charlie Ford and Bob Ford stayed all night at the home of my grandmother, Mrs. Samuels, near Kearney, Mo. My grandmother had known Charlie Ford for years, but this was the first time she had met his brother. Bob. She did not like the looks of Bob and she told my father that she did not believe Bob Ford was true. Father laughed at her and said

"Mother, I don't set much store by him either, but he has got into some trouble and Charlie wants him to go with us till he can get a chance to leave the country. I'll keep my eye on him." The last time that my father was at his birthplace was an ideal spring day. The grass and flowers were just coming up green and fresh, and the leaves were budding on the big coffee bean tree in the corner of the yard where he lies buried now. Father was in a good humor that day and he sat all of the afternoon with my grandmother in the shade of the porch run and they talked together of old times. While they were sitting there a pretty red-headed woodpecker alighted on a tree fifty yards away and clung to the bark. My father pulled his revolver and said to my grandmother

"Mother, have you heard about my being a good shot; I will show you." He threw the revolver down on the little bird, pulled the trigger and it fell dead.

My father was a wonderful marksman. I have heard his old comrades tell that seated on horseback with a revolver in each hand, he would ride at full speed between two telegraph poles, or two trees and begin firing at them when he was a few yards away, and before he was more than a few yards beyond them, he had emptied the chambers of both revolvers, and the six bullets from the revolver in his left hand were buried in the pole to the left of him, while the six bullets from the revolver in his right hand were in the pole to his right. I think this story of his marksmanship was true, because several different men in whom I have great faith told me they saw it done more than once. I have heard other stories of his great skill with his revolver that are equally as wonderful as this. I have seen my father at practice shooting with a revolver. That was while we were living at St. Joseph and when he had taken me on a horseback ride to a lonely part of the country.

But I was too young then to pay much attention to it, and I recall only that he was shooting at a mark on a tree.

After spending the day at the home of my grandmother, my father and the two Ford boys rode away on horseback to St. Joseph. Father carried with him a small dog that was given him by his half-sister as a present to my sister and me. Father carried that dog in his arms all the way to St. Joseph.

The Ford boys killed my father for the reward that was offered for his apprehension. This reward was $5,000 for the apprehension of Jesse James and $5,000 additional reward for his conviction in any court. There has been a great deal of misunderstanding about this reward. It is generally believed that the reward was offered for the capture of Jesse James alive or dead. This was not the case. I have read the proclamation of Governor T. T. Crittenden offering the reward, and it was as I have stated.

The Ford boys had the confidence of my father. Charlie Ford had been with him off and on for years, and father had befriended him and protected him and fed him when he was penniless. Father had not the slightest suspicion that the Fords meant to harm him.

This is proven by the fact that after breakfast that morning father took off his belt and revolvers and threw them upon the bed and threw his coat over them. He did this because it was a very warm morning, and the belt and revolvers were tiresome to carry. Another reason was that it was necessary to have the doors and windows open, and father thought that people passing the house might be suspicious if they saw him armed.

After my father put the revolvers upon the bed he noticed that a picture on the wall was hanging awry. He placed a chair beneath the picture and stood upon it to straighten it and then he started to brush the dust from it. Standing thus, his back was turned to the Ford boys, who were in the room.

This was the opportunity the Fords had been waiting for. It was the very first time they had seen him unarmed since they knew him. Bob Ford drew his revolver, aimed it at the back of my father's head and cocked it. Father heard the click of the hammer and made a movement as if to turn around.

But before he could do so Ford pulled the trigger and father fell backward dead. The Fords ran out and across the back yard fence, and went down town and surrendered to the authorities, telling that they had shot and killed Jesse James. Years afterward the Fords, who found themselves despised of all men because of this murder, denied that they shot my father for the reward, but that they learned that Jesse James suspected them of treachery and meant to kill them, and they shot him for self protection.

That this story was absolutely false is proven by the fact that immediately after the murder Charlie Ford sent the following telegram to the Governor of Missouri

"I have got my man." Charlie Ford practically admitted in my presence and hearing that he killed my father for the reward. That conversation was held under the following circumstances.

Nearly three years after the murder, when I was nine years old, I was in Kansas City with my grandmother. We were walking up Main Street. I had hold of my grandmother's hand. Suddenly I saw and recognized Charlie Ford coming down the street toward us. I knew him the instant I saw him, and I was very much excited. I said to my grandmother.

"Here comes the man who killed my father." It was the first time my grandmother had seen him since that day he was at her home with father, ten days before the murder. The sight of him made her weak and she sat down on a box in front of a shoe store. Ford saw her and went to walk past with his head turned the other way, but she called to him
;

MY FATHER   JESSE JAMES

"You don't know me, Charlie?"

He stopped and said "Yes, I know you. You are Mrs. Samuels."

"Yes, and you killed my brave boy; you murdered him for money. I ought to kill you," she said to him.

He threw up both his hands in front of his face and answered: "Mrs. Samuels, don't say that. If you only knew what I am suffering, you wouldn't talk to me that way."

"And what have you made me and mine suffer?" she said.

"Mrs. Samuels, I have been in the blackest hell of remorse ever since it was done. But I didn't kill him. It was Bob did it," Ford said.

"Yes, and you knew Bob intended to do it when you brought him to my house. You ate bread under my roof with blackest murder in your heart, and murder for money, too. There will come a day of terrible reckoning for you."

I heard Charlie Ford tell my grandmother in that talk that he did not know that Bob intended to kill my father till they got to St. Joseph, and then Bob told him if he did not consent to it, he would kill him along with Jesse. Ford repeated over and over again, that he was suffering the worst agonies of remorse. The perspiration streamed down his face and there were tears in his eyes. He begged my grandmother to forgive him and she said "If God can forgive you, I will."

My grandmother asked him what he did with the $10,000 he got for murdering my father, and he replied

"Mrs. Samuels, before God, we never got but a few hundred dollars of that reward."

I watched Charlie Ford closely while he was talking. I was only nine years old but I understood it all. I said nothing until he had gone on down the street. Then I said to my grandmother "If ever I grow to be a man I'm going to kill him."

My grandmother said to me "You will never live long enough my son; God will never let an onery man like that live until then." Eleven months after that day, Charlie Ford committed suicide in Richmond, Mo., by shooting himself.

Bob Ford was shot and killed later in a gambling house in Colorado.

A great many persons have asked me in recent years if I would have sought revenge on the Fords if they had lived till I grew up. I have never given a direct answer to that question. I answer it now by saying that I would not have troubled the Fords or sought an encounter with them or any of the other enemies of my father. I realize that the feelings and prejudices of the days of border warfare have almost passed away, that the times and conditions have changed and that it was a certainty that with a price of $10,000 on his head it was only a matter of time till some traitor would kill my father to get it, and that if the Fords had not done it some other would have.

Every member of the James family has proven to the world in the seventeen years since my father's death that they are good citizens, and honest men and women.

The conditions and events and prejudices that led my father to become a member of Quantrell's guerrilla band, and the story of the persecutions and proscriptions that prevented his honorable surrender at the close of the war, and made him an outlawed and hunted man, are told of in the succeeding chapters.

MY FATHER   JESSE JAMES

CHAPTER THREE

THE JAMES FAMILY

My grandfather, Robert James, was a Baptist preacher of wide renown in the early days in Western Missouri. He was born and raised in Kentucky, and was a graduate of the Georgetown, Ky., college. His family was one of the old families of Logan County, Ky. My grandfather was married to my grandmother. Miss Zerelda Cole, one year before he graduated. He was then 23 years old, and she was 17. They met first at a religious gathering and it was a case of love at first sight. My grandmother's people lived in Lexington, Ky., and she was educated in a Catholic convent in that city. The Cole family, of which my grandmother was a member, was of old Revolutionary stock. Her grandfather was a soldier in the war of the Revolution. My grandmother's mother was a Lindsay, of the famous old Lindsay family of Kentucky. Senator Lindsay is a member of this family.

My grandfather and grandmother were married December 28, 1841. The following August they came to Clay County, Mo., to visit the mother of Mr. James, who had married her second husband and was living in that county. He left my grandmother in Clay County and returned to Kentucky. He was to have returned the next Christmas, but the Missouri river was frozen and he had to postpone the trip. He came in the spring. My grandfather liked Clay County and he remained there, settling near Kearney. He combined farming with preaching and was very successful at both. He acquired a large and valuable farm, on which my grandmother yet lives, and from the product of this farm he supported his family, because he never asked money for preaching and the good farmers to whom he broke the bread of life gave him very little.

He was a great exhorter and a fervid expounder of the Gospel. He founded the Baptist churches at New Hope and at Providence, which are yet in existence, He was a wonderful revivalist and he baptized many of the old settlers of Clay County who are yet living and many more who are dead. I have had old men and women tell me of seeing him go into the water and baptize sixty converts at one time. At this time when my grandfather baptized sixty converts without leaving the water, my father, Jesse James, was fourteen months old, and he was held up in his mother's arms and saw the ceremony.

Years afterward, when my father had returned desperately wounded from the border wars, he was baptized not very far from the same place.

In 1851 my grandfather, the Rev. Robert James, went to California. The day he started, Jesse James was four years old. He clung to my grandfather and cried and pleaded with him not to go away. This affected my grandfather very much, and he told my grandmother that if he had not already spent so much money in outfitting for the trip, and if he had not promised the other men who were going with him, he would give up the trip. It was a great desire to get money to educate his children, that led him to undertake the journey to the gold fields of California. My grandmother had a presentiment then that she would never see him again, and she never did. The overland trip from Clay County to California lasted from April 12 to August 1, three months. My grandfather lived only eighteen days after reaching California, and was buried there.

He had preached the gospel for eight years and received in all that time less than $100 for his services. He was a good Christian and a noble man.

The children of my grandfather were:

Alexander James, born January 10, 1844.
Robert James, born July 19, 1845, died in infancy.
Jesse W. James, born September 5, 1847, died April 3, 1882.
Susan L. James born November 25, 1849, married November 24, 1870, to Allen H. Palmer, died 1889.

My grandmother remained a widow for four years. She married Dr. Reuben Samuels in 1855. The children born of that marriage were:

Sarah L. Samuels, born December 26, 1858, married November 28, 1878, to William Nicholson.
John T. Samuels, born May 25, 1861, married July 22, 1885, to Norma L. Maret.
Fannie Quantrell Samuels, born October 18, 1863, married December 30, 1880, to Joseph Hall.
Archie Payton Samuels, born July 26, 1866, murdered by Pinkerton detectives, January 26, 1875.

My grandmother had eight children. Two of them were murdered.

My grandmother lives yet on the old homestead near Kearney, Mo. Dr. Samuels, her second husband, lives with her, but is old and quite feeble. My grandmother is seventy-four years old, is vigorous and in good health.

MY FATHER   JESSE JAMES

CHAPTER FOUR

THE BORDER WARS

The Kansas Jayhawkers and Red Legs made the Missouri guerrilla possible. When the civil war broke out, Eastern Kansas was filled with abolitionists who formed themselves into marauding bands, called Jayhawkers and Red Legs, who invaded Western Missouri, ostensibly in the interests of the Union cause, but really for the purpose of plunder, making war an excuse for robbery. Jackson and Clay Counties were settled mostly by people of Southern sympathies, many of them from Kentucky.

The marauding bands from Kansas stole and drove off horses and cattle, enticed negro slaves away, robbed and burned houses, hanged and shot men and insulted women. These outrages led to the organization of the Missouri guerrillas under Quantrell.

Charles William Quantrell was born in Hagerstown, Md., in 1836. In 1855 Quantrell came to Kansas and joined his only brother and they started on a trip overland to California, with a negro as cook and hostler. Although there was peace at that time, Western Missouri and Kansas were at war. Armed bands which called themselves "patriots" roamed over Kansas and made frequent dashes into Missouri.

One night in the summer of 1856, when the Quantrell brothers were camped on the Little Cottonwood River, on the way to California, one of these bands of thirty-two armed men rode deliberately up and attacked the little camp. The elder Quantrell was killed instantly and Charles William Quantrell was left for dead. But he did not die. He lay in great agony for two days, scarcely able to move, keeping the coyotes and buzzards from the body of his brother. Early in the morning of the third day an old Shawnee Indian found and rescued Quantrell and buried his dead brother, and nursed Quantrell back to life.

The experiences and sufferings of those two awful days and nighs made a fiend of Quantrell.

When he recovered he taught school long enough to pay the old Indian for his board and then he went to Leavenworth, and under the name of Charles Hart, he joined the Jayhawkers. He was promoted to the position of orderly sergeant, and held the esteem and confidence of all. But it was revenge he was after, and he bided his time. In the four years he was with the Jayhawkers, he killed thirty out of the thirty-two men who had murdered his brother, and each one of them was shot mysteriously in the very center of the forehead. Quantrell was discovered by his comrades at last and then he fled to Jackson County, Mo., and organized Quantrell's band of guerrillas.

Major John N. Edwards says of Quantrell "One-half of the country believes Quantrell to have been a highway robber crossed upon the tiger; the other half that he was the gallant defender of his native South; one-half believes him to have been an avenging nemesis of the right; the other a forbidding monster of assassination. History cannot hesitate over him, however, nor abandon him to the imagination of the romancers. He was a living, breathing, aggressive, all-powerful reality-riding through the midnight, laying ambuscades by lonesome roadsides, catching marching columns by the throat, breaking in upon the flanks and tearing a suddenly surprised rear to pieces; vigilant, merciless, a terror by day and a superhuman if not a supernatural thing when there was upon the earth blackness and darkness."

Major Edwards, in his wonderful book, 'Noted Guerrillas, or the Warfare of the Border,' speaks thus of the men who formed the guerrilla band under Quantrell. "As strange as it may seem, the perilous fascination of fighting under a black flag-where the wounded could have neither surgeon nor hospital, and where all that remained to the prisoners was the absolute certainty of speedy death-attracted a number of young men, born of higher destinies, capable of sustained exertion in any scheme or enterprise, and fit for callings high up in the scale of science or philosophy. Others came who had deadly wrongs to avenge, and these gave to all their combats that sanguinary hue which yet remains a part of the guerrilla's legacy. Almost from the first, a large majority of Quantrell's original command had over them the shadow of some terrible crime. This one recalled a father murdered, this one a brother waylaid and shot, this one a house pillaged and burned, this one a relative assassinated, this one a grievous insult while at peace at home, this one a robbery of all his earthly possessions, this one the force which compelled him to witness the brutal treatment of a mother or sister, this one was driven away from his own like a thief in the night, this one was threatened with death for opinion's sake, this one was proscribed at the instance of some designing neighbor, this one was arrested wantonly and forced to do the degrading work of a menial; while all had more or less of wrath laid up against the day when they were to meet face to face, and hand to hand, those whom they had good cause to regard as the living embodiment of unnumbered wrongs. Honorable soldiers in the Confederate army -amenable to every generous impulse and exact in the performance of every manly duty-deserted even the ranks which they had adorned, and became desperate guerrillas because the home they left had been given to the flames, or a gray-haired father shot upon his own hearth-stone. They wished to avoid the uncertainty of regular battle and know by actual results how many died as propitiation or a sacrifice. Every other passion became subordinate to that of revenge. They sought personal encounters, that their own handiwork might become unmistakably manifest. Those who died by other agencies than their own were not counted in the general summing up of a fight, nor were the solacements of any victory sweet to them unless the knowledge of being important factors in its achievements. As this class of guerrillas increased, the warfare of the border became necessarily more cruel and unsparing. Where at first there was only killing in ordinary battle, there became to be no quarter shown. The wounded of the enemy next felt the might of his individual vengeance-acting through a community of bitter memories-and from every stricken field there began, by and by, to come up the substance of this awful bulletin : Dead such and such a number, wounded none. The war had then passed into its fever heat, and thereafter the gentle and the merciful, equally with the harsh and revengeful, spared nothing clad in blue that could be captured."

At the outbreak of the civil war my people lived near Kearney, in Clay County, Mo. My grandmother being a native of Kentucky, was naturally a Southern sympathizer, as was her husband. Dr. Samuels.

In that neighborhood at that time were a great many sympathizers with the Northern cause. Many of these had formed themselves into organizations known as 'Home Militia' or 'Home Guards,' and these often operated in conjunction with the raiders from Kansas who came into Missouri to pillage and kill. Members of these organizations hated my grandmother because she was a Southern sympathizer and outspoken in her loyalty to the cause of the Confederacy.

MY FATHER JESSE JAMES

The feeling in those days was very intense against Southern sympathizers. Northern spies in Southern uniforms would go to families and get a drink of water or something to eat, and the families would be persecuted for it and sometimes put in jail.

In the spring of 1863 a band of Northern militiamen came to the home of my grandmother and demanded to know where Quantrell was. Quantrell's band had been in that neighborhood shortly before this, and these militiamen thought, I suppose, that my folks could be frightened into telling where they were, if they knew. My father was ploughing corn with Dr. Samuels when the militiamen came up. They took Dr. Samuels from the plough and drove him at the points of their bayonets to a tree near the barn and put a rope around his neck and hung him to a limb until he was nearly dead. Then they lowered him, loosened the rope, and demanded that he tell where Quantrell was. He did not know, and of course could not tell. He would not have told if he had known. Three times they strung him up to the limb and lowered him. The rope cut into his neck until it bled.

The militiamen drove my father, who was a boy of fifteen, up and down the corn rows, lashing his back with a rope and threatening him with their bayonets. They forced him up to the mulberry tree to witness the cruel treatment of his stepfather. When they were through torturing Dr. Samuels with the rope, they went to the house and pointing their guns at my grandmother, said:

"You had better tell what you know." My grandmother answered: "I am like Marion's wife, what I know I will die knowing." Captain Culver was commanding the squad of militiamen. He shouted to the men under him, who were at the rear of the house with Dr. Samuels:

"Bring him around here and let him bid his wife good bye." My grandmother asked him what he intended doing with her husband.

"I'm going up here to kill him and let the hogs eat him," was the reply.

They took him away and had been gone a short while, when three shots were heard in the direction they had gone. My grandmother thought they had killed him, and believed so for days afterward. But they did not kill him. They rode with him until midnight and lodged him, hungry and suffering great pain with his neck, in the jail at Liberty.

After the militiamen had gone with his stepfather, Jesse James said to his mother:

"Ma, look at the stripes on my back."

My grandmother took off his shirt, and his back was livid with long stripes. My grandmother wept at the sight and he said to her:

"Ma, don't you cry. I'll not stand this again" "What can you do?" she asked him.

"I will join Quantrell," he said.

"But they have stolen all the horses, and you have no money," she said.

"Time will bring both," was the reply of my father.

Soon after this my grandmother and her daughter were arrested and taken to St. Joseph and thrown into jail, and kept there twenty-five days. No charge was made against her. She was imprisoned in this shameful way simply because she and her sons were Southern sympathizers. Is it to be wondered at that her sons, beaten, imprisoned, tortured, persecuted at every turn, and driven from home joined Quantrell's avenging band? That same spring after Jesse James had been beaten by the militiamen, Fletcher Taylor, a member of Quantrell's guerrillas, and one of the most desperate fighters the world ever saw, came for him and took him to join Quantrell.

The exciting life and the horseback riding with Quantrell agreed with my father. He had been a delicate boy, but in one winter he grew so stout and strong that when he returned home the following spring for a short visit, his mother did not know him at first. Fletcher Taylor came home with him on that visit. He said to my grandmother:

"You didn't know the boy, did you?"

"No, I did not," his mother said.

Taylor pointed to my father and said:

"There is the bravest man in all Quantrell's command."

"Yes, anyone would be brave if they had done to them what the militiamen did to him," was the answer my grandmother made to this.

In his book, "Noted Guerrillas, or Warfare of the Border," Major Edwards says of the causes that drove my father to be a guerrilla:

"His mother and sister were arrested, carried to St. Joseph and thrown into a filthy prison. The hardships they endured were dreadful, often without adequate food, insulted by sentinels who neither understood nor cared to learn the first lesson of a soldier-courtesy to women-cut off from all communication with the world, the sister was brought near to death's door from a fever which followed the punishment, and the mother-a high spirited and courageous matron-was released only after suffering and emaciation had made her aged in her prime. Before she returned to her home Jesse had joined the dreaded Quantrell."

"Jesse James had a face as smooth and as innocent as the face of a school girl," says Major Edwards in his book. "The blue eyes-very clear and penetrating were never at rest. His form-tall and finely moulded-was capable of great effort and great endurance. On his lips there was always a smile, and for every comrade a pleasant word or a compliment.

Looking at the small, white hands with their long, tapering fingers, it was not then written or recorded that they were to become with a revolver among the quickest and deadliest hands in the West. Jesse's face was something of an oval. He laughed at many things. He was light hearted, reckless, devil-maycare. He was undaunted."

CHAPTER FIVE

JESSE JAMES AS A GUERILLA

Whether or not my father was in the Lawrence raid I am unable to say. I have heard some of his comrades say that he was there and some of them say he was not there. Jesse James was at Centralia, September 27, 1864. A train from St. Louis reached there at 11 o'clock that morning having on board twenty-four Federal soldiers. Quantrell's guerrillas were there to meet it. As the train slowed up the soldiers looked out of the windows and saw the waiting guerrillas on the platform. One of the federals recognized Bill Anderson, one of Quantrell's bravest men, and said to his comrades:

"Lord! Lord! There is Bill Anderson! Boys, go to praying." Bill Anderson's sisters had been killed by Federal soldiers, and over their dead bodies he had sworn a solemn oath to never spare a Federal, and he never spared one. When he was killed the silken cord on which he tied a knot each time he killed a Federal soldier had fifty-four knots on it.

The twenty-four soldiers were taken off the train, stood in line and shot.

Later in the day, Major Johnson and three hundred Federal soldiers went three miles southeast of Centralia and attacked the two hundred and sixty-two guerrillas who were encamped there in the timber. The guerrillas came out to meet them. The story of the fight is best told by Major Edwards and it is a true account of it, as follows:

"Major Johnson halted his men and rode along his front speaking a few calm and collected words. They could not be heard in the guerrilla ranks, but they might have been divined. Most battle speeches are the same. They are generally epigrammatic, and full of sentences like these: 'Aim low,' 'keep cool,' 'fire when you get loaded,' 'let the wounded lie till the fight is over. ' But could it be possible that Johnson meant to receive the charge of the guerrillas at a halt? What cavalry books had he read? Who had taught him such ruinous and suicidal tactics? And yet monstrous as the resolution was in a military sense, it had actually been taken, and Johnson called out loud enough to be heard from opposing force to opposing force: 'Come on, we are ready for the fight.'

"The challenge was accepted. The guerrillas gathered themselves up together as if by a sudden impulse, and took the bridle reins between their teeth. In the hands of each man there was a deadly revolver. There were carbines also, and yet they never had been unslung. The sun was not high, and there was great need to finish quickly whatever had need to be begun. Riding the best and fastest horses in Missouri, the guerrillas struck the Federal ranks as if the rush was a rush of tigers. Jesse James, riding a splendid race mare, led by half a length, then Arch Clements, then Peyton Long, then Oil Shepherd. There was neither trot nor gallop; the guerrillas simply dashed from a walk into a full run. The attack was a hurricane.

Johnson's command fired one volley and not a gun thereafter. It scarcely stood until the interval of three hundred yards was passed over. Johnson cried out to his men to fight to the death, but they did not wait even to hear him through. Some broke ranks as soon as they had fired and fled. Others were attempting to reload their muskets when the guerrillas, firing right and left, hurled themselves upon them. Johnson fell among the first. Mounted as described, Jesse James singled out the leader of the Federals. He did not know him then. No words were spoken between the two. When Jesse James reached to within five feet of Johnson's position, he put out a pistol suddenly and sent a bullet through his brain. Johnson threw out his hands as if trying to reach something above his head and pitched forward heavily, a corpse. There was no quarter. Many begged for mercy on their knees. The guerrillas heeded the prayer as a wolf might the bleating of a lamb. The wild rout broke away toward Sturgeon, the implacable pursuit, vengeful as hate, thundering in the rear. Death did its work in twos, in threes, in squads-singly. Beyond the first volley, in which three were killed and one mortally wounded, not a single guerrilla was hurt.

"Probably sixty of Johnson's men gained their horses before the fierce wave of the charge broke over them, and these were pursued by five guerrillas, led by Jesse James, for six miles at the dead run. Of the sixty, fifty-two were killed on the road from Centralia to Sturgeon. Todd drew up his command and watched the chase go on. For three miles nothing obstructed the vision. Side by side over the level prairie the five stretched away like the wind, gaining step by step and bound by bound, upon the rearmost riders. Then little puffs of smoke arose. No sounds could be heard, but dashing ahead from the white spurts terrified steeds ran riderless. Night and Sturgeon ended the killing. Five men had shot fifty-two. Johnson's total loss was two hundred and eighty-two, or out of three hundred only eighteen escaped. History has chosen to call this ferocious killing at Centralia a butchery. In civil war encounters are not called butcheries when the combatants are man to man and where over either rank there waves a black flag. Johnson's overthrow, probably, was a decree of fate. He rushed upon it as if impelled by a power stronger than himself. He did not know how to command, and his men did not know how to fight. He had, by the sheer force of circumstances, been brought face to face with two hundred and sixty two of the most terrible revolver fighters the American war or any other war ever produced, and he deliberately tied his hands by the act of dismounting, and stood in the shambles until he was shot down. Abject and pitiful cowardice matched itself against reckless and profligate desperation, and the end could only be just what the end was. The guerrillas did unto the militia just exactly what the militia would have done unto them if fate had reversed its decision and given to Johnson what it permitted to the guerrillas."

Father was with Todd a few days after Centralia when they made a raid from their camp on the Blackwater into Lafayette County to break up a German Federal military organization. The militia knew Todd and his guerrillas were coming and they formed an ambuscade of one hundred men in some hazel brush near the road and sent fourteen cavalrymen down the road to meet the guerrillas, and to fire upon them and to fall back past the ambush. Jesse James and ten men rode ahead of the main body of one hundred and sixty-three guerrillas. These ten men met the fourteen cavalrymen and charged them, driving them past the ambuscade. Todd and his one hundred and sixty-three guerrillas heard the firing in front and rushed up, and his command received the fire from the ambush full in the teeth. Todd and his men dismounted and rushed into the brush and killed all but twenty-two of the one hundred militiamen hiding there. While this was going on Jesse James and the ten guerrillas with him had killed ten of the fourteen cavalrymen farther down the road and were pursuing them when they ran at full speed into the advance of a Federal column two hundred strong. There was nothing for the eleven guerrillas to do but turn and run for dear life pursued by the two hundred Federals shooting and yelling. My father's splendid race mare, that had borne him so well in the Centralia fight, was killed beneath him. Father was shot in the left arm and side. He fell behind his dead horse and fought from there, shooting down five of the Federals closest to him. The balance of the guerrilla company came up at this critical time and drove off the Federals. In this day's fight one hundred and seventeen militia were killed and Jesse James killed ten of them.

MY FATHER JESSE JAMES

There is not room in a book of this size to tell one-hundredth part of the adventures, the comings and goings, the hot battles, the victories and the hairbreadth escapes of Quantrell's guerrilla band, of which my father was a member. Only a few of these events, in which my father took a prominent part will be mentioned here.

The attack of Plattsburg, Mo., by the guerrillas was one of these most thrilling events. The court house in the center of the square in Plattsburg was held by forty-six Federal soldiers heavily armed. Twelve guerrillas marched to the town in the night. Three hundred yards from the square they formed fours and made a charge forward. The garrison in the court house was warned of their coming, and every window was full of guns, and the square was swept by minnie balls. The twelve guerrillas attacked the court house in the face of a pitiless fire and captured it. Forty-six Federal soldiers surrendering to twelve guerrillas, who broke to pieces the two hundred muskets they found in the court house and appropriated $10,000 in Missouri defence bonds they found there. The forty-six Federal soldiers were paroled under sacred promise that in the future they would treat non-combatants and Southern sympathizers with more mercy than they had done in the past.

Leaving Plattsburg, the guerrillas crossed the Missouri river to Independence. Four miles from Independence there was a disorderly house kept by several women, and it was a resort for the officers of the Federal garrison at Independence. The guerrillas set a trap to catch these officers.

Jesse James, dressed as a young girl, rode on horseback up to this house and called its mistress out. Imitating the voice and manner of a girl my father told her that he lived not far away, that he was a girl fond of adventure, and would like to come to the house that night, bringing two or three neighbor girls, "to have a good time." The mistress of the house consented, and the supposed girl on horseback said he and the other girls would be there that night.

The mistress sent word at once to the Federal officers in Independence that four new girls would be at her house that night.

It was after dark when Jesse James and the other guerrillas rode up to the house, and dismounting, crept up and peered in at the windows. Twelve Federal officers were in there with the women. No guards or sentinels were out. The Federals felt secure. All the company was in one room, five women and twelve men. A cheery fire blazed and crackled on the hearth of the old-fashioned fire place.

Jesse James, with five men, went to one window. Bill Gregg, with four men, went to another. Each of the nine guerrillas in the darkness outside selected his man. At a signal that had been agreed upon there was a crack of nine revolvers that sounded like the discharge of a single gun. The glass, shivered in a thousand bits, crashed, and nine of the Federal soldiers fell dead at that first volley. The remaining three fell dead an instant later. The guerrillas mounted and rode away.

The next fight of these guerrillas was in June, 1863. Todd led the command of seventy guerrillas, and the plan was to capture and burn Kansas City. But on the way to Kansas City these seventy guerrillas met in the old Sante Fe trail near Westport a column of two hundred Federals. These were soldiers from Kansas, on their way to Kansas City. Todd drew his men up in line and said to them:

"These Kansas soldiers are the fellows we want. They had better be fought out here in the open than behind brick walls."

Todd formed his men behind a knoll near Brush Creek, and himself rode forward to reconnoitre the advancing column. The signal for the guerrillas to advance was when Todd lifted his hat. Todd mounted on a superb horse, stood in the middle of the road and watched the advancing Federal column. At the proper moment he turned to the knoll behind him and lifted his hat, at the same time hitching his revolvers around to his front. The seventy guerrillas came over the hill and galloped down like a whirlwind into the faces of the two hundred soldiers who were a part of the Ninth Kansas cavalry under Capt. Thatcher. It was a hot day. The dust rose in clouds from under the hoofs of the horses and rolled above them. The battle was a hand to hand conflict. The guerrillas with their bridle reins in their teeth and a big revolver in each hand, rode right into the Column, firing with the right and left hand at once and never missing a man. In this fight my father, although he was only a boy, won this remarkable compliment from old Bill Anderson:

"For a beardless boy he is the keenest and cleanest fighter in the command."

Eighty Federals were killed before their column wheeled in a mad, clattering rout back to the Kansas prairies they had just left. The seventy guerrillas chased them, firing and killing as they went. The fleeing Kansas cavalry ran straight into a solid regiment of the Federal infantry and formed behind it. The guerrillas had to retreat but they had lost only three men.

After this the guerrillas were unusually active. Eight of them came upon eight Federals and drove them into a barn and then set it on fire, and as the eight soldiers ran out to escape the flames each was killed in turn.

Twelve guerrillas came to a tavern west of Westport, in Kansas, and killed eight Federal soldiers who were stopping there.

Todd, with ten guerrillas, met eighteen Kansas Red Legs on the road to Independence, and killed fifteen of them.

Poole and thirty guerrillas hid in the woods on a hillside that overlooked a spring on the road three miles west of Napoleon. Eighty-four Federal cavalry came along and stopped there to water their horses. Thirty-three of the eighty-four Federal cavalry were killed and eleven badly wounded.

Jesse James was in all of these combats.

In July, 1863, Major Ransom and four hundred Federals, with two pieces of artillery, were met on the road between Blue Springs and Pleasant Hill by twenty guerrillas under Todd, who was one of Quantrell's lieutenants. The twenty guerrillas made a whirlwind charge into the ranks of the four hundred Federals and killed fifteen of them and wounded a dozen, and then fell back, and kept charging and then retreating down the road. Ransom pursued slowly, firing his cannon from every hill top. Quantrell's full command joined Todd and formed in line of battle beyond a ford of the Sni that Ransom would have to pass. Quantrell charged down upon the Federals as they were crossing this ford and forced Ransom to retreat to Independence, leaving seventy-three of his men dead behind him.

Anderson, one of Quantrell's officers, and twenty guerrillas, circled Olathe, Kas., and killed thirty eight Federal infantry they found in a foraging party.

After the Lawrence raid, in which the guerrillas killed a number of Kansans variously estimated to be between one hundred and forty-three and two hundred and sixteen, the Federals began scalping the guerrillas they killed in fair and foul fights. There had been no scalping before that. The first body scalped was that of Ab. Haller, a guerrilla of great courage and fighting energy. He was hiding, desperately wounded, in some timber near Texas Prairie, near the eastern limits of Jackson County. Seventy-two Federal soldiers found him there and demanded his surrender. But a guerrilla never surrendered at any time or place. Desperately wounded as he was, Haller, single handed and alone, fought from the brush the seventy-two soldiers and killed five of them before they succeeded in killing him. In the fight he was wounded eleven times. The fatal bullet went fair through his heart. His slayers were so infuriated at the gallant fight he made that they scalped him and cut off his ears. An hour or two later the body was found by Andy Blunt and a small party of guerrillas. When they saw the mutilated body of their brave comrade they took this oath:

"Hereafter it is scalp for scalp."

Thereafter a few of the more desperate guerrillas scalped their victims, and a few of the Federals did the same. But in truth it must be said that most of the guerrillas and most of the Federals never mutilated a body. My father never did this, it is needless for me to say, and he disapproved of it most emphatically, but a few of the guerrillas had been desperately and shamefully wronged by the Kansas militia, and when they saw the bodies of their dead comrades mutilated they took an eye for an eye and a tooth for a tooth.

There is not space here to tell of the many savage combats that occurred between guerrillas and Federals all over Jackson, Clay and Lafayette Counties in Missouri, and Johnson County in Kansas, in these years of the war. The guerrillas were not always cruel. Sometimes they were merciful. An instance of this was when a company of guerrillas surrounded eleven Federals in a house of ill repute four miles west of Wellington in Lafayette County. The Federals were ordered to come out and they came. Ten of them were shot down. The eleventh could not be found. A search of the house was made and he was found dressed as a woman in one of the beds. He had hoped by this ruse to escape. This soldier fell upon his knees when he was discovered and begged piteously for his life. He promised, if he was spared, to desert the army and throw his gun away and go home to his mother. He prayed and wept. When he talked about his mother, and begged to be spared for her sake, Arch Clements, the most desperate of them all, took pity on him and said to him:

"Come, get up off your knees and go outside with me."

Arch Clements led him out into the woods under the shade of a huge oak near the roadside.

"For the sake of my dear mother do not kill me," he begged. He was almost a boy, with a fair, honest face. Clements halted him under the oak tree, out of sight of his guerrilla comrades and said to him, pointing down the road:

"You are free ; go, and go quick."

The Kansas boy ran out into the darkness, and Clements discharged his pistol in the air and returned to his comrades, who believed that the pistol report they heard had sent a bullet through the young man's heart.

My father was badly wounded and almost killed August 13, 1864, at Flat Rock Ford, over Grand River.

Sixty-five guerrillas were camped there. A mile away lived a northern sympathizer who notified a body of Federals. Three hundred militia and one hundred and fifty Kansas Red Legs under Col. Catherwood were guided up to the foot of a ravine, where they dismounted and crept up to within range of the guerrillas before the Federals were discovered. Jesse James and Peyton Long saw the Federals first and gave the alarm. Bill Anderson, who was in command, shouted clear and loud:

"Hurry up, men; half of you bridle up and saddle up the horses, while the other half stand off the devils."

The guerrillas answered with a cheer. While half of them were saddling the horses the others formed in the brush and with an incessant and unnerving revolver fire kept the four hundred and fifty Federals at bay. As soon as the horses were ready the guerrillas leaped into their saddles and charged the Federals. Sixty-five men against four hundred and fifty, but those sixty-five were whirlwind fighters and not one of them ever knew what it was to be afraid of anything. That charge was a death grapple. Peyton Long and Arch Clements fell each with a horse killed. Anderson and Tuck Hill each went down with slight wounds. Jim Cummings took Anderson up behind him, Oil Shepherd picked up Arch Clements and Broomfield took up Peyton Long, but Long's revolver was shot from his hand. Broomfield's horse was shot beneath him. Jesse James, Cave Wyatt, William Reynolds and McMacane charged clear through the four hundred and fifty Federals and then charged back again. Dock Rupe, a boy of seventeen, fell dead alongside of Jesse James.

My father fell next, just as he was leading a third charge upon the Federals. He was hit twice. The first wound made him reel in his saddle and his pistol dropped from his right hand. He recovered himself and drew another pistol with his left hand and fired several shots. But a Spencer rifle ball struck him in the right breast, tore a great hole through the lung and came out his back near the spine. No man could bear up under such a wound as that. My father fell. Arch Clements sprang to his side and was standing over him fighting, when Clements was shot again in the face and again in the left leg and fell beside my father.

The desperate and bloody grapple went on. Never did a handful of men fight against such terrible odds. The whole Federal force, cut to pieces by the guerrillas charges, retreated to heavy timber and reformed there, leaving behind seventy-six killed and one hundred wounded. The guerrillas took advantage of this to get away, taking every one of their wounded with them. This they did in all their fights. A wounded guerrilla was never left behind, because the Federals showed no quarter to even wounded guerrillas. My father was sent to the home of Captain John A. Rudd, in Carroll County, and Gooly Robertson, Nat Tigue, Oil Shepherd and Peyton Long were detailed to guard him with their lives. It was not thought that my father would live through the night. Bill Anderson kissed him fondly as he parted with him, and my father, who did not think he had long to live took from his finger a plain gold ring and gave it to Peyton Long to be delivered to his sister Susie.

My father was nursed to life and strength by Mrs. Rudd and Mr. and Mrs. S. Neale.

The guerrillas who were in this desperate fight escaped with a loss of five or six and scattered out to reunite at an appointed rendezvous.

The success of the guerrillas in such encounters as this at Flat Rock Ford was due to their own peculiar training, tactics and methods of fighting. The guerrillas were trained, as Major Edwards has said, "solely in the art of horseback fighting. To halt, to wheel, to gallop, to run, to swing from the saddle, to go at full speed horseback, to turn as upon a pivot - to do all these things and to shoot either with the right hand or the left while doing them - this was guerrilla drill and guerrilla discipline. Taking the first Federal fire at a splendid rush, they were to stop for nothing. No matter how many saddles were emptied, the survivors -

MY FATHER   JESSE JAMES

relying solely upon the revolver were to ride over whatever stood against the whirlwind or sought to check it in its terrible career."

In September, 1864, my father had recovered from the terrible wounds he had received in the fight, at Flat Rock Ford. He left the Rudd home against the earnest protests of his nurses and physician, who said he was not strong enough to travel; crossed the Missouri river on a raft, and joined Todd in Jackson County. He was thin and pale as a ghost. Jesse James was in Todd's camp near Bone Hill when General Sterling Price sent Capt. John Chestnut to Todd with a communication asking Todd, who was operating with Quantrell, to gather up all the guerrillas he could and stir up the militia in North Missouri. Price was then preparing for his Missouri campaign. Todd immediately sent my father to Dave Poole in Lafayette County with orders to gather up his men at once. This order was executed and my father returned to Todd, who sent him with eleven men under Lieut. George Shepherd to cross the river into Clay County to harass the militia there. These men could not find a boat, and they crossed the river in an old horse trough, using fence rails for oars. Todd crossed the river a few days later. He surprised forty-five militia in camp and killed them all. The guerrillas went to Keytesville, which was held by a garrison of eighty militia. Todd and his men surrounded the fort and the eighty militiamen surrendered without firing a shot. The prisoners were paroled.

A few days later Todd's command came upon one hundred and fifty Federal soldiers escorting seventeen wagons. Ninety-two of the one hundred and fifty were killed. In this fight my father, as he galloped on horseback, killed a Federal lieutenant two hundred yards away. The lieutenant had just lifted his carbine to his face when a bullet from my father's heavy dragoon pistol crushed into his head. This remarkable shot was the talk of the command for a long time thereafter.

This battlefield was described afterward in the following language:

"The scene after the conflict was sickening. Charred human remains stuck out from the mouldering wagon heaps. Death, in all forms and shapes of agony made itself visible. Limbs were kneaded into the deep mud of the roadway, and faces, under the iron feet of the horses, crushed into shapelessness."

The march against Fayette began the morning of September 30, 1864. The town was reached at eleven o'clock that forenoon and the attack began at once. Four hundred Federal soldiers were garrisoned there. Todd had two hundred and seventy seven men altogether. The Federals were behind such strong fortifications that they repulsed the guerrilla attack. When the guerrillas retreated Lee McMurtry was left wounded under the shadow of the stockade. Todd called for volunteers to bring him out. My father and Richard Kinney returned and ran in under a heavy fire from the stockade and carried McMurtry out to safety. McMurtry is now sheriff of Wichita County, Texas.

The guerrillas under Poole joined General Price in his famous Missouri raid and remained with him, scouting and picketing and fighting with the advance until Price started Southward from Mine Creek. After Mine Hill they returned to Bone Hill, Jackson County, some going afterward into Kentucky with Quantrell, and some to Texas with George Shepherd. From that time on the days of the guerrillas in Missouri as an organized band were over.

CHAPTER SIX

CLOSING DAYS OF THE BORDER WARFARE

After the death of Todd, near Independence, and the retreat of General Price from Missouri, the guerrilla band was broken up. Lieut. George Shepherd, taking with him Jesse James, Matt Wayman, John Maupin, Theo. Castle, Jack Rupe, Silas King, James and Alfred Corum, Bud Story, Perry Smith, Jack Williams, James and Arthur Devers, Press Webb, John Norfolk, James Cummings, William Gregg and his wife, Dick Maddox and his wife, James Hendrick and his wife, and others to the number of twenty-six, started south from Jackson County to Texas, November 13, 1864.

November 22, 1864, Shepherd and his twenty-six veterans were riding southward on Cabin Creek, in the Cherokee nation. They met Capt. Emmet Goss of Jennison's old command, riding northward with thirty-two Kansas Jayhawkers. My father had a special grievance against Goss, who was six feet tall and had red hair and was a desperate fighter. My father had encountered him before and had sworn to kill him if he ever met him again. When the two commanders lined up and charged each other my father rode straight for Capt. Goss. Goss fired at him point blank four times while my father was trying to control his horse, which became unmanageable in the melee, owing to the fact that my father was suffering with a wound in his left arm. My father got close to Goss at last and shot him through and through. Goss reeled in his saddle but held on and refused to surrender. My father fired again and killed him. Of the thirty-two Kansans, twenty-nine were killed and only three escaped.

At Sherman, Texas, Shepherd disbanded his men December 2, and took a part of them into Western Texas. My father and seven others remained to take service with Arch Clements and the remainder of Bill Anderson's guerrillas.

March 1, 1865, Clements and his command started on a march for old Missouri again. They had many fights and skirmishes on the way and after they got into Missouri.

March 14, 1865, the guerrillas in Missouri held a conference to talk over a plan of surrender. The Confederate armies everywhere had surrendered, with the exception of Shelby's brigade, which was going into Mexico to espouse the cause of Maximilian. The guerrillas at this conference decided to surrender, with the exception of Clements, Jesse James and several others, and bearing a flag of truce, they marched into Lexington, Mo., to allow all who wanted to surrender to do so. My father rode at the head of the column and bore the white flag of truce. They held a conference with Major Rodgers and were marching out again, my father yet in front carrying aloft the white flag, when eight Federal soldiers fired point blank at them and were charged in turn by the guerrillas and routed. Four of the Federals were killed and two wounded. These eight who had charged the guerrillas were the advance of a body of sixty Federals, thirty Johnson County militia and thirty of the Second Wisconsin cavalry. A Wisconsin trooper singled my father out and charged him. At the distance of ten feet both fired together and my father's dragoon pistol bullet went through his heart. Another Wisconsin trooper charged my father, firing as he came. My father killed his horse and the trooper sent a pistol ball through my father's right lung, the same lung that had been torn through by a bullet not so long before at the Flat Rock Ford fight. My father fell and his horse fell dead on top of him. As the Federals galloped past, five of them fired at my father as he lay pinned to the ground. My father pulled himself from beneath the horse and ran for the timber. Five Federals pursued him firing as they ran. My father turned once and at a distance of two hundred yards killed the Federal who was leading the chase. This caused a momentary halt of his pursuers, and during it he pulled off his heavy cavalry boots which were nearly full of blood. Before he started again to run in his stockinged feet he fired at his pursuers and shattered the right arm of one of them. The other three Federals were pressing him close. My father was getting weaker and weaker from loss of blood. The leader of the three pursuers yelled at him:

"Damn your soul, we've got you at last. Stop and be killed like a gentleman."

My father, at bay, tried to lift his heavy dragoon pistol but was too weak to lift it with one hand alone. He grasped it in his two hands and killed the Wisconsin trooper who had cursed him.

The remaining one of the five turned and ran. My father staggered five hundred yards further and fell fainting upon the bank of a creek.

This encounter occurred March 15, 1865. That night, the next day and all of that night and till sunset of the third day, my father lay alone on the banks of the creek, bathing his wound and drinking the water. He had a burning fever, and the bullet hole through his lung gave him the most intense pain. At sunset of March 17, he crawled to a field where a man was ploughing and this man proved to be a friend of the Southern cause. This new-found friend carried my father on horseback that night to the home of Mr. Bowman, a distance of fifteen miles. There my father was tenderly nursed by his inseparable companion Arch Clements, till the surrender of Poole, March 21, with one hundred and twenty-nine guerrillas. It was well understood by these guerrillas and also by Major Rodgers to whom they surrendered, that my father was considered one of the number who surrendered, although his wounds kept him from actually surrendering. Major Rodgers understood this so well, and he was so fully convinced that my father would die, that he thought it unnecessary to parole him when he paroled the other guerrillas, and Major Rodgers declared then that this was why he did not parole him, because he thought it an unnecessary formality to go through with in the case of a dying man.

I have gone thus into detail about this because it has been published thousands of times and is generally believed, that my father did not surrender at the close of the war. He did surrender, and surrendered in good faith. The attack upon him and the handful of guerrillas with him when they were returning with a white flag after negotiating the terms of surrender with the proper official, shows how bitter was the prejudice against the guerrillas. It was a prejudice that developed into a persecution most cruel and which prevented my father from surrendering or from living at home, and which made him a hunted man, with a price on his head, for sixteen long years and finally caused his murder. Arch Clements refused absolutely to surrender on any terms; he preferred to fight to the death.

To enable my father to reach his mother, who had been banished by Federal militia from her home in Clay County, to a home among strangers in Nebraska, Major Rodgers furnished my father with transportation, money and a pass on a steamboat.

To show how genuine was the surrender of my father, and that the Federal forces thereabouts looked upon it as genuine, I will state, as a matter of fact, that while waiting at Lexington for a steamboat up the Missouri river, my father became acquainted with the soldier who had shot him through the lung. He was John E. Jones, Company E, Second Wisconsin cavalry. My father and he became fast friends and exchanged photographs.

At the time of this surrender my father had the scars of twenty-two wounds on his body.
At this point I will quote again from the writings of Major John N. Edwards, that faithful historian of the guerrilla warfare of the border. He says in extenuation of the things the guerrillas did:

"Was it justifiable? Is there much of anything that is justifiable in civil war? Two civilizations struggled for the mastery, with only that imaginary thing, a state line, between them. On either side the soldiers were not as soldiers who fight for a king, for a crown, for a country, for an idea, for glory. At the bottom of every combat was an intense hatred. Little by little there became prominent that feature of savage atrocity which slew the wounded, slaughtered the prisoners, and sometimes mutilated the dead. Originally the Jayhawkers in Kansas had been very poor. They coveted the goods of their Missouri neighbors, made wealthy or well-to-do by prosperous years of peace and African slavery. Before they became soldiers they had been brigands, and before they destroyed houses in the name of retaliation they had plundered them at the instance of individual greed. The first Federal officers operating in Kansas - that is to say, those who belonged to the state were land pirates or pilferers.

"Stock in herds, flocks, droves and multitudes, were driven from Missouri into Kansas. Houses gave up their furniture; women their jewelry; children their wearing apparel; storerooms their contents; the land its crops; the banks their deposits. To robbery was added murder, to murder arson, and to arson depopulation. Is it any wonder, then, that the Missourian whose father was killed should kill in return? Whose house was burned should burn in return? Whose property was plundered should pillage in return? Whose life was made miserable, should hunt as wild beast and rend accordingly? Many such were in Quantrell's command-many whose lives were blighted; who in a night were made orphans and paupers; who saw the labor and accumulation of years swept away in an hour of wanton destruction; who, for no reason on earth save that they were Missourians, were hunted from hiding place to hiding place; who were preyed upon while a single cow remained or a single shock of grain; who were shot at, outlawed, bedeviled and proscribed, and who, no matter whether Union or Disunion, were permitted to have neither a flag nor a country."

While quoting on this subject from the writings of Major Edwards, I wish to use one more extract from them, which gives Major Edwards' estimate of Cole Younger. He says:

"The character of this man to many has been a curious study, but to those who knew him well there is nothing about it of mystery or many sideness. An awful provocation drove him into Quantrell's band. He was never a bloodthirsty or a merciless man. He was brave to recklessness, desperate to rashness, remarkable for terrible prowess in battle; but he was never known to kill a prisoner. On the contrary there are alive to-day fully two hundred Federal soldiers who owe their lives to Cole Younger, a man whose father had been brutally murdered, whose mother had been hounded to her death, whose family had been made to endure the torment of a ferocious persecution, and whose kith and kin, even to most remote degrees were plundered and imprisoned. At Lawrence he was known to have saved a score of lives; in twenty other desperate combats he took prisoners and released them; when the steamer Sam Gaty was captured, he stood there a protecting presence between the would-be slayers and their victims, at Independence he saved more lives; and in Louisiana probably fifty Federals escaped certain death through

Younger's firmness and generosity. His brother James did not go into the war until 1864, and was a brave, dauntless, high-spirited boy who never killed a soldier in his life save in fair and open battle. Cole was a fair-haired, amiable, generous man, devoted in his friendships, and true to his word and to comradeship. In intrepidity he was never surpassed. In battle he never had those to go where he would not follow, aye, where he would not gladly lead. On his body to-day there are scars of thirty six wounds. He was a guerrilla, and a giant among a band of guerrillas, but he was one among three hundred who only killed in open and honorable battle. As great as had been his provocation, he never murdered; as brutal as had been the treatment of every one near and dear to him, he refused always to take vengeance on those who were innocent of the wrongs, and who had taken no part in the deeds which drove him, a boy, into the ranks of the guerrillas, but he fought as a soldier who fights for a cause, a creed, an idea, or for glory. He was a hero and he was merciful.

"John Thrailkill, another of Quantrell's band, who fought with Jesse James along all the border side, was a Missourian turned Apache. He slept little; he could trail a column in the starlight; his only home was on horseback, and he had already mixed with the warp and woof of his young life the savage agony of tears. Thrailkill, when the war began, was a young painter in Northwest Missouri, as gentle as he was industrious. Loving a beautiful girl, and loved ardently in return, he left her one evening to be absent a week. At its expiration they were to be married. Generally the woman who is loved is safe, but this one was in peril. Her father, an invalid of fifty, was set upon by Federal militia and slain, and the daughter, bereft of her reason at the sight of the gray hairs dabbled in blood, went from paroxysm to paroxysm, until she too was a corpse. The wildest of her ravings were mingled with the name of her lover. It was the last articulate thing her lips lingered over or uttered. He came back as a man in a dream. He kissed the dead reverently. He went to the grave as one walks in his sleep. It was bitter cold and someone remarked it to him. 'Is it,' he said; 'I had not felt it.' Another friend, tried to fashion something of a solacement. The savage intensity of the answer shocked him: 'Blood for blood; every hair in her head shall have a sacrifice!' The next day John Thrailkill began to kill. He killed over all Northwest Missouri; of the twenty militia who were concerned in the murder of his sweetheart's father, and, indirectly in the murder of his sweetheart, he killed eighteen.

William Anderson was another of Quantrell's men who had a wrong to avenge. He was a strange man. If the waves of the civil war had not cast him up as the avenger of one sister assassinated and another maimed, he would have lived through it peacefully, the devil that existed in him sleeping on, and the terrible powers latent there remaining unaroused. It is probable that he did not know his own nature. He certainly could have not anticipated the almost miraculous transfiguration that came to him on the eve of his first engagement - that sort of transfiguration which found him a stripling and left him a giant.

"He was a pensive, brooding, silent man. He went to war to kill, and when this self-declared proposition was once well impressed upon his followers, he referred to the subject no more. Generally those who fought him were worsted; in a majority of instances annihilated. He was a devil incarnate in battle, but had been heard over and over again to say: 'If I cared for my life I would have lost it long ago; wanting to lose it I cannot throw it away.' And it would appear from the history of his career up to the time of his death, that what in most men might have been regarded as fatalism was but the inspiration of a palpable destiny. Mortal bullets avoided him. At desperate odds fortune never deserted him. Surrounded, he could not be captured. Outnumbered, he could not be crushed. Surprised, it was impossible to demoralize him. Baffled by adversity, or crippled and wrought upon often by the elements, he wearied no more than a plough that oxen pull, or despaired never so much as the granite mass the storms beat upon and the lightning's strike. Shot dead from his saddle at last in a charge reckless beyond all reason, none triumphed over him a captive before the work was done of the fetters and the rope. His body, however, remained in the hands of the enemy, who dragged it for some distance as two mules might draw a saw log, and finally propped it up in a picture gallery in Richmond, Mo., and had pictures taken of the wan, drawn face of the dead lion and his great mane of a beard that was full of the dead leaves and the dust of the highway."

MY FATHER   JESSE JAMES

CHAPTER SEVEN

AFTER THE WAR

During the war my grandmother, Mrs. Zerelda Samuels, was banished from her home in Clay County by the Home Guards. These Home Guards were Northern sympathizers whose chief business it was to harass and torment people living in the same neighborhood who were Southerners. As a sample of the persecutions of these "patriots" I have heard my grandmother tell that once during the war, when my father was with Quantrell, a band of Home Guards came to her home and after plundering the barn came to the house and began nosing around. One of them said to my grandmother:

"Just show me a southern man and I'll show you a thief."

My grandmother noticed hanging from beneath his overcoat the straps of a bridle of hers that he had just stolen from the barn. She pointed to it and asked sternly:

"What is that you have under your coat"

"Oh, that is only a bridle that I pressed into the service," he replied.

"Well, I will just press you" my grandmother said, and she grabbed him and backed him up into a corner and choked him until he was blue in the face and his tongue hung out. One of his comrades ran to the door and yelled:

"Help! help!"

One of his comrades up by the barn shouted the inquiry:

"What's the matter down there?"

"Mrs. Samuels is choking Sam to death," was the answer.

A month or two after this happened this same soldier returned to my grandmother's house. She saw him coming and threw a shovel full of hot coals from the fireplace into his face and he ran away.

My grandmother was warned by these Federal soldiers to leave Clay County and to go South, "where she belonged," or she would be killed. She went away but she did not go South. My father told her not to go South, because, he told her, when the war closed times would be so hard she would find it difficult to get

North again, and if she did finally get back to Clay County she would find some Kansas Jayhawker squatted on her place. So my grandmother and her family moved North. She was first imprisoned in the jail at Weston for two days. Then she was released on her promise to leave the country. She hired a man to drive her to Nebraska and paid him $1 a mile for eighty-five miles. She and her family went in an open wagon in the bitter winter weather of February. The sleet often froze on her and her two little children as they drove northward. She went to Rulla, Neb., and her husband practised medicine there.

When my father surrendered at the close of the war so badly wounded with a bullet through his lung that he could scarcely walk, he went on a steamboat from Lexington, Mo., up the Missouri river to my grandmother at Rulla, Neb. Richard West, one of Quantrell's guerrillas went with him and cared for him on the way. He reached Rulla in April. He stayed there with my grandmother eight weeks, and in that time he was often so near death that my grandmother would bend over his bed and put her ear to his heart to see if it was yet beating. One day at the end of eight weeks he drew the face of his mother down to his and said to her:

"Ma, I don 't want to be buried here in a Northern state."

"My son, you shall not be buried here," my grandmother told him.

"But, ma, I don't want to die here."

"If you don't wish to you shall not," my grandmother told him, and at once she announced to the members of her household:

"We are going back to old Missouri if the trip kills every one of us. Jesse don't want to die here."

She began preparing immediately for the trip and the very next day my father was put aboard of a boat bound down stream. He was so weak and sick that four men carried him to the boat as he lay on a lounge. He fainted while they were carrying him to the boat, and the people of Rulla tried to persuade my grandmother to abandon the trip. But she would not listen to it. Her son wished to die on Missouri soil and that was enough for her.

On the steamboat my father recovered consciousness enough to ask:

"Ma, where am I?"

"On the boat, honey, going home," my grandmother told him.

"Thank the Lord," he said, and fainted again.

The trip down river seemed to help him a little. He was landed at Harlem, across the river from Kansas City, and was carried to the home of John Mimms, who kept a boarding house there.

He was wounded so badly that for months he could not even sit up in bed. He was nursed by Zerelda Mimms, my mother, and his sister, Susie James, she nursed him from early August till late in October, and then he was strong enough to be moved and he begged to be taken to his old home near Kearney. When he left it was agreed between him and Miss Zerelda Mimms that if ever he recovered, they would be married.

MY FATHER   JESSE JAMES

He was carried home in a wagon. When he reached home he could not walk a step. After a week or two of nursing he could walk across the room and used to say to my grandmother:

"Ma, if I only get so I can walk through the whole house I will be happy."

At that time his wounds discharged so that at stated intervals he had to lean over and allow the pus to drain into a vessel.

He did not tell his mother of his engagement to marry until he was strong enough to ride out a little on horseback. Then he said to her one day:

"Ma, I am going to marry Zee"

My grandmother was opposed to him marrying anyone and she told him so, but he replied in a way that convinced her and silenced all her opposition to it:

"Ma, Zee and I are going to be married."

As soon as my father was strong enough to get around he attended a revival service held in the Baptist church in Kearney and was converted and confessed religion, and was baptised and joined the church. His was a sincere conversion. No one who is acquainted with the life and doings of my father will accuse him of hypocrisy in this act because a hypocrite is a coward, and even the worst enemy my father ever had never accused him of cowardice. He would not stoop to hypocrisy to convince his enemies that his surrender at the close of the war was sincere, and that his only wish was to live a clean, honest, God-fearing life, and at peace with all the world.

But the hatred of the Southern people that rankled in the hearts of the Northern militia and home guards during the war did not die down at its close. They yet hated the Southern soldiers who had honorably surrendered. Even in his desperately wounded condition my father was not permitted to stay at home. He was warned by friends and threatened by enemies.

One night while he was sleeping upstairs at the home of his mother the family was aroused by the sound of signal whistles outside, as if someone was calling and answering. My father got painfully out of bed and crawled to the window and looked out.
He saw six horses tied to the fence in front of the house and he saw that they had on United States government saddles and he divined instantly that they were Home Guards. He got the heavy dragoon pistols he had carried through the war and came down stairs and said to his mother:

"Ma, the house is surrounded, but don't be scared, I have been in tighter places than this and come out all right. I will fight my way out."

The six men came upon the front porch and demanded the surrender of Jesse James. He asked them through the door what they intended to do with him.

"Hang you, by God," their leader answered.

Thereupon my father, sick and weak as he was, threw open the front door, and, with pistol in each hand

stepped out on the porch, and the six armed Home Guards backed away as the wounded Jesse James advanced, and finally broke into a run, regained their horses and galloped away. One printed account has it that my father killed three or four of the Home Guards that night, but this is untrue.

My father knew well that after this repulse the Home Guards would return with a larger gang and would surely kill him if he stayed at home. So that very night he mounted a horse and rode away. There was snow on the ground and it was a bitter cold night. It was the night of February 18, 1867. He made a long ride that night to the house of a friend. His enemies were searching for him everywhere, however, and they kept him dodging around. This caused his wound to open again and he became so ill that he could not be moved. He was hiding in a house in the timber and Dr. Woods attended him and nursed him so well that in the spring he was able to travel to New York City, and there he took steamer and went to California by way of the Isthmus of Panama. He went to the home of his uncle, Woodson James, who owned a hotel near a hot spring of wonderful medicinal qualities and there he stayed for a year, and then returned quietly to his mother's home in Clay County, hoping that in that time the old prejudices and hatreds had died down and that he would not be molested if he stayed close to home and worked the farm for his mother.

But he had been home but a short time when his old enemies, the Home Guards, smelled him out and came after him again. There had been a bank robbery in Gallatin, Mo., and one of the robbers, in escaping, had narrowly missed being killed, and had left behind a horse that had once been the property of my father. This horse had been sold by my father to James Anderson, a brother of Bill Anderson. But it was identified as having once belonged to Jesse James, and that gave his persecutors a chance to accuse him of the robbery and to swear out a warrant for his arrest. Sheriff Thomason and a posse went to my grandmother's house to arrest my father, who knew full well that if they ever got hold of him they would kill him. Jesse James was at home when the posse came, and saw them in time to get out the kitchen window at the rear of the house and run to the barn for his horse. The posse saw him as he mounted and they chased him up through the pasture. When he thought he had gone far enough he turned in his saddle and shot the sheriff's horse dead and warned the posse that the first man who came a step nearer would be shot in his tracks. They knew he would do as he said and they returned to the house, and Sheriff Thompson took out of the barn my father's favorite horse Stonewall, and rode him away. My father returned in a few minutes, and when he found they had stolen his horse it made him very angry. He started after the whole posse but they got away. He rode on to Kearney and there he wrote a letter to the sheriff and mailed it, telling him that he did not wish to kill him because he had been a Southern soldier, but if he did not return Stonewall to his stall before the end of three days there would be trouble sure enough. Two days later the horse was returned and Sheriff Thomason never tried to arrest my father again.

This incident forced my father to leave home again. That night he went to the home of General Jo Shelby, in Lafayette County, and stayed there six weeks. At the end of that time he became homesick. General Shelby sent Dave Poole, a veteran ex guerrilla, to my grandmother's house to test the loyalty of the negro servants and see if it would be safe for my father to return. Neither my grandmother nor the servants knew Poole. My grandmother had two servants, Ambrose, called "Sambo," and Charlotte. Both had been slaves in our families from their birth, and when freedom came to them with the Emancipation Proclamation they refused to accept it, preferring to remain at the old home, and they spent the rest of their days there and died there.

Poole came to the house pretending to be a detective. He first went to the barn where Sambo was currying the horses, and shoved a big revolver up against his face, and backing him into a corner demanded:

"Tell me where Jesse James is or I'll blow your damn brains out,"

"I can't tell you, boss. I haven't seen him," the negro answered, and he stuck to it.

Poole then went to the house and put a revolver to Charlotte's face and demanded:

"Now tell me where Jesse James is or I'll kill you."

"Why, I haven' seen him since the war," she replied.

Poole went back to General Jo Shelby's and reported that the negroes were true blue. My father went home and almost the first thing he said to my grandmother was:

"Ma, don't ever let Aunt Charlotte and Ambrose want for a thing as long as you have a crust of bread."

Old Aunt Charlotte was a sincere Christian, and the falsehood she had told Poole worried her considerably, and she asked my grandmother if she thought God would mark down the lie against her.

"No, my dear; you will wear a crown in glory for that," my grandmother told her.

My father was home only a short time when the home guards smelled him out again and drove him away. From that time to the day of his death, fourteen years later, he was a hunted and an outlawed man.

As a fitting close to this chapter I will quote again from the book by Major John N. Edwards, "Noted Guerrillas, or the Warfare of the Border." This book was published in 1877, and has long been out of print. It is a graphic and faithful account of the doings of the guerrillas and some of the happenings in Western Missouri immediately after the war. In this book Major Edwards says:

"To the great mass of the guerrillas the end of the war also brought an end to their armed resistance. As an organization they never fought again. The most of them kept their weapons; a few had great need of them. Some were killed because of the terrible renown won in the four years' war; some were forced to hide themselves in the unknown of the outlying territories; and some were mercilessly persecuted and driven into desperate defiance and resistance because they were human and intrepid. To this latter class Jesse James belonged. No man ever strove harder to put the past behind him. No man ever submitted more sincerely to the result of a war that had as many excesses on one side as on the other. No man ever went to work with a heartier good will to keep good faith with society and make himself amenable to the law. No man ever sacrificed more for peace, and for the bare privilege of doing just as hundreds like him had done - the privilege of going back again into the obscurity of civil life and becoming again a part of the enterprising economy of the commonwealth. He was not permitted to do so, try how he would, and as hard, and as patiently.

"Jesse James, emaciated, tottering as he walked, fighting what seemed to everyone a hopeless battle of 'the skeleton boy against skeleton death' - joined his mother in Nebraska and returned with her to their home near Kearney, in Clay County. His wound would not heal, and more ominous still every once in a while there was a hemorrhage. In the spring of 1866 he was barely able to mount a horse and ride a little. And he did ride, but he rode armed, watchful, vigilant, haunted. He might be killed, waylaid, ambuscaded, assassinated; but he would be killed with his eyes open and his pistols about him. The hunt for this maimed and emaciated guerrilla culminated on the night of February 18, 1867. On this night an effort was made to kill him.

"Jesse James had to flee. In those evil days bad men in bands were doing bad things continually in the name of law, order and vigilance committees. He had been a desperate guerrilla; he had fought under a black flag; he had made a name of terrible prowess along the border; he had survived dreadful wounds; it was known that he would fight at any hour or in any way; he could not be frightened out of his native state; he could be neither intimidated nor robbed; and hence the wanton war waged upon Jesse James, and hence the reason why to-day he is an outlaw, and hence the reasons also that - outlaw as he is and proscribed in county or state or territory - he has more friends than the officers who hunt him; and more defenders than the armed men who seek to secure his body, dead or alive.

Since 1865 it has been pretty much one eternal ambush for this man - one unbroken and eternal hunt twelve years long. He has been followed, trailed, surrounded, shot at, wounded, ambushed, surprised, watched, betrayed, proscribed, outlawed, driven from state to state, made the objective point of infallible detectives, and he has triumphed. By some intelligent people he is regarded as a myth; by others as in league with the devil. He is neither, but he is an uncommon man. He does not touch whiskey or tobacco in any form. He never travels twice the same road. He never tells the direction from which he came nor the direction in which he means to go. There is a design in this - the calm, cool, deadly design of a man who recognizes the perils which beset him and who is not afraid to die. He trusts very few people, two probably out of every ten thousand. He comes and goes as silently as the leaves fall. He never boasts. He has many names and many disguises. He speaks low, is polite, deferential and accommodating. He does not kill save in stubborn self defense. He has nothing in common with a murderer. He hates the highwayman and the coward. He is an outlaw, but he is not a criminal, no matter what prejudiced public opinion may declare, or malignant partisan dislike make noisy with reiteration. The war made him a desperate guerrilla, and the harpies of the war - the robbers who came in the wake of it, and the cut-throats who came to the surface as the honorable combatants settled back again into civilized life - proscribed him and drove him into resistance. He was a man who could not be bullied - who was too intrepid to be tyrannized over - who would fight a regiment just as quickly as he would fight a single individual - who owned property and meant to keep it - who was born in Clay County and did not mean to be driven out of Clay County and who had surrendered in good faith, but who, because of it, did not intend any the less to have his rights and receive the treatment the balance of the Southern soldiers received. This is the summing up of the whole history of this man since the war. He was hunted, and he was human. He replied to proscription by defiance, ambushment by ambushment, musket shot by pistol shot, night attack by counterattack, charge by counter-charge, and so he will do, desperately and with splendid heroism, until the end."

The foregoing was written by Major Edwards in 1877, five years before my father's death.

MY FATHER   JESSE JAMES

CHAPTER EIGHT

OUTLAWED AND HUNTED

For sixteen years of his life, beginning with 1866 and ending April 3, 1882, when he was killed, my father was outlawed, and police officials and detectives were searching for him everywhere, except in the right place to find him. In these long years he had many thrilling adventures, some amusing ones, and many narrow escapes none of which have ever been told in print before. Owing to the fact that my father had only two photographs ever taken and that these were in the hands of his family and were never seen by those who were searching for him, no correct picture of him was ever printed, and consequently his features were unknown to all except a few, and nearly all of these were loyal friends who could be depended on never to betray him under any circumstances. My father used to live in Kansas City and other cities, and go and come on the busiest streets in broad daylight, as any other citizen would, even when a large reward was offered for his capture. Of course he was in great danger of discovery at all times, and he was always heavily armed.

While the officers were hunting for him at one time there was an agricultural county fair held in Kansas City, and among the prizes offered was one for the best lady's saddle horse, which must be shown in action before the judges at the fair. My father attended this fair and entered his favorite horse, "Stonewall," for the prize. In the competition for the prize "Stonewall" was ridden by Miss Annie Ralston, and the horse took first prize. At that very moment there was a big reward offered for my father's capture.

At another time my father entered a horse in the races at the Jackson, Miss., fair. The race was in three heats. My father was quite sure that his was a better horse than any in the race, but in the first heat he failed to win. My father suspected that the jockey was holding the horse in deliberately and for the purpose of making him lose the race, so my father himself rode the horse in the last two heats and won the race and the purse.

A year or two after the close of the war my father and a companion who had been with him in Quantrell's command, were riding on horseback through the mountain districts of Tennessee. They stopped for dinner at a house along a country road, and while resting there learned that the woman of the house was a widow whose husband had also been a guerrilla with Quantrell, and had died a short time before of wounds received in one of the skirmishes of the last days of the war. My father noticed that the widow was very despondent, and he supposed it was because of the death of her husband. He talked to her in a consoling way, and she told him that what worried her most just then was that her house and little farm was mortgaged for five hundred dollars, the loan fell due that very day, and she expected the sheriff and the money-lender to come that afternoon, and foreclose the mortgage and order her off the place. My father had fought in the same company with her husband in the war. He had five hundred dollars with him, but it was about all he did have, and he was a stranger in a strange land and could not spare the money. But he was determined to aid the widow of his old comrade in some way. He said to her:

"Suppose you had the five hundred dollars to pay the money-lender when he came, would you know how to sign up the papers and get your receipts all correct so there would be no flaw in it?"

She told him she did. He then gave her five hundred dollars, with instructions to be very particular to see that the mortgage was taken up. My father inquired from her the road by which the sheriff and mortgagee would drive out, and then he and his companion bade the woman good-bye and rode away. But they did not go far. They dismounted not far from the widow's home, and led their horses into the brush and concealed themselves. They saw two men go past in a buggy driving in the direction of the widow's home. In an hour or two when these two men came driving back over the same road they were halted by my father and his companion.

"Are you sheriff so and so?"

"Yes."

"And money-lender so and so?"*

"Yes."

"Throw up your hands."

The sheriff and the money-lender obeyed and were relieved of the five hundred dollars, and then were told to drive on. This act of my father's was certainly open to criticism, but by it the widow's home and farm were saved to her and my father regained the money which he had to have to continue his journey. I give this as an example of how desperate chances Jesse James would take to aid the widow of a comrade in distress.

In the later years of his life my father stopped at the home of General Jo Shelby in Lafayette County, to rest himself and his horse from a long journey. General Shelby had a negro boy whom he thought a great deal of. This boy was a waif of the war who had drifted into General Shelby's camp during the war to get something to eat, and Shelby had adopted him. This boy had gone that day to a near-by town with a load of firewood to sell. On a former trip to town this negro boy had been set upon and beaten by the white boys of the town, and this time he took with him an old army pistol that he had taken from the General's room. When he reached town the boys set upon him again, and the negro boy pulled out his pistol and shot one of them in a leg. The wounded boy ran away howling, and the other boys followed him. The negro boy knew that the white folks would get after him for this, so he hurriedly unhitched his mules, mounted one of them and started on a run for General Shelby's house. He was within a mile of the house when a posse of white men on horseback hove in sight on his trail. The boy urged his mule into a faster run, and had just reached the gate at the foot of the lane leading to General Shelby's house when the mob caught him, and dragged him from the mule and started away with him.

My father had taken one of General Shelby's shotguns and was out beyond in a pasture hunting quail when he saw the mob ride up to the gate. He very naturally supposed that the mob had discovered that he was there and had come after him. He went on a run for the stable to get his horse, but before he reached there he saw the mob riding away with the negro boy.

General Shelby was not at home, but his wife was there and she was almost distracted when she saw the mob capture her negro boy and ride away with him. My father declared that he would go and rescue the boy. She begged him not to do it. But he felt in duty bound, as the guest of his friend General Shelby, to protect his servants in his absence, so he saddled his horse and went on a gallop after the mob. There were more than a dozen men in the mob. My father overtook them as they had halted on a high bridge over a creek and were getting ready to lynch the young negro. All of these men were armed, but my father rode right in among them and demanded:

"What are you going to do with that boy?"

"Lynch him," answered a dozen men in chorus.

"What has he done?"

"He shot a white boy. The niggers are getting too bold and we're going to make an example of this one."

"No, you are not," my father said. "That is General Shelby's boy and I am General Shelby's friend. If that boy has harmed a white man he must have a fair trial for it."

The argument might have lasted longer and become more pointed and animated but a man in the mob recognized my father and exclaimed:

"That's Jesse James."

The men in the mob grew respectful at once, and asked what had better be done.

"The best thing for you to do is to take this boy to Lexington and turn him over to the sheriff and have him put in jail, and let him get the same sort of a fair trial that a white boy would get. That will satisfy General Shelby, it will satisfy me, and it ought to satisfy you."

The men in the mob agreed to it and went to Lexington and did as agreed. My father rode behind them to the outskirts of Lexington, and then rode away.

The negro boy was tried by a jury and acquitted.

Henry Clay Campbell was a soldier in Marmaduke's brigade of Price's army. He surrendered at Shreveport, La., and returned to his former home in Cooper County, Mo. A man who lived four miles from Butler, in Bates County, owed Campbell $1,000 since before the war, and at the close of the war Campbell went there to collect the debt. This man who owed him had been a soldier in the Federal army, and when Campbell came to collect the $1,000 this rascal set a gang of fifteen Federal soldiers upon him to kill him. These soldiers, on horseback, were pursuing Campbell, who was also on horseback, along a country road. My father. Arch Clements, Oil Shepherd, and two others saw the pursuit and they ambushed themselves near the road, and as the Federals rushed by six of them were shot and killed, and the rest gave up the chase of Campbell and escaped.

As narrow an escape as my father ever had from capture was in the 70 's when he and a companion were riding through Jackson County one warm day in August. They had been riding all day and were tired and dusty when they came to the Little Blue river, and decided to halt there and take a plunge bath. They tied their horses in the brush, undressed and left their clothing on the bank and plunged into the water. They were in the water up to their necks and were talking to each other, and never dreaming of danger, when suddenly from the bank came the stern command:

"Throw up your hands."

Jesse James and his companion turned their heads quickly, and there on the bank was standing a man with a double-barreled shot gun to his shoulders and the two muzzles pointing fair at the men in the water. There was nothing for the two naked men to do but to obey the command, and up went their hands. It was the first and only time my father ever put up his hands at the command of anyone, and it was the first and only time that he was ever captured. This time he was caught sure enough. His clothing and revolvers were on the river bank behind the determined looking man with the shot gun.

"Come out here" was the next command.

There was not time to form a plan of operation. But my father and his companion were used to surprises and to the necessity of quick action. Experience together in different "tight places" had sharpened their wits so that each almost divined what was going on in the mind of the other, and without either having spoken a word to the other they acted in concert on a plan of escape.

At the command of the man behind the shot gun my father waded slowly ashore, talking and arguing all the time with the man on the bank to distract and confuse him. The other man stayed in the water with his hands above his head, watching father and the man with the shot gun. My father walked up the bank, demanding earnestly all the while to know why two gentlemen enjoying a quiet bath after a day's horseback ride should be disturbed in this rude manner.

As soon as my father reached the side of the man on the bank, his companion, who was in the water, gave a shrill war whoop and dived beneath the surface. This shrill yell so surprised and disconcerted the man with the shot gun that he turned his head quickly away from my father, and looked at the man in the water. That was the chance my father had been waiting for. Quick as a flash he sprang upon the man, grabbing his shot gun and him at the same time, and they rolled over in the weeds locked together in a fierce wrestling match. They had hardly grappled each other before the man in the water was out and got hold of one of his own revolvers, and the rest of it was easy.

The man turned out to be a country constable who was out hunting for horse thieves. He came upon the two horses in the brush and jumped at the conclusion that the two men in the water were horse thieves, and determined to capture them. He never once suspected who the men really were that he had captured. My father dipped his shot gun in the water so it could not be fired, took away all his ammunition, and gave him a good ducking in the Blue and let him go his way.

My grandmother was greatly harassed in these times by detectives who came to her home searching for my father. She learned to suspect every stranger who came there, and to be very wary in her talks with them. At one time during the war Fletcher Taylor and eight guerrillas who were traveling through Clay County near her home were very tired and hungry. They knew of only one house to which they might safely go and ask for food, and that was my grandmother's. Taylor had been there before with my father, and he supposed, of course, that my grandmother would recognize him and it would be all right. It was late at night when he and his eight companions rode up to the house and knocked at the door. My grandmother inquired from within:

"Who is there?"

"It is Fletcher Taylor and eight guerrillas, Mrs. Samuels; we are very hungry."

In those perilous times Federal soldiers often went in the guise of guerrillas to the homes of Southern patriots and asked for food or water, and if it was given them the people who gave it were reported and punished for giving aid and sustenance to the rebels. So my grandmother was very suspicious and cautious.

"I don't know you," she said. "Go away and do not bother me."

"But I am Fletcher Taylor, who was here with your son Jesse."

"That is a good lie. I never saw or heard tell of Fletcher Taylor," she answered.

"But don't you remember, Mrs. Samuels, the good gooseberry pie and clean pair of socks that you gave me."

My grandmother knew then that it was all right, and she threw open the door and prepared a meal for the hungry soldiers.

One time after the war my father was at home and was lying on the floor reading a book, when his mother discovered three men coming up on horseback. She called to my father; he got up and looked out the window and saw that it was the sheriff. He went out the back door, and as he went my grandmother said to him:

"My dear boy, if it is necessary, fight till you die. Do not surrender."

She gave him that advice because a little before that time two men who had been with Quantrell were arrested and put in jail at Richmond, and a mob had taken them out and hanged them.

My father got to his horse and was so closely chased that he had to turn in his saddle and shoot the collar off the sheriff's neck. That ended the pursuit.

Among the many cruel falsehoods that have been told and retold, and printed and reprinted about my father, is that he murdered Whicher, a Pinkerton detective, near my grandmother's home and then carried the body to the banks of the Missouri river, fourteen miles distant, and ferried it across the river and left it in Jackson County. Some writers have embellished this story and made it the more horrible by telling that my father hobbled the detective first and started him to running and then shot at him as he ran, clipping off pieces of his flesh; and that after the man was dead, my father sliced off his ears and carried them around in his vest pocket.

This story is absolutely false; and not only that, it is so ridiculous that any one would know it was false who cared to look at it in a fair way. It is a fact that Whicher was found dead in Jackson County, twenty miles or more from my father's home and on the other side of the river. He had simply been shot without any mutilation. If he had been shot near my father's home, is it likely that whoever killed him would have gone to the trouble of carrying the body away across to where it was found? It would have been much easier to have buried the body where it was killed.

That story of Whicher's killing was concocted by Pinkerton detectives, who knew my father had no hand in the killing. The man who killed Whicher is living in Texas today.

Pinkerton's detectives, in the pursuit of my father and their harassment of my grandmother, were guilty of as wanton and cruel a murder as was ever done anywhere. I can deny that my father ever killed a Pinkerton detective, and my denial bears the evidences of truth to substantiate it. But the Pinkerton detectives cannot deny that they murdered my father's half-brother, and shot off the right arm of my grandmother. They cannot deny it because the proofs of the murder are plain.

I recently heard my grandmother give the following account of this murder:

"It was long after the war, while my boys were hunted everywhere and detectives were coming to my home every little while. One dark midnight while only me and the doctor, and my colored woman and my eight-year-old son, Archie, were alone, a bomb came crashing through the kitchen window. It was thrown with such force that it smashed the whole sash out and fell on the floor. We ran into the kitchen and there it lay blazing. It was wrapped around with cloth and soaked in oil. We rolled it into the fireplace to keep it from setting the house on fire. Then it exploded. A piece of the shell struck little Archie in the breast, going nearly through him and killing him almost instantly. Another piece tore my right arm off between the wrist and elbow. We rushed out doors but could see no one in the darkness. We found the house had been set afire and was blazing fiercely, but we put it out. Those fiends had intended to kill us all with the bomb and then burn us up. There was a light snow on the ground and the next morning we tracked the cowardly hounds, and it appeared there were eight of them. We found a revolver one of them had dropped, and it was stamped with the Pinkerton name."

My grandmother has yet at her home the half of this iron bomb-shell, and visitors to her home may see it there. It is wrought iron with a shell about one-fourth of an inch thick, and it is eight inches in diameter. The edges are torn and jagged by the force of the explosion that burst it asunder. A photograph of Archie Samuels, who was murdered by the Pinkertons, hangs in a corner in the parlor of my grandmother's home and it shows a bright, sweetfaced boy. Beside it on the wall, hanging in a faded frame, is a piece of exceedingly delicate needlework made by grandmother when she was a school girl in a Catholic convent in Kentucky. On the other side of it hangs the picture of a gravestone, and beneath the monument is this inscription:

> In Loving Remembrance of My Beloved Son,
> JESSE W. JAMES.
> Died April 3, 1882.
> Aged 34 Years, 6 Months, 28 Days.
> Murdered by a Traitor and Coward
> Whose Name is Not Worthy to Appear Here.

Before my father was killed, my grandmother did not know he was living in St. Joseph. She never knew where he lived at any time after the war, nor anything of his comings and goings. He came often to see her, but would never talk to her about himself. Once, shortly after his marriage, he visited his mother and she asked him where he was living, and he told her:

MY FATHER JESSE JAMES

"Ma, don't ever ask me where my family is."

"Why?" she inquired.

"Because if you knew where we were living, every wind that blew from that direction would make you uneasy."

A year or two ago my grandmother told in my presence and hearing the following to a reporter for the Kansas City Star; and it was printed in that paper:

"A few days ago," said Mrs. Samuels, "a man came here to look around and said to me he believed my boys were after him once,

"No, sir;" I told him, "my boys were never after you. If they had been they'd have got you. If my boys ever started after a man they always got him.

"My boys were brave. I saw enough of it." Mrs. Samuels laughed heartily and went on: "I remember one day during the war, Jesse and three more of Quantrell's men rode up here to wash up and change shirts. They told me they were hard chased and while they were washing my colored boy held their horses back of the house and I watched from the front. By and by I saw about forty Federal soldiers going up through the field over there toward old Dan Askew's house. Dan was a Northern spy. I shouted to Jesse:

"'I see some Federals'"

"'How many, mother?'" asked Jesse.

"'About forty.'"

"'Where are they?'"

"'Going up through the field to old Dan Askew's.'"

"'Well, keep your eye on them, mother,' said Jesse, and they went right on washing.

"In a minute I saw them coming down toward our house and I shouted:

"'Boys, they're coming to the house.'"

"Jesse was spluttering with his face down in the water basin and he stopped long enough to say:

"'Let 'em come, mother; there are four of us, and I guess we can whip forty Federals all right enough.'

"I got scared and I ran back to where the boys were washing and begged them to run.

"'Do go, Jesse' I said. 'They're crossing the branch and will be right here in half a minute.'

"Jesse just laughed at me and said: 'Don't get rattled, mother. I'm not going away from here with a dirty neck if I have to fight two hundred and forty Federals instead of forty.'

"Well, sir, those four boys did not mount their horses till the soldiers were at the front gate and they heard the latch rattling. Then they sprang into their saddles, and leaped the back fence and rode across the pasture like mad. The Federals galloped around the house, part one way and part the other, and pulled their cavalry pistols, and such shooting and cursing you never heard. Our boys shot back as they ran, and the last I saw of them was a waving line of horses going over the top of the hill. I waited half an hour and then I could stand it no longer. I got on my horse Betsy, and went up over the hill expecting to find the bodies of four boys shot full of holes. About a mile from the house some one hailed me from the brush.

"'Where are you going, ma?'

"It was Jesse, and he and the boys were coming down from the old school house leading their horses and looking for their caps they had lost during the fight. They wouldn't listen to anything I'd say, but rode back to the house with me after they'd found their caps. They washed up again and then rode away.

"Jesse seemed to take delight in getting me scared and playing jokes on me. You know I was always watching out for detectives, and we had plenty of them spying around here. That was long after the war, when Jesse was accused of every bank and train robbery that was done. One day a big man rode up to the gate, hitched his horse and stalked right up to the house and demanded to know where Jesse James was. He said he was a detective and he pulled out a big revolver and threatened to kill him on sight. He took Jesse's gold watch out of his pocket and showed it to me, and said he had killed Jesse and took his watch. I told him I knew he was lying. He searched the house and barn, bulldozed my colored man and woman, and I followed him around, daring him to harm a hair of anyone around the place. At last he sat down in a chair and laughed until I thought he'd split. He told me he was Dave Poole, a friend of Jesse's, and he handed me a letter from Jesse, who had told him to pretend he was a detective and give me a scare. Jesse had said to him:

"'The old lady may take a shot at you, but if she doesn't hit you, go right in.'

"Some of the detectives that came prowling around here had narrow escapes," continued Mrs. Samuels. "You see, they were all cowards; I never saw a detective in all my life who wasn't a coward, and Jesse knew that well enough, too. The detectives used always to come when they thought my boys were away, but two of them missed it once and came very near getting killed. Jesse was here one day when I saw two men coming down the road. We could tell a detective on sight, and we knew they were detectives. They stopped at the gate and hallowed. Jesse stepped just inside the door to the stairway leading to the attic and stood there with his revolvers in his hands. Jesse said:

"'Go to the door, mother.'

"I opened the door and one of the men said they were cattle buyers, and asked if we had any fat cattle.

"'Tell them yes, mother,' said Jesse. 'Tell them the cattle are here and for them to come in and get them.'

"'The cattle you are looking for are in the house; come in and get them!' I shouted. They talked together awhile in whispers and then went on. I guess that was as near as I ever came to seeing shooting right here in the house.

MY FATHER   JESSE JAMES

"But the funniest thing that ever happened was one day when a sheriff - I won't mention his name, because he is living yet - came here alone after Jesse.
I had ten harvest hands at work in the field, and Jesse was hiding in the attic. When dinner was ready I brought Jesse down to eat first before the hands came in at noon. Just as he came down stairs there was a knock at the door. Jesse peeped out the window and said it was the sheriff. He drew his revolver and said:

"'Open the door, mother.'" I opened it and the sheriff walked in.

"'Your gun, please,' Jesse said, as cool as could be, and the sheriff took out his revolver.

"'Throw it over on the bed,' ordered Jesse, and he did so.

"'Now, sit down and have dinner with us,' commanded Jesse, and the two sat down at the table and chatted like old friends while they ate a hearty meal. After it was over Jesse handed the sheriff his revolver and bid him good-bye. The sheriff never came back. He was always a great friend of my boys after that."

As an instance of the courage displayed by the survivors of Quantrell's guerrilla band, who were persecuted and driven from pillar to post after the war, I will tell here of an adventure of Clel. Miller, who was hounded by officers because he had been seen in company with my father. Miller had broken his leg in a fall from his horse and was lying at the home of his cousin near Carrollton, Mo. While he was there the sheriff of the county with a posse rode up and surrounded the house. The sheriff dismounted and came to the door and inquired:

"I understand that Clel. Miller is here?"

"No, he is not here;" answered Miller's cousin, who had answered the knock at the door.

"Yes, he is here. I have the information from a most reliable source. Unless you surrender him at once we will set fire to the house and smoke you all out."

Clel. Miller was lying on a sofa in the parlor and overheard every word of this conversation. Suddenly he sang out:

"Yes, I am here in the front room with a broken leg and unable to move. Come in sheriff, and I will talk over terms of surrender." The sheriff knew that Miller's leg had been broken only a few days before. He had no fear of Miller, and he walked boldly in.

"Take a chair and sit down, sheriff, I want to talk to you," said Miller.

The sheriff sat down and Miller said:

"Give me a chance to fight the whole posse, and you can take me, dead or alive"

"No; I will listen to no propositions. You must go along and take your chances at a trial in the court."

"All right; I will go with you if you will give me your promise to protect me from violence at the hands of the posse."

"I will do that. I will be personally responsible for your safety." the sheriff said.

"That is satisfactory. Help me put my overshoe on my good leg and I will go with you."

The sheriff had no reason to suspect that Miller was not sincere. Miller reached under the sofa as if to get his overshoe, but instead of bringing out a shoe he jerked out a revolver and put it to the sheriff's ear. His manner changed instantly from one of politeness to fierceness. He threatened the sheriff with instant death if he did not obey. He took away the sheriff's revolvers and put them in his own pockets. Then he put his left arm around the sheriff's shoulders and leaned upon him for support and with the muzzle of his huge revolver stuck in the sheriff's ear he hobbled on one foot outside the front door. Standing there, in full view of the posse, he called out that if one man advanced a step toward him he would kill the sheriff and then shoot into the posse and kill all he could before he himself was killed. He made the sheriff order the posse to stand back and obey orders. Then the sheriff assisted Miller to the sheriff's horse and helped him mount, the sheriff himself getting up in front of him. Miller ordered the posse to stay where they were, threatening to kill the sheriff if one of them stirred. He rode with the sheriff for three miles and then made him dismount, thanked him, bade him goodbye, and rode away alone in the gathering darkness and escaped.

My father was anxious at all times to surrender to the proper authorities, upon proper guarantees of protection from violence at the hands of his enemies and fair treatment at the hands of the officers of the law. These overtures on his part were spurned. My grandmother and friends of the family went to three different governors of Missouri and begged and pleaded for fair terms upon which he could surrender. My father said to his mother shortly before his death:

"I would be willing to wear duck clothing all my life if I could only be a free man."

But all his pleadings for a fair chance to surrender were spurned. His old enemies were working constantly to prejudice the public and the officers against him. For twelve years every train robbery and every bank robbery in the country was attributed to him. I have looked through the old files of the daily papers published in Kansas City during those years, and it is really ridiculous to see what crimes were charged up to the account of my hunted and outlawed father. This week there would be a bold robbery somewhere in Missouri, and the newspapers in great head lines charge it to "The James Gang Again." The next week there would be a robbery in Texas, and again it would be the "James Gang." To have committed one-fourth of the crimes charged to him my father would have to have been equipped with an air ship or some other means of aerial flight, for no known method of terrestrial transportation could have made it possible for him to rob a bank in West Virginia Monday night and hold up a train in Texas three nights later.

Yet the credulous public believed the most of these stories. And the gangs who were doing these robberies wished the public to so believe, and in most of these robberies the leader always took pains to inform the robbed people that he was Jesse James, or to write a notification to that effect and leave it where it could be found.

The very day upon which my father was killed there was a peculiarly bold and successful hold up and robbery of a train in Texas, and the newspapers over all the country attributed it to Jesse James. If there is anyone who doubts this to be true, he may prove it true by turning back to the files of the daily papers of that date and find the account of this train robbery upon the first page. In most of the newspapers the name "Jesse James" is the first and most prominent headline, and the succeeding headlines tell of how he and his "gang" held up and robbed the train.

And at the very moment this train was robbed my father was lying dead in St. Joseph.

The death of my father did not bring a cessation of train or bank robberies. This nefarious method of robbery went right on and has continued to the present time, and probably will go on, like Tennyson's brook, forever.

The death of my father created one of the greatest sensations that the West had ever known. He was killed April 3, 1882. I have clipped from the Kansas City Journal of April 4, 1882, the news account, head lines and all, of that tragedy, and here reproduce a part of it as a bit of history that will be found deeply interesting to all who have been interested enough in the story this book tells to have read this far into it:

GOOD-BYE, JESSE!

The Notorious Outlaw and Bandit, Jesse James, killed at
St. Joseph by R. Ford, of Ray County, a Young Man But
Twenty-one Years of Age. - The Deadly Weapon Used Presented to
His Slayer by His Victim But a Short Time Since. -
Jesse in Kansas City During the Past Year and Residing on
One of the Principal Streets. - Kansas City Excited Over the Receipt of the News.
Talks With People. - Life of the Dead Man.

"I've got him, sure," was the telegram that came to the city yesterday. It was meaningless to almost everybody, yet it contained news of the greatest importance. Jesse James was the person referred to, and as he was a corpse, the sender of the dispatch was confident that he had him, sure.

At 9 o'clock yesterday morning Jesse James was shot dead at St. Joseph, Mo., by Robert Ford, a young man about twenty-one years of age, from Ray County. Ford, being acquainted with the James gang, recently planned the death of Jesse. This plan was concocted in this city, and was, as it has been seen, successfully carried out. His brother Charles was with him at the time of the killing, and the wife of Jesse was in the kitchen of the house in which they were living. At his death, Jesse was hanging pictures. He had but a few minutes before being killed, divested himself of his coat and his revolvers. He never spoke a word after falling to the floor. The slayers gave themselves up soon after the killing, and an inquest over the remains was begun.

THE KILLING IN DETAIL

Special Dispatch to the Kansas City Journal:

St. Joseph, Mo., April 3.-Between eight and nine o'clock this morning Jesse James, the Missouri outlaw, before whose record the deeds of Fra Diavolo, Dick Turpin and Shinterhannes dwindle into insignificance, was killed by a boy twenty-one years old, named Robt. Ford, at his temporary residence on Thirteenth and Lafayette streets, in this city. In the light of all moral reasoning the shooting was wholly unjustifiable, but the law is vindicated, and the $10,000 reward offered by the state will doubtless go to the man who had the courage to draw a revolver on the notorious outlaw when his back was turned, as in this case. There is little doubt that the killing was the result of a premeditated plan formed by Robert and Charles Ford several months ago. Charles had been an accomplice of Jesse James since the third of last November, and entirely possessed his confidence. Robert Ford, his brother, joined Jesse near Mrs. Samuels (the mother of the James boys), last Friday a week ago, and accompanied Jesse and Charles to this city Sunday, March 23.

Jesse, his wife and two children, removed from Kansas City (where they had lived several months until they feared their whereabouts would be suspected) to this city, arriving here November 8, 1881, coming in a wagon and accompanied by Charles Ford. They rented a house on the corner of Lafayette and Twenty-first streets, where they stayed two months, when they secured the house No. 1381 on Lafayette Street, formerly the property of Councilman Aylesbury, paying fourteen dollars a month for it, and giving the name of Thomas Howard.

The house is a one-story cottage, painted white, with green shutters, and is romantically situated on the brow of a lofty eminence east of the city, commanding a fine view of the principal portion of the city, river and railroads, and adapted by nature for the perilous and desperate calling of Jesse James. Just east of the house is a deep, gulch-like ravine, and beyond that a broad expanse of open country backed by a belt of timber.

The house, except from the west side, can be seen for several miles. There is a large yard attached to the cottage, and a stable where Jesse had been keeping two horses, which were found there this morning.

Charles and Robert Ford have been occupying one of the rooms in the rear of the dwelling, and have secretly had an understanding to kill Jesse ever since last fall. Ever since the boys have been with Jesse, they have watched for an opportunity to shoot him, but he was always so heavily armed that it was impossible to draw a weapon without James seeing it. They declared that they had no idea of taking him alive, considering the undertaking suicidal. The opportunity they had long wished for came this morning. Breakfast was over. Charlie Ford and Jesse James had been in the stable currying the horses preparatory to their night ride. On returning to the room where Robert Ford was, Jesse said: "It's an awfully hot day." He pulled off his coat and vest and tossed them on the bed. Then he said, "I guess I'll take off my pistols for fear somebody will see them if I walk in the yard." He unbuckled the belt in which he carried two 45-calibre revolvers, one a Smith & Wesson and the other a Colt, and laid them on the bed with his coat and vest. He then picked up a dusting brush with the intention of dusting some pictures which hung on the wall. To do this he got on a chair. His back was now turned to the brothers, who silently stepped between Jesse and his revolvers. At a motion from Charlie both drew their guns. Robert was the quickest of the two, and in one motion he had the long weapon to a level with his eye, and with the muzzle not more than four feet from the back of the outlaw's head.
Even in that motion, quick as thought, there was something which did not escape the acute ears of the hunted man. He made a motion as if to turn his head to ascertain the cause of that suspicious sound, but too late. A nervous pressure on the trigger, a quick flash, a sharp report and the well directed ball crashed through the outlaw's skull. There was no outcry; just a swaying of the body and it fell heavily backwards upon the carpet of the floor. The shot had been fatal and all the bullets in the chambers of Charlie's revolver still directed at Jesse's head could not more effectually have decided the fate of the greatest bandit and free booter that ever figured in the pages of a country's history.

The ball had entered the base of the skull and made its way out through the forehead, over the left eye. It

MY FATHER   JESSE JAMES

had been fired out of a Colt's 45 improved pattern, silver mounted and pearl handled pistol, presented by the dead man to his slayer only a few days ago.

Mrs. James was in the kitchen when the shooting was done, separated from the room in which the bloody tragedy occurred by the dining room. She heard the shot, and dropping her household duties ran into the front room. She saw her husband lying extended on his back, his slayers, each holding his revolver in his hand, making for the fence in the rear of the house. Robert had reached the enclosure and was in the act of scaling it when she stepped to the door and called to him: "Robert, you have done this, come back." Robert answered: "I swear to God I didn't." They then returned to where she stood. Mrs. James ran to the side of her husband and lifted up his head. Life was not yet extinct, and when she asked him if he was hurt, it seemed to her that he wanted to say something, but could not. She tried to wash away the blood that was coursing over his face from the hole in his forehead, but it seemed to her that the blood would come faster than she could wipe it away, and in her hands Jesse James died.

Charlie Ford explained to Mrs. James that "a pistol had accidentally gone off." "Yes," said Mrs. James, "I guess it went off on purpose." Meanwhile Charlie had gone back in the house and brought out two hats, and the two boys left the house. They went to the telegraph office, sent a message to Sheriff Timberlake, of Clay County; to Police Commissioner Craig, of Kansas City; to Governor Crittenden, and other officers, and then surrendered themselves to Marshal Craig.

When the Ford boys appeared at the police station, they were told by an officer that Marshall Craig and a posse of officers had gone in the direction of the James residence and they started after them and surrendered themselves. They accompanied the officers to the house and returned in custody of the police to the marshal's headquarters, where they were furnished with dinner, and about 3 p. m. were removed to the old circuit court room, where the inquest was held in the presence of an immense crowd. Mrs. James accompanied the officers to the house, having previously left her two children, aged seven and three years, a boy and a girl, at the house of a Mrs. Terrel, who had known the Jameses under their assumed name of Howard ever since they had occupied the adjoining house. She was greatly affected by the tragedy, and the heart-rending moans and expressions of grief were sorrowful evidence of the love she bore for the dead desperado.

The report of the killing of the notorious outlaw spread like wildfire throughout the city, and as usual the report assumed every variety of form and color. Very few accredited the news, however, and simply laughed at the idea that Jesse James was really the dead man.

Nevertheless the excitement ran high, and when one confirming point succeeded the other, crowds of hundreds gathered at the undertaking establishment where lay the body. At the city hall, at the court house, and in fact on every street corner, the almost incredible news constituted the sole topic of conversation, to the exclusion of the barely less engrossing topic of the coming election.

Coroner Heddens was notified, and Undertaker Sidenfaden instructed to remove the body to his establishment. This was about 10 o'clock. A large crowd accompanied the coroner to the undertaker's, but only the wife and the reporters were admitted. The body lay in a remote room of the building. It had been taken out of the casket and placed upon a table. The features appeared natural, but were disfigured by the bloody hole over the left eye. The body was neatly and cleanly dressed; in fact, nothing in the appearance of the remains indicated the desperate career of the man or the many bloody scenes of which he had been the hero. The large, cavernous eyes were closed as in a calm slumber. Only the lower part of the face, the square cheek bones, the stout, prominent chin covered with a soft, sandy beard, and the thin, firmly closed lips, in a measure betrayed the determined will and iron courage of the dead man. A further inspection of the body revealed two large bullet wounds on the right side of the breast, within three inches of the nipple, a bullet wound in the leg and the absence of the tip of the middle finger of the left hand.

THE NEWS IN KANSAS CITY

The news of the killing of the famous outlaw created such an excitement on the streets of Kansas City as had not existed since the assassination of President Garfield. Everybody was talking of it yesterday afternoon, and it was frequently heard that it was "decidedly too thin." People would not believe it, and it is probable that when the patrons of the Journal read the account of it this morning that many of them will be unable to realize that the famous bandit, whose name is better known in Missouri than that of any statesman in America, has ended his eventful career. Groups gathered on the street corners to discuss the matter, and even the all absorbing question of city politics was abandoned to ask "who killed him?" "when did it happen?" etc. The most ignorant as well as the wisest of the citizens were interested in the matter, and every representative of the press, as well as the members of the police force, were besieged with anxious inquiries. Occasionally a man is seen who denounces the deed as cowardly, and the wish was heard to be expressed that the man who did the killing might hang. At the station there was a crowd all the afternoon anxious to hear the very latest news. Mayor Frink and a crowd of the clerks and city officials were engaged in an animated discussion of the affair. Said the mayor: "I fully believe that he is dead this time."

The Kansas City Times on this day printed the following description of Jesse James;

Jesse James was about 5 feet 11 inches in height, of a rather solid, firm and compact build, yet rather of the slender type. His hair was black, not overly long; blue eyes, well shaded with dark lashes, and the entire lower portion of his face was covered by a full growth of dark brown or sun browned whiskers, which are not long and shaggy, but are trimmed and bear evidence of careful attention. His complexion was fair, and he was not sunburnt to any considerable extent, as the reader is generally led to suppose. He was neatly clad in a business suit of cassimere, of dark brown substance, which fit him very neatly. He wore a shirt of spotless whiteness, with collar and cravat, and looked more the picture of a staid and substantial business man than the outlaw and desperado that he was.

The widow of Jesse James was a neat and rather prepossessing lady, and bears the stamp of having been well brought up and surrounded by influences of a better and of a holier character than the reader would at first suppose. She is rather slender, fair of face, light hair, blue eyes, with high forehead and marks of intelligence very strikingly apparent. The two children, a little boy and girl, were neat and intelligent, and seemed to grieve much over the deed which had in one short moment deprived them of a father's love and protection.

The Kansas City Times of April 7, 1882, published the following account of the funeral of Jesse James:

Special to the Kansas City Times.

Kearney, April 6. - Yesterday was a holiday at Kearney, near which is the home of Mrs, Samuels, mother of the noted Jesse James. Kearney is a town of between four hundred and five hundred inhabitants, situated on the Hannibal and St. Joe railway, twenty-four miles from Kansas City. At an early hour from all directions came people on the trains, on horseback and in vehicles, anxious to gaze upon the remains of the dead bandit. The metallic casket containing the body was taken to the Kearney house upon its arrival at 2:45 a. m. It was placed upon chairs in the office, and during the forenoon and a portion of the afternoon was surrounded by friends, relatives and strangers anxiously peering into the pallid features. No one who claimed to know him in life doubted that the remains were those of Jesse James. Photographs of the deceased in possession of the Times correspondent were compared with the corpse, and admitted by many of his friends to be genuine. No ill will was engendered or if any existed those possessing it were careful not to let their passions get the better of them. It seemed to be understood by everyone that the solemnity of the occasion demanded that everything be done decently and in order.

THE FUNERAL PROCESSION

Long before noon the town was full of people. The funeral procession started for the Baptist church, in which Jesse was converted in 1866. The edifice was filled, and for many there was standing room only. The pall bearers were J. D. Ford, Deputy Marshal J. T. Reed, Charles Scott, James Henderson and William Bond. There was another, a sixth pall bearer, a rather mysterious character, whom none of the other five seemed to know. He seemed to have charge of the cortege and directed the movements, but neither his fellow pall bearers nor the bystanders knew who he was. He was a stout and well preserved man, of perhaps forty years, and seemed to understand what he was about, but no one could say who he was or where he came from.

The relatives, consisting of Mrs. Samuels, Mrs. James and two children, Mr. and Mrs. Luther W. James, Mrs. Hall and Mrs. Mimms, were seated beside the coffin, placed in front of the altar. The services were opened by singing the hymn, "What a Friend We Have in Jesus." Rev. R. H. Jones, of Lathrop, read a passage of scripture from Job, commencing, "Man born of woman is of few days and full of trouble." Also the fourth and fifth verses of the 39th Psalm, beginning, "Lord, make me to know mine end." He offered up a touching and pathetic prayer for the grief stricken mother, wife and children, asked the Lord to make their bereavement a blessing to them, by leading them to a true knowledge of himself.

THE FUNERAL SERMON

Rev. J. M. P. Martin, pastor of the church, as an introduction to his discourse said: We all understand that we cannot change the state of the dead. Again, it would be useless for me to bring any new information before this congregation respecting the life and character of the deceased.

The text which I have chosen to-day is the 24th chapter of Matthew, 44th verse: "Therefore be ye ready, for in such an hour as ye think not the Son of Man Cometh" First, I wish to call special attention to the certainty of the coming of Christ to each of us. There is a certainty of a grave before each of us. We cannot jump over it or pass it by. God's word is written on His tablets for our instruction and guidance. It takes it for granted that there is a certainty of death. It is constantly warning us of this solemn fact. We talk of death to others, and dwell upon its terrors and are stricken down with grief when it lays its hand upon those we love, but seem unwilling to regard its certainty to ourselves. The truth I wish you to take home with you to-day is that Christ is sure to come to each of us. In the second place, Christ is sure to come at such an hour as we think not. He comes like a thief in the night. As the thief comes when we are least expecting it, so Christ comes. Whatever the past has been, we all have our idle dreams of the future. We all in our imagination have fancy pictures, and are apt to forget the evils that are likely to befall us. If we could at all learn a lesson from the past, we would not expect the future as our fancy paints it. Though we are assured that others shall die and not live, we feel for ourselves we shall live and not die. Shall we not set about for a future which is as real as life is real? Our expectation then of the lengthening out of our lives will not keep away the coming of the Son of Man. Let us remember that He comes as a thief in the night, and not delay our preparations. But it seems idle to try to get men to make preparation for what seems imaginary.

We will not entertain the fact as it is. It is necessary for us to prepare to meet our God. If men are so careful to prepare for things that pertain to this life, how much more important is it to prepare for things that pertain to the life to come? If we accept Christ our account will be acceptable to our Lord. How would we feel if God should come and we should be compelled to stand before Him unprepared? As I said before, we cannot change the past life or condition of the dead. I ask you to take your eyes off from that coffin; I ask you to take your eyes off from the open grave and look higher. Let us not forget our duties and responsibilities in life. A true prophet is not without honor save in his own land, and those who point the way to righteousness are often unheeded. Notwithstanding the many unheeded warnings, God is constantly reminding us and calling us to Him. At the same time that He points us to the grave and tells us to look into it, He says to us it is not all of death to die, not all of life to live. But we need not die spiritually. All we need do is to look and live. Yet we turn away, and turn away until our hearts become hard as stone. He asks us to turn to Him and promises us everlasting life. What more could he say? Let us see that we make ready and stand ready when He calls to us.

Before the coffin is taken from the house, I have been asked to make one or two requests. As John Samuels is very low on account of the shock caused by the death of his brother, and as the grave is very near the house, Mrs. Samuels asks that those who are here will not go out to the house. It is feared that the excitement of seeing so many persons present will injure him. It is therefore requested that none but the friends and relatives go to the grave.

My father was buried in a corner of the beautiful yard that surrounds my grandmother's home, the house in which he was born. The grave is beneath a giant coffee bean tree, and it is covered by flowers that are tended by his mother. A monument of white marble marks the grave.

MY FATHER   JESSE JAMES

CHAPTER NINE

JESSE JAMES, Jr.

Come now to where I must speak of myself and the family left when my father was killed. Not long after his death, my mother and her two children moved to Kansas City to live and to earn a living. I was eleven years old when I answered an advertisement of a "Boy wanted," and it led me to the office of Thomas T. Crittenden, Jr., son of the T. T. Crittenden who was governor of Missouri when my father was killed. T. T. Crittenden, Jr., was in the real estate business, and it was to his office that I unwittingly went in reply to the advertisement and applied for work. He was greatly surprised, I have learned since, when I, together with other boys who were applicants for the place, wrote my name upon a sheet of paper to give him a sample of my handwriting. He employed me in preference to any other boy who was there, and I found in him the best and truest friend that I have ever known. He sold to my mother a lot of ground in Kansas City and loaned us the money to build a modest house upon it, taking my notes for the amount and assuring us that the notes should never go out of his hands, and that we should have our own time in which to pay them off. He kept his word. I remained with him as his office boy for one year. I went to school until I was fifteen years of age. Then I went to work in the Armour packing plant, and remained there six and one-half years, when I opened a cigar stand in the county court house.

In all those years that I was working for wages I was paying a part of my earnings each month taking up the mortgage on our home. The balance of my wages went to help support my mother and sister, and to keep my sister at school. She graduated from the High School in the class of '98.

The most gratifying thing to me in all my life was when I was under arrest on a false charge of train robbery and men whom I had worked for, and men of well known integrity and honor in the community, who had lived near me and watched me grow up, took the witness stand voluntarily and testified under oath that they knew no young man in the city whose character was better than mine or whom they would trust farther. Since I was old enough to know anything I had striven industriously to build up and establish just that kind of a character and reputation, and when a set of unscrupulous detectives sought by false charges to tear down in a day what I had spent the few years of my life in building up, it was peculiarly satisfying to me to see that I was trusted and believed in by men whose regard I would rather have than the good will of all the detectives who ever lived and lied.

I come now to an account of that conspiracy which was intended to be my utter ruin, and the ruin of my mother and sister as well. , This conspiracy, hatched in the brains of detectives, was intended by ruining me and mine to pay off old scores that the detective fraternity had against the James family for years past.

CHAPTER TEN

THE LEEDS HOLD-UP

What is known in the criminal annals of Jackson County, Missouri, as "The Leeds Hold-up" occurred the night of September 23, 1898, on the Missouri Pacific road near Leeds, Mo., eight miles south of Kansas City. In order to understand the events that followed this hold-up, resulting at last in my arrest and trial for the crime, it is best to give here the account of the robbery as it was published the next day in the Kansas City Star. That account, written by one of the most graphic writers on that great newspaper, follows:

The dull explosion that was heard throughout the southeastern part of the city last night was the work of train robbers. It was not much after ten o'clock when the robbers dynamited the express car of a southbound Missouri Pacific train a few miles beyond Leeds and eight miles from Kansas City. That they did not blow off their own clothing was a wonder, for the car was razed, the great iron safe was shattered, and, for a distance of two miles, waybills and papers and fragments of baggage were scattered along the track. The party of masked bandits, thinking they had cut the telegraph wires to Kansas City, used no stint in the application of dynamite. They left a card with the express messenger stating that the supply of quails was good.

A MERRY LITTLE TRAIN ROBBER JOKE

Chief Hayes has in his possession the only tangible clue of the man who did the work. It is a card handed to Express Messenger E. N. Hills by one of the robbers after they had finished. On one side is printed: "Vote for Robert W. Green, Republican nominee for county collector of Jackson County." On the reverse side this is printed with a dull lead pencil:

We, the masked knights of the road, robbed the M. P. train at the Belt Line junction tonight. The supply of quails was good. With much love we remain,

John Kennedy,
Bill Ryan,
Bill Anderson,
Sam Brown,
Jim Redmond.

Whoever the robbers are, one of them, the author of the printed card, evidently has a smattering of Latin, as the last line on the card is "we are ex comspert to." This is undoubtedly intended for ex conspectu, meaning "out of sight." So the last words would read, "we are out of sight."

MY FATHER JESSE JAMES

The Pacific Express company declares it lost nothing except smashed express matter. Last night officials of the company said that everything of value in the safe had been blown to pieces.

The whole affair took only a few minutes. At 9:40 o'clock the Wichita-Little Rock express stopped at the Pittsburgh & Gulf junction, fewer than eight miles south of Kansas City, and in thirty minutes the sound of the explosion was heard in the city.

Word of the hold-up reached police headquarters between 10:30 and 11:00 o'clock. It was more than an hour past midnight when a special train bearing railroad and express officials, and police officers, started for the scene.

After an hour of rushing and jerking through the inky darkness, the lights of a train were made out. Standing just across a trestle at what is most commonly known as "P. & G. Junction," was the southbound Little Rock and Wichita express. It swarmed with passengers. They were loud in their praises of the dispatch and nerve of the robbers. It was all over before they knew anything about it.
Leaning out of the mail car, which had the front of the train, was John Nelson, the mail clerk.

"How did it happen?" "Hanged if I know," he explained. "I heard a shot and looked out, and then I stayed inside my car."

"Where's the engine?"

"Took it west of Swope Park and blew it up."

THE OPERATOR'S STORY

Beside the trestle and the train, the only other things to be made out in the darkness were the lights of a little shanty, a hundred yards away. Therein a blonde mustached man labored patiently with a battered telegraph apparatus.

"The tall man smashed it," he explained, "while the short man covered me with a Winchester!"

Between his efforts to make the instrument work the operator added that the place was "P. & G, Junction" sometimes called Brush Creek junction and Belt Line junction, where the Kansas City, Pittsburg & Gulf crosses the southbound Missouri Pacific, between Leeds and Dodson. He was D. M. Hisey, the Pittsburg & Gulf railway operator.

"It was just before the Missouri Pacific No. 5 was due," he said, "that they came in. By they I mean the tall man and the short man. The short man had a black mask over his face. He shoved a Winchester into my stomach and ordered me to throw up my hands. The tall man had a cloth tied over his face. The mask on the short man slipped down, and I saw his nose and the upper part of his face. He had a big red nose.

"The tall man had a revolver and a pair of wire pliers. He tried to cut the wires and smashed at the switchboard with his revolver when he was unable to cut the cables."

To appreciate this scene it should be understood that the little telegraph room is just big enough to contain three men and a gun.

"Just then the train crossed the trestle, and as it always does, stopped," continued Hisey. "The short man shoved me along at the muzzle of the Winchester, down the track to the train. I noticed that the mouthpiece of his mask was down over his chin. Around the engine were several men with black masks. They had the engineer and fireman down from the engine. They swore horribly. I think I saw seven of them. There was a shot. I was ordered, along with the engineer, to uncouple the engine and express car. We complied! Did we comply quickly? You bet we did! Then they said to us:

"Get on the train and stay on there, or we'll kill you!"

"Then they whistled for a flagman and went off with the engine. About twenty minutes afterward we heard a tremendous explosion. The express messenger came running back and said the express car had been blown up. I began fixing my instruments and sent a message to Kansas City. The big fellow who tried to cut off telegraphic communication was a lobster and didn't know how to do it."

The engine of the relief train pushed the robbed and engineless express car ahead, for it was impossible to pass it. It held the track. It was a slow, noisy procession. About one-half mile further on the caravan of coaches came upon a strange scene.

WRECKAGE ALONG THE TRACK

Looming up in the flare of torches were two Kansas City policemen, Sergeant Caskey and Officer Harry Adams, who had driven out in a buggy and beaten the train. The conductor of the ill-fated train, Hans Carr, several deputy marshals, and a number of negroes with guns, were delving in a mass of debris by the track side in the weird torchlight. Broken trunks, women's finery, fragments of car roofs, a bicycle, men's underclothing, blackened valises, and a pulpy mass of a hundred different things were piled and scattered in the ditch along the left hand side of the track. The telegraph wires were festooned with wreckage. Here the express car had been blown up, but where was the car?

"We're from the coal camp," said the armed negroes. "We heard the explosion and came over to find out about it."

The railway and express officials fell to heaving the fragments of baggage and express matter into the empty baggage car brought with the relief train. They found half of a 32-caliber revolver twisted as if given a wrench when heated redhot. A little lantern was found in the grass, intact, not a crack in its dainty glass. A section man picked up a sack of tobacco, dry and sweet. Working hardest of all was E. N. Hills, the express messenger. He had lost his hat, and a child's soldier cap, picked up in the wreckage, hung over a bump on his head where a robber struck him with the butt of a revolver. The express officials had a long talk with him before he talked of his experience. Then he denied being given a card with the message from Kennedy and Kedmond, saying: "We are the quail hunters."

THE MESSENGER'S EXPERIENCE

"I was working away," said Hills, a smooth faced, nervous young man, "when I felt that my car was starting without the rest of the train. I looked out and saw some figures of men. I realized it was a hold-up and ducked in. Then they came to the side door and beat on it with their guns.

"'Let us in or we'll blow you up!' they said."

"Where was your riot gun?" asked Mr. Moore.

"I got a shell jammed in it," explained Hills.

"And you let them in?"

"To be plain about it," replied Hills to his chief, "I didn't feel justified in losing my life. I had no chance to put up a fight. I opened the door and three got in. They were masked and carried sacks over their arms. One man got the drop on me. They cursed me and asked how much money there was in the safe. I lied to them good and plenty.

"They didn't ask me for the combination of the through safe, because they knew I didn't have it we had a good deal of talk. The mask of the man with the Winchester slipped and I tried to get a good look at him. Quick as a flash he hit me on the head with the butt of his revolver.

"Meanwhile we were moving away. They put seven sticks of dynamite on top of the safe, set the small portable safe, the local safe which I showed them was empty, on top of the dynamite. The car stopped and they set a fuse. I saw a match struck. They jumped out leaving me in the car.

"'You stay and see how it goes!' they told me.

"It was an awful moment. I begged for my life. I pleaded with them and they let me jump down. We all moved up on the other side of the engine. It seemed an age and there was no explosion. They explained that the fuse had gone out. I was afraid they would order me to go inside to investigate. Instead they told me to uncouple the car from the engine. Just as I was doing it there was a flash and roar. It seemed to me I was within a foot of it! I fell down.

"'Git!' somebody said, and I got down the track!"

THE WRECKED CAR AFIRE

The caravan went on through the darkness. It was now three o'clock in the morning. Somebody said that men had been seen driving rapidly through the darkness toward Kansas City in a buggy, just after the robbery. Employees of the Diamond Brick works asserted they heard two explosions following the first great explosion. At a point which the railway men said was about three and one-half miles beyond the junction, burned a fitful, sullen fire. It was the wrecked express car and the killed engine.

What a wreck it was! The car was literally razed to the flat car. Twisted irons and a flat, tangled mass of baggage, express matter and timbers, burned like a gigantic spent fire cracker or a huge bit of "punk." On the left side of the wreck, on the ground, lay the great iron safe. Its top was stove in and it was shattered as if riddled by a thirteen inch shell. The crowds pulled out lumps of the fire proof cement lining as mementoes.

City police, deputy marshals, sections hands, railway officials, passengers in dishabille from the sleeper, tall, thin strangers who came out of the darkness, gathered about the shattered safe helplessly.

FAMILIAR WITH RAILROADING

Charles Slocum, the engineer, and G. L. Weston, the fireman, said that they found the engine without water in the boilers and the crown sheet in danger of blowing out. They had drawn the fire to save the engine. They did not think the robbers were railroad men.

"Even farmers can throw a throttle nowadays," they said.

Nevertheless, it was strange that the robber engineer blew five blasts for a flagman as he pulled out with the engine, notifying the train crew to send back a flagman, if he was a railroad ignoramus.

When the train crew came up to the wreck they found it burning fiercely, and pulled off a good deal of debris to stop the fire. The big safe hung on one side by its iron stanchions, and the train crew and section men pushed it off. Such a joker dynamite is! The fierce shock that razed a staunch car did not harm its trucks, and it was brought to Kansas City at daylight this morning. The small, portable safe was not in sight anywhere. It seemed to have been blown into inky space. Yet a barrel - a mere flimsy barrel - from which stuck whisps of straw, stood unharmed and untouched in a corner wherefrom the walls had been ripped to the floor! Several trunks were uninjured, while the contents of others made a soft, pulpy carpet of the floor of the wrecked car.

Scattered over the whole face of the scene were these cards:

ALBERT HAMILTON DENTON
AND
ALICE EMILY YOUNG,
Married, Tuesday, September 27, 1898,
Arkansas City, Kas.

"If there was anything in that safe," said Superintendent Moore of the Pacific express, "it was blown into smithereens! The robbers did not get a cent!"

Two days after this robbery Governor Stephens offered three hundred dollars reward, and the County Court offered five hundred dollars reward, for the capture and conviction of any one of the robbers, making eight hundred dollars reward in all, a prize well worth working for by detectives.

MY FATHER JESSE JAMES

About this time there came upon the scene Thomas Furlong, of the Furlong Secret Service Agency, and Del Harbaugh, his chief assistant. Furlong was the detective of the Missouri Pacific railroad. Harbaugh was a man who had been a hack driver, and all around tough and "disreputable," for years in Lawrence, Kas., until he had been picked up by Furlong and given a commission as a private detective. Furlong turned over to Harbaugh the job of running to earth the robbers, and gaining thereby the reward, and whatever fame and glory would come from the achievement of such a clever detective feat.

Harbaugh made his headquarters at the Savoy hotel. The following newspaper account of his doings, printed in the Kansas City Star, September 30, shows how his work was looked upon by a newspaper reporter:

Headquarters for operations against the robbers have been transferred to the Savoy hotel, where Thomas Furlong, Del Harbaugh and other railroad detectives are staying. The movements of these men are exceedingly mysterious. Bell boys are kept on the jump delivering telegrams to the sleuths. The doors to their private apartments are locked and the keyholes stuffed with paper. There isn't a bell boy in the hotel who has read a line of "Old Cap Collier" or "Young Sleuth" for a week. Fiction has been discarded to watch the movements of real live detectives working on real live clues.

UP STAIRS AND DOWN AGAIN

Chief Hayes and Marshal Chiles pay hourly visits to the big sleuths at the hotel. They go up and down stairs silently and talk in whispers. The mystery of it all is enough to drive bell boys and chambermaids to distraction.

Last night Chief Hayes paced the length of the hotel office mopping the sweat from his face. Harbaugh and Furlong tip-toed down stairs and then the trio tip-toed up stairs. They were followed by John DeLong, the Missouri Pacific detective, who long ago acquired the sobriquet of "Gum Shoes." Later J. H. Schumacher, manager of the Pinkerton agency, came along and found his way on tip-toes to Furlong's room. There they deliberated while a row of bell-boys stood in the hall expecting every minute to hear shots, shouts, screams and a wild denouement of the daring robbery. Even Sam Campbell, the hotel clerk, has grown nervous watching the mysterious actions of his guests.

After last night's conference Furlong took a late train out of town. Harbaugh had been out of town during the night before.

At the county marshal's office this morning telegrams came and went thick and fast. Mr. Chiles said he had nothing to give out, but that the robbers would be under arrest very soon. Chief Hayes said the same thing. Detectives who have not been "let in" on the case declared that this talk was all without foundation and was a ruse to gain time. They say the trail is getting cold. However, the story comes from sources of reliability that one suspect is actually in the hands of the officers.

A search of the hotels failed to find the prisoner, but there are thousands of places where the police could hide a prisoner and keep him safe from reporters. The man under arrest is said to be a former railway employee. Detectives hint that the sweating process applied to the prisoner has been fruitful. They promise that other arrests are to follow quickly.

THE THEORIES NOW

The theory of the detectives is that two of the robbers did not come to the city after the robbery; that they were countrymen and that they live not far from the place where the train was robbed. The railroad detectives say the Leeds robbery was the best planned of its kind that was ever committed in Missouri. Every detail was so carefully carried out as to leave no doubt that old hands did the work.

The story that the thieves got only twenty-nine dollars for their work is hooted at as absurd. The Pinkertons insisted upon knowing exactly how much money was taken before they went to work on the case. It goes out now that the robbers got at least twenty-five thousand dollars.

A telegram was received at police headquarters this morning from Constable Withers of Mayview, Mo., saying that he had arrested two suspicious looking men who he thought might be train robbers. The men carried Winchester rifles and large caliber self-acting revolvers, and displayed plenty of money. Chief Hayes will send two detectives to Mayview tonight to bring the men to Kansas City.

SMITH'S TALE

J. D. Smith, a man whom no one seems to know, came to Kansas City last night with Detective De Long ("Gum Shoes") of the Missouri Pacific railway secret service. Mr. Smith has harrowing and hair splitting details to tell of how he overheard the planning of the recent hold-up in a box car at Ottawa, Kas., by three men whom he can positively identify. The story, coming as it does from a man in close touch with Detective DeLong, who is noted for being able to supply necessary details when no one else can furnish them, is given little attention by those who are given to taking the train robbery seriously.

Mr. Smith is a man of medium height, dark complexion and shrewd little eyes. He has a small, dashing mustache, and a little wisp of hair on his under lip. He hinted his story to a reporter for The Star this morning in an apparently very reluctant manner, with promises of the details tomorrow morning. In answer to vigorous questioning he said about the following:

"It was in a box car at Ottawa, Kas., on the Tuesday night before the hold-up. Shortly after midnight three men got in the car and planned the hold-up. I saw them when they left the car at daylight, and can positively identify them. Later in the morning I saw them on the streets of Ottawa, and at noon I ate dinner at some restaurant with one of them. I learned from the conversation in the box car that one of the men is a bandit and outlaw from the Indian Territory.

HE KEPT HIS SECRET

"I went to Omaha to see the exposition, and while in a barber shop I read in a paper of the holdup. I kept the secret until I was on my way home, and somewhere between Omaha and Pattonsburg I told the

Missouri Pacific conductor what I knew. I was on my way home to Halstead, Kas. The conductor telegraphed for Mr. DeLong, and he met me at Hiawatha, Kas., and brought me here."

"Have you identified the man who is under arrest? "he was asked.

"I cannot talk to-day. Wait until to-morrow."

"How do you identify the men you heard in the box car."

"I can't talk today."

"What is your business?" Mr. Smith was asked.

"I am a house painter by trade."

Chief Hayes was asked what he thought of Smith's story.

"What Smith? Who is Smith?" he answered.

"The man who was brought here by Detective DeLong," he was told.

"Oh," said the chief, with a look and a smile that meant worlds, "Oh, rats."

September 27, William W. Lowe, a railroad switchman, was arrested by the detectives with great secrecy and hidden away at the police station in Westport, and kept there for weeks, until he finally made what he purported to be a full and complete confession of his part and the part of others in the Leeds hold-up. This confession was as follows:

"The following is my true statement of the train robbery on the Missouri Pacific railway at Belt junction on September 23, 1898, at or about the hour of ten p. m.:

"The said robbery was planned and arranged for September 21, 1898, but was postponed on account of rain until Friday night, September 23, 1898. The robbery was planned by myself, Andy Ryan and Jesse James, Jr. We three did not want to go alone, so Jesse James, Jr., said he had some friends, who he called Charlie and the old man, and also a large man by the name of Evans.

On the night of September 23, I left my home about 6:50 p. m., and took a Summit street car, and rode to the end of the Troost avenue line, from where I went to Thirty-fourth and Tracy avenue and met Jesse James, Jr., and he told me that there was a buggy hitched in front of the two little brick houses south of his place, unoccupied. I went there and got the buggy. I drove around on Troost avenue and then back on Thirty-fifth street by a little clump of three or four small trees, and there I met another rig with a dark horse. They drove by me and stopped, and this man they called Charlie got out and came over to me and asked me where was the 'Kid.' The old man was fixing something on the right shaft of the buggy that he was afraid would let go.

"There were four of us then that showed up - the big man would not get there before 8 p. m. Jesse James, Jr., brought the sack which contained the costumes and guns. The costumes consisted of overalls, old hats, jackets and masks. This big man came, that made five, and then came Andy Ryan, which made up the party of six men.

Jesse James, Jr., Andy Ryan and myself got in the first buggy; Charlie and the old man and the big man got in the other buggy. Then we all drove east on Thirty-fifth street till we came to the rock road (Indiana avenue is known as the rock road), went south on the rock road to a point close to Brush creek, took the first road east after crossing Brush creek, for some distance, then turned into an old field, turned the buggies around facing the south and dressed, putting on masks and disguises.

"I had on a pair of blue overalls, a check jacket, white hat and black mask; I had on a canvas belt with a big brass buckle, on one side of the buckle were three cartridge holders cut off. I cut them off myself. I had two revolvers stuck in the belt. I had in the hip pocket of my pants a 38-caliber revolver belonging to Henry Simms. I also had a 44 caliber revolver, which I carried in my hand; belongs to Dick Spaw.

THE OLD MAN UNARMED

"When we were dressed it was arranged for the old man to hold the horses. He said he had no gun. I gave him a little Colt's revolver, 38-caliber, that shoots a rim fire cartridge; it was an old style powder and ball, with a cartridge cylinder. To load it you had to knock a pin out and take the cylinder off. The sight was knocked off the end of the barrel. This gun was not returned to me.

"We five went through the weeds to the railroad track, cat-a-corner, and cut a wire fence; went north on the Missouri Pacific track opposite the telegraph office.

"Andy Ryan and Jesse James, Jr., went over to the telegraph office and took charge of the operator and destroyed all communication with Kansas City.

"Myself, Charlie and the big man went down to capture the train. As the train came to a stop, with the air applied, and before the air was released, I shut off the cock at the forward end of the baggage car, holding the air set so he could not release it from the engine. I was then standing on the left side of the train going south.

"I crossed over the platform of the baggage car to the right hand side and got up to the engine, and drove the engineer and fireman down to the big man. Charlie searched them to see if they had any guns.

"I took possession of the cab and blew the whistle five times, a signal for the flagman to protect rear end of train.

Andy Ryan and Jesse James, Jr., then came up with the operator. Charlie was on the engine with me; the big man, engineer and fireman and operator went and cut the baggage car loose from the train. I started the engine and when the cars were separated about ten feet, the air set; I got down on the cab and shut off the cock at back end of the tank and 'bled' the car; that released the brake on the car.

"I then boarded the engine and pulled out. We stopped at the whistling post for wagon crossing. I stayed on the engine and filled the toiler with water. I got down off the engine and joined the party with the express messenger on the 'Frisco' track.

MY FATHER   JESSE JAMES

"I put a gun to the messenger's head and told him, 'God damn you, you got a key to that little safe and I want it.' He said he had given it to them, meaning the members of the party who robbed the train.

"This messenger was taking a good look at one of the men with his mask off; his attention was directed to it and he made the messenger about face.

"The dynamite did not go off. I and the big man got into the car; there are two doors in the car - double doors. The safe was north of the door on the east side of the car. Dynamite was laid on top of the safe; the little safe was placed on top of the dynamite. I took my pocket knife and split the fuse. Then I struck a match and lit it, jumped out of the car, and then we thought it was not going to go again, so I got on the engine.

"They ordered the express messenger to cut the engine off, and then the dynamite went off and blowed the safe. We went back to the car and found it all dark and full of smoke.

"There was a lot of silver dollars in a pine box. After the explosion it was scattered all over the floor. What was got out of the safe was put in a sack and carried away by the big man.

"I supposed the engine was cut off from the car. I pulled up to the road crossing and there we burned up in the fire box of the engine all the costumes, masks, etc., except my overalls and belt. We then went to our buggies and left in the same order we went out in.

"Between the hold-up and Leeds I threw away my overalls and belt. We came on the rock road to Thirty-fifth street, turned west and went to Tracy Avenue. There Jesse James, Jr., got out and left the shotgun and revolvers in the weeds. My 44 was left there also - this is the gun that belongs to Dick Spaw. Jesse said he would leave it in the weeds or put it in the cellar of one of the vacant houses.

"The shotgun Jesse had was a double barrel, breech loader, with hammers, and the case found in the buggy belonged to this gun. It was a heavy gun.

"We all got back in the buggy and drove to one block of the end of the Holmes street line, where Ryan got out. Jesse and I drove to the corner of block east of stable, where I got out and took the laprobe and rubbed the sweat off the horse.

"I went through a vacant lot cat-a-corner. About midway of the block I threw away a handful of 38-caliber cartridges. I came out of the vacant block at the north-west corner through a gate which I found open, boarded a Holmes street car, got on front end on right side of car. Sat on the seat facing east. Andy Ryan was on the car, sitting beside me. We got off the car at Fourteenth street and Grand avenue and went to Fourteenth and Main, and got a glass of beer. We then went up Fourteenth street to Broadway and parted, Ryan going west on Fourteenth and I south on Broadway to Sixteenth and thence west on Sixteenth to my home, arriving at home at 11:15 p. m.

"The old man I refer to is about my height; weight about 150 pounds. From conversation I inferred that this old man is a relative of Polk's, and lives with Polk or near him. The big man known to me as Evans is described as follows: About six feet tall, weight 175 to 190 pounds, said to have come from Texas, and is a friend of Polk's. I understand he is a friend of Seth Lowe, in Crackerneck.

The inducements that were offered to Lowe to make this confession will be shown in the following chapter, as it was proven at my trial. There is no doubt in the minds of anyone who heard the trial that Lowe was really in the hold-up. He was promised immunity if he would connect me with the robbery, and this promise was kept, because, immediately after my honorable acquittal by a fair and intelligent jury of twelve of the best citizens of the county, the indictment against Lowe was dismissed, and this self-confessed train robber walked out of the court room a free man. The cases against all of the other alleged train robbers were also dismissed and they were discharged from custody. This is positive proof, to me at least, that the detectives were after me alone, and failing to convict me, did not wish that justice be done, and did not seem to care whether train robbers ran at large in the community or not.

I was arrested October 11, 1898, charged with being the leader of a gang of robbers who held up the train at Leeds. The arrest created a great sensation, of course. I quote again from the Kansas City Star, my motive in giving newspaper accounts of this matter being that the public cannot then accuse me of distorting the facts to favor myself, and certainly no one who read the accounts of this affair in the Star would ever suspect that paper of being biased in my favor. The Star said of my arrest:

"The arrest of young Jesse James aroused and stirred up that element in the community which is linked by old memories and associations with the border days, when the people of this country were divided on the issues of the civil war. Old men with excited faces and eyes flashing with anger appeared at police headquarters and around the jail early this morning and demanded to know where Jesse James was and by what authority he was held. The voices of these men trembled with excitement as they talked about the case.

"At the court house the police were denounced for arresting James. Many of the people employed there made light of the police claim that they had a strong case, and it was evident that Jesse James, guilty or guiltless, had friends there. The arrest was spoken of by some as a very serious mistake, for it would be 'bad for the party.'

JUDGE HENRY CALLS IT AN OUTRAGE

"Judge Henry was very indignant at the manner in which Jesse James had been arrested. He said to a reporter for The Star this morning:

"'The manner in which this boy was kidnapped by the police was a damnable outrage. You must bear in mind that young Jesse James is not like other boys. He occupies a peculiar position in this community. His father was a bandit and was killed for a reward. Young Jesse has grown up here, watched by everybody. Many watched over him with solicitude for his welfare, advising him, guiding his footsteps in the right, anxious for him to get along and be a good, clean man.

"'Many others watched him askance to see how soon he would show a tendency to follow in his father's footsteps. Many wished him ill. I have watched this boy closely. I know that no boy in the county has led a cleaner life. He has worked and slaved and saved, and alone and unaided has paid for the home in which he, his mother and sister live. It was his wages that clothed his sister and paid for her music lessons. No one ever saw this boy in a saloon. Who ever saw him out late at night? Who ever heard of him being in a brawl or scandal? Here he has grown up with us, with his father's past to live down, and I say he has shown himself a well balanced, worthy boy.

"'To brand that boy as a train robber, if he were innocent, would be a crime that would merit hanging. So I say that the police should have waited till they were sure he was guilty, and then they should have gone in open daylight and sworn out a warrant and arrested him, and placed him in jail so that his mother and sister could see him. Instead of that they kidnap him and hide him away. That is evidence to me that they do not know he is guilty. They kidnap him to put the thumb-screws upon him in secret and try and extort something from him. That is unlawful and unfair.'

"Chief Hayes said this afternoon that Jesse James was not even locked up last night. He was kept in a well furnished room, and was allowed to telephone to his mother and to his friends. The chief said he had talked very little to him about the case during the night.

"HAD A RIGHT TO KILL THE OFFICERS"

'

"Finis C. Farr, lawyer for Jesse James, said: 'The grand jury has been in session for weeks. If the police have evidence against the boy why didn't they have him indicted. Jesse knew they were shadowing him. He had no intention of running away. He was tending his cigar stand in the courthouse when he was kidnapped. Why did the police spirit him away unless it was to bulldoze and browbeat him into saying something that would hurt him? That is the Pinkerton way of doing things: It was the Pinkertons who threw the bomb into the house of this boy's grandmother and blew her arm off and killed her baby. The Pinkertons hate the whole James family. But I'll tell you they can't kidnap people in this community with impunity, no matter whether they are train robbers or not. Jesse had a right to kill those officers who took him without a warrant and he ought to have done it."

R. L. YEAGER AS HIS LAWYER

"R. L. Yeager, a lawyer and president of the school board, went to see Chief Hayes this morning, and demanded that Jesse James be released within an hour. Mr. Yeager said:

"I have been employed to defend Jesse James, who was kidnapped by the police unlawfully. He must be released or properly apprehended and held.

"Ex-Governor T. T. Crittenden said: 'The arrest of Jesse James is a greater crime than train robbery. If I were governor I would have the men who arrested him indicted.'"

The Star said of my arrest upon this day:

JESSE JAMES'S GOOD RECORD

"Jesse James' friends - and the young man has many, some of them among the responsible citizens of the town - are loth to believe the suspicions gathering about him. He has always been known as a steady, industrious and home-loving youth, fond of his mother, and willing to be guided by her wishes. To his mother any suggestion that Jesse has been guilty of wrong will come as a heavy blow. The same may be said of his grandmother, the aged Mrs. Samuels, who lives near Kearney. Mrs. Samuels lives in talking and thinking of her boy Jesse, and Jesse, Jr., she idolizes, but, although her son was a bandit, she would not have Jesse, Jr., go the same way. Jessie never has looked upon his father as the criminal that the world pictures him, yet the fact that there is a stain upon his father's name has always served as a governor in his actions. His employers liked him and always spoke in the highest terms of his steadiness and unremitting application to duty. They say, too, that during the several years he was stock taker in the cured meat department he never was caught in a mistake. His salary was not large, but it sufficed for the modest needs of the family of three, and by careful economy permitted the saving of the money that paid for the home at 3402 Tracy Avenue."

Later on in the day I was admitted to bond in the sum of $2,500, furnished by E. F. Swinney, cashier of the First National Bank, and Finis C. Farr.

CHAPTER ELEVEN

THE TRIAL FOR TRAIN ROBBERY

My trial on a charge of being the leader of the band which held up the train at Leeds, began in the criminal court of Jackson County, Mo., February 23, 1899. Of the five cases against men under arrest and indictment for this robbery, my case was selected for trial first, although I was many years younger than any of the others and had a reputation in the community that was spoken of by all the newspapers as good. The prosecution claimed that my case was selected for trial first because I was the planner of the robbery and the leader of the band. I believe that my case was selected for trial first because there was no case against any of the other men who were indicted for this robbery except W. W. Lowe, who confessed this robbery. My theory of the conspiracy to convict me is that Lowe actually was in this robbery, that his wife, who was anxious to get rid of him, informed the detectives, and he was at once arrested and very damaging evidence accumulated against him by the detectives. I believe that every pressure that the ingenuity of the detectives could devise was brought to bear on him to make him confess who his accomplices were, but he steadfastly refused to confess, owing to some sense of honor that he might have had or because he was afraid that his accomplices might kill him if he did confess. The detectives then, either by inference or by direct statements made to him, gave him to understand that they believed I was in the robbery. Lowe saw by their statements that the detectives were anxious to fasten the crime on me. Lowe then intimated that I was in the robbery, and at once the detectives promised him immunity if he would confess, and not only that, but Del Harbaugh, the Missouri Pacific detective, promised that his case would be dismissed and he given a good position on the Missouri Pacific railroad if he would tell all. Lowe then confessed, not all at once, but piecemeal, that I was with him in the robbery. Of course he had to give the names of others who were in the robbery too, and he selected the names of men known to be acquainted with me. They were Andy Ryan, Charles Polk and Caleb Stone. Andy Ryan I had known almost from my infancy, owing to the fact that he lived in Kansas City and was a member in good standing of the city fire department, and as his brother, Bill Ryan, had been an acquaintance of my father, I came naturally to know Andy Ryan, and I never knew wrong of him. Andy Ryan was by no means an associate of mine; I simply had a passing acquaintance with him. Polk I knew very well. He worked at Armour's packing house when I worked there. I had a little acquaintance with Caleb Stone, an old man of seventy years. The detectives knew that I knew all of these men, and in casting about in their minds for men to associate with me in Lowe's false confession of the train robbery, they probably selected these men almost at haphazard, simply because they knew that I knew them. Certain it is that not a scrap of evidence was ever produced to show that Ryan, Polk or Stone had the slightest connection with the Leeds robbery, and they were discharged from custody as soon as I was acquitted.

My theory as to why the detectives sought to convict me of the robbery, takes in several causes and motives on their part. There had been a number of train robberies recently in Jackson County. The detectives were unable to capture the robbers. The railroad companies who employed these detectives, were naturally dissatisfied with their failure to do so. This incensed the detectives. When Harbaugh was brought into the case a man came who was wholly unscrupulous. He was found not to fail. He would catch someone. Harbaugh knew that if he could convict Jesse James for the robbery, after the failure of all the detectives who had gone before him and failed to convict anyone, it would win him a great reputation. This is why he sought, by a conspiracy, to convict me.

The detectives even claimed that a man named Jennings, who was in jail at Springfield, was really Bill Ryan, and that Bill Ryan was in the robbery at Leeds. The detectives knew this to be absolutely false. Jennings is not Bill Ryan.

The reader who will take the trouble to follow the trial as I will outline it here, will see how this theory of mine is borne out by the facts as they developed, and at the end of the trial, which resulted in my acquittal, the reader will see the cases against all of the other men dismissed, and even Lowe was allowed to walk, a free man, out of the court room.

As bearing out my theory of the conspiracy to convict me, I quote as follows from the Kansas City Star of October 12, 1898:

"Lowe was kept locked up. He was continually harassed by detectives, who plied him with questions. Lowe is a Free Mason, and so is Harbaugh, the detective. Harbaugh promised Lowe that if he would confess he would guarantee that he would be given the lowest penalty, his child would be put in the Free Masons home and cared for while he was in the penitentiary, and when his term was up he would be given a permanent job on the railroad, Lowe has a brother who is an engineer on the Missouri Pacific railroad, and the detectives sent for him and had him urge Lowe to make a confession. Then Lowe confessed that Jesse James was in the robbery."

The twelve jurors who heard my trial and returned a verdict of acquittal, were King R. Powell, William Ewing, Albert L. Miller, Eugene McEntee, John J. Durrett, William S. Rodgers, Leonard Veugelen, Samuel E. Spence, Joseph M. McConnell, William E. Mullens, J. E. Broughal and Harry G. Clark.

Of these jurors the Star of February 22, 1899, said:

"The jurors are regarded as excellent men, who will do their duty as their consciences see it."

The Journal of the same date said;

"Neither side has been able to find a blemish upon the name and character of any of the jurymen."

The Kansas City World of February 23 said:
:

"Both sides consider the jury an exceptionally fine one. Every man on it resides in Kansas City and is apparently a man of more than ordinary intelligence."

While the jurors were being selected in the court room, it developed that detectives had questioned them and attempted to influence them against me.

My lawyers were Frank P. Walsh, Finis C. Farr, R. L. Yeager, president of the Kansas City school board, and

Milton J. Oldham. The magnificent management of my case is due to the skill, ability and legal learning of these four splendid men.

The county prosecutor who represented the state at the trial was James A. Reed, and he was assisted by Frank G. Johnson.

Of the interest which my trial excited, the Kansas City Star said during its progress:

"In all the history of criminal courts in this country there has probably never been a trial in which there was so much strained attention by the spectators in the court room to every word and to everything done, as there is in the trial of Jesse James for train robbery, now on in the criminal court here. There have been many trials in which the public took a deep interest. In this same court room a woman was tried for her life not long ago; it was a most interesting trial and the court room overflowed day after day. There have been other remarkable trials. But in all these other trials the court room filled with a hodge-podge audience of all sorts of persons, who seemed to have come from mere curiosity, and were ready to laugh at the most trivial thing.

"But in this trial of Jesse James every one of the hundreds in the court room seems to have a personal interest in it. They watch things so closely. The feelings of suspense that seem to fill the very air of the crowded room, the looks of deep and attentive concern on every face, are quite wonderful to see. There is no levity, no laughter, and there are no interruptions.

"This deep interest is probably because of the fact that the young man on trial is the son of Jesse James, the old rough riding bandit who kept the newspapers of the country well filled with news of his doings hereabouts for a good many years, and it is a thing quite remarkable that this young man, if he is guilty, should have taken up the desperate calling of his father. It is equally remarkable, if this son of a bandit is innocent, and the victim of a gigantic conspiracy on the part of the authorities either to hang him or send him to the penitentiary.

"The jurors seem to be more deeply interested in the trial than jurors usually are in cases they are trying. They do not miss a word or an act of the proceedings. They are thought by court house officials to be jurymen of average intelligence and probable integrity. There are four old men on the jury with gray hair and beards. None of the other eight men appear to be more than forty nor less than twenty-five years old.

"If Jesse James is innocent, he is the victim of one of the most gigantic conspiracies ever concocted to convict a man."

The proceedings on the first day of the trial were reported as follows in the Kansas City Star. I prefer to use the newspaper accounts of the trial because I cannot then be accused of making misrepresentations:

William W. Lowe the principal witness against Jesse James in his trial on the charge of robbing a Missouri Pacific train near Leeds on the night of September 23 last, was on the witness stand in the criminal court all yesterday afternoon and a part of this forenoon. Lowe told how he had known Jack Kennedy and Andy Ryan for many years when Lowe lived in Independence, and they lived near there. He told about meeting Kennedy here in Kansas City last winter, and said he was an alibi witness for Kennedy in Krueger's court, and that Jesse James was a witness there for Kennedy, too; that Lowe and Jesse met there for the first time, became acquainted and kept up this acquaintance, which led up to the train robbery.

Lowe told every detail of the robbery with great minuteness, giving little incidents, such as whom they met, what routes they traveled, what conversations were held, and every little thing that was done. They planned first to rob the train in the early part of September, he said, but Jesse postponed it because his uncle was in town then. They planned it next for September 21, but it rained hard that day and it was postponed again.

Lowe said that while planning the robbery he was at the home of Jesse James several times, and the night of the robbery the party started from near there. He described the interior of the James home and drew with a pencil before the jury what purported to be a plan of the interior of the place. He said there were in the robbery himself, Jesse James, Andy Ryan, a man who was called Evans, who was a stranger to him, whom he had never seen before or since, and two other men, one an old man, who were introduced to him by Jesse; they were called Charlie and Harry.

The police claim that the man Evans was Bill Ryan, in jail at Springfield for the Macomb robbery, and that the men called Charlie and Harry were old Caleb Stone and Charles Polk, both under indictment now. But Lowe would not identify Caleb Stone yesterday in the court room. That was a dramatic incident of the trial. It was during the cross-examination of Lowe by Mr. Walsh, lawyer for Jesse James. Caleb Stone sat at the end of the lawyer's table, right behind Jesse James, and facing Lowe and the jury.

"Whom do you say were in this robbery with you besides Jesse James, Ryan and Evans?" asked Walsh.

"Two men called Charlie and the 'Old man.'"

"Describe them."

"Charlie was about my size."

"What sort of a looking man was the 'Old man?'"

"He was an oldish man."

"Would you know him if you saw him again?"

"I don't know." Mr. Walsh turned to where Caleb Stone sat and said:

"Stand up, Mr. Stone." Caleb Stone stood up and looked sharply at Lowe. He is an old man, small in size, bent and slightly stoop shouldered, with gray mustache and chin whiskers, and rather plainly dressed.

"Is that the man?" asked Walsh.

Lowe merely glanced at Stone, and said:

"I wouldn't identify him."

"Do you think it's he?"

"I wouldn't say."

MY FATHER JESSE JAMES

"Does it look like the man?"

"I can't say; I don't know."

"You saw the 'old man' plainly the night of the robbery, did you not?"

"I saw him there."

"Did he have a mask on?"

"No."

"And you don't know whether this is the man or not?"

"No."

"Why did you go into a robbery with three men you did not know, and had never seen before?"

"Jesse told me they were all right, and Jack Kennedy told me I could bank on anything Jesse said, because he was all right"

Another interesting point in the trial late last evening was when Mr. Walsh asked Lowe why he confessed to the police.

"I refused for fourteen days to tell a thing. They tried to get me to tell, but I wouldn't. I waited for these men who were in the robbery with me to help me out, and I waited fourteen days in jail and they never did a thing for me. I made up my mind that they had 'ditched me,' and I was up agin it anyway, and I just told the whole business from start to finish."

A surprising development was when Lowe denied last evening that he had ever made a written confession or statement, or had ever signed his name to one.

Mr. Walsh had a copy of The Star of last October, with Lowe's confession in full printed on the first page. Mr. Walsh questioned him about it, and questioned him again closely this morning. Mr. Walsh read the printed confession. It tallied in every particular with the story told yesterday and to-day by Lowe on the witness stand. Lowe said when asked about it:

"I never did write down a word about the robbery; I never dictated a statement to a stenographer or to anyone else, and I never signed my name to any statement or confession."

Lowe stuck to it in spite of all questioning, that he never made a written confession or statement.

"I told the police and detectives the whole truth," he declared, "and if they wrote it down that's their business."

"Did they write it down in your presence?"

"No, sir."

The cross-examination of Lowe by Frank P. Walsh, attorney for Jesse James, gave an idea of what the plan of the defense would be in regard to his testimony. Mr. Walsh questioned Lowe for two hours last evening, and resumed the cross-examination when court opened this morning. It was a very skillful arrangement of questions. The impression sought to be conveyed by these questions was that Lowe was really in the robbery; that after he was arrested the railroad and express companies' detectives and the police tried to get him to confess; that Lowe would not tell anything about it; that they used every inducement they could to get him to confess, promising him immunity and part of the reward, and convincing him that they had him "dead to rights," and threatening to convict him sure unless he confessed; that the detectives kept asking him if he knew Jesse James and Jack Kennedy, and gave him to understand if he would implicate Jesse James in it he would be given immunity; that then Lowe did make an alleged confession, protecting the men who were really in the robbery, and telling that Jesse James, Ryan, Polk and Stone were in it.

"When did you first see any of these detectives?" asked Mr. Walsh.

"One came to my house and represented that he was working for the claim department of the street railway, and that I was witness to an accident on the Twelfth street incline, and that he wanted to talk with me about it. I knowed right away that he was a detective."

"When did you see him next?"

"When they came to arrest me, some time after that."

"Where did they take you?"

"To the Savoy hotel."

Lowe told this story this morning in answer to questions of how he came to confess to the police:

"They took me from the Savoy to No. 3 police station and locked me up. I was there several days, and then they took me to the Westport station. For fourteen days they kept after me, telling me each visit they made the evidence they had against me, and it was good, straight evidence, too. They kept getting after me stronger and stronger all the time. They brought my wife down to see me, and she told me she had told the police all she knew. They wouldn't let me see an attorney, nor no one else, and they kept telling me what they had agin me. Finally I asked to see my brother, and he came and advised me to tell all, and I did so."

"Didn't they promise you immunity?"

"No, sir."

"Didn't they promise you a reward?"

"No, sir."

"Weren't you indicted for this train robbery jointly with Jesse James?"

"I don't know."

MY FATHER JESSE JAMES

"Do you mean to say you don't know?"

"No, I don't know."

"Wasn't a copy of the indictment served on you?"

"It might have been. I don't remember."

"Didn't you know that under that first joint indictment, the state would have to discharge you before you could go on the stand and testify?"

"No I didn't know."

"You know that they had you and Jesse and the others indicted separately afterward, and that now they can use you as a witness without first discharging you?"

"I don't know."

The theory of the defense on this point is that Lowe and Jesse James were indicted separately so that the state could use the indictment as a club over Lowe's head to force him to testify.

"Where have you boarded in Westport since your arrest?" asked Walsh.

"I've taken my meals at the Harris house."

"Haven't you gone out bird hunting since your arrest?"

"I went down the railroad track with an officer. I had a little cartridge gun and was shooting grasshoppers."

"Did Detective Harbaugh tell you that a reward was offered for the conviction of the robbers or one of them, and that he would divide it with you?"

"No, sir."

"Didn't they promise you immunity?"

"No, sir."

"Didn't Chief Hayes advise you to confess?"

"Yes."

"Did he make any promises?"

"He said if I would confess it would go light with me. He said he would make no promises except that he would use his influence. My brother came and advised me to tell it all, too."

"Didn't the officers keep asking you before you confessed, if you knew Jesse James?"

"Yes; they asked me once and I told them I knew him."

"Didn't they tell you they had evidence against Jesse James and Jack Kennedy?"

"No: I think not."

"When you first told about this robbery, did you tell the names of all who were in it?"

"Yes."

Mr. Walsh here began a new series of questions on a point which the defense thinks is a strong one in its favor.

"Who was it took the stuff out of the safe that night after you had set off the dynamite?"

"The man they called Evans."

(Evans is the alias of the man supposed to be Bill Rvan.)

"Did he get any money out of the car?"

"I saw him get packages out."

"How big packages?"

Lowe pointed to two law books on a table and said "As big as the two of them together."

"You say that several times before this robbery you stood at the Union depot and saw them transferring money packages from an Omaha express car to this one you robbed?"

"I said I saw them transfer packages I thought was money."

"Was the package Evans took out the same shape and size?"

"Yes; it looked just like it."

"What did Evans do with the package he took from the safe?"

"Put it in a sack."

"How big a sack?"

"About a two bushel sack."

"What did he do then?"

MY FATHER   JESSE JAMES

"He swung the sack over his shoulder and left."

"Did he go with you?"

"No."

"Do you suppose it was money he got in that package?"

"Yes."

"And you had never seen this man Evans before in your life?"

"No."

"And never since?"

"No."

"And you didn't know who he was?"

"No."

"You let a stranger walk away with what you thought was the money after you had risked so much to rob the train?"

"I supposed he was all right."

Mr. Walsh questioned Lowe further about what occurred at and near the home of Jesse James when Lowe went there the night of the robbery. Lowe said he went to the house and inquired of Jesse's sister for Jesse. She told Lowe he had gone to put his aunt, Mrs. Palmer, on a street car to go to the Union depot. Lowe sat down on the porch and in a little while Jesse came in the back door and called him out to the back and pointed to a clump of trees and said the horse was tied there and for him to go over. Lowe went and found the horse, which was restless. Lowe unhitched the horse and drove it around the block. Jesse came and said he had been to a drug store to show himself, so as to fix an alibi. Jesse and Lowe started in the buggy and picked up Andy Ryan at Thirty-Fifth Street. They drove out a ways and caught up to the other two men in a buggy. One of these said everything was all right, the big man meaning Evans, would be out at the scene of the robbery.

That ended the cross-examination by Mr. Walsh. Prosecutor Reed asked Lowe if he and Jesse and Ryan talked on the drive back to town about the money got in the robbery.

"Yes," said Lowe; "Ryan told me they didn't get anything. He said too much dynamite was used and it blew everything to the devil. I told him I didn't believe Evans got nothing. I believed he got something."

Lowe said that he went to the jail last August, when this robbery was planned, in response to a letter from Kennedy.

"Is this the letter?" asked Mr. Reed, handing him an envelope and letter.

"Yes, sir; that's it."

The letter was shown to the jury. The envelope was addressed in ink: "Mr. Bill Lowe, 1001 West Sixteenth Street, Kansas City, Mo." It was stamped and had passed through the mail and had been delivered to Lowe: It bore the postmark: "Kansas City, Mo., August 15, 10 P. M., '98. The letter was written with a lead pencil on a sheet of note paper and was as follows:

>8:15, '98. K. C, Mo.
>Mr. Wilum lowe.
>dear frend bil i thoght at i wuld write
>you a few lines unce for the first time say bil
>when you get this please cum down if you can.
>yours as ever
>J. F. Kennedy.

This is important evidence for the state if it is actually proved to be Kennedy's writing. The lawyers for the defense realized this and examined the letter closely. Mr. Farr showed it to Major Blake L. Woodson, who had once defended Kennedy on a charge of train robbery and was in the court room. Woodson said he thought it was not Kennedy's writing.

Prosecutor Reed showed Lowe a card on the back of which this was written:

"We the masked knights of the road, robbed the Missouri Pacific at the Belt Line junction tonight. The supply of quails was good. With much love, we remain, John Kennedy, Bill Ryan, Bill Anderson, Sam Brown, Jim Redmond. We are ex com spect to."

This card was handed to the express messenger by one of the robbers the night of the robbery. Prosecutor Reed asked Lowe:

"Did you ever see that card before?"

"Where?"

"The Sunday night before the robbery we were at Andy Ryan's house and Jesse showed me that very card."

Edwin E. Hills, the express messenger who was held up, was the next witness, and part of his testimony was quite dramatic. He told what has never been made public before-exactly how much money was on the express car and how much the robbers got. It has always been a matter of speculation with the public as to how much was stolen that night. Hills, the messenger, says they got only $30. Hills is a man of about thirty, with a sandy mustache. He talked in a very loud tone, giving straight, direct answers to questions. He said he was in charge of the express car the night of the robbery. Then he went on:

"As we stopped at the Belt Line crossing the night of the robbery I heard some talk outside and a flag signal of five blasts. I heard the word 'injector' spoken outside the car. In a minute or two the car started again and I noticed it was not the usual motion of the train. I looked out and saw the balance of the train behind us and just the express car attached to the engine. I made up my mind we were being held up. I got my shot gun and laid it on my box and hid my personal valuables. The car stopped and some one knocked on the door and with an oath, said:

"'Open the door or we'll blow your car to hell.'

"I parleyed with them and looked out. I saw the forms of several men. I heard some one say: 'We'll get the dynamite and blow him up.' I told them never mind, boys, I'll open up. They ordered me to put up my hands. I put them up. One climbed up and ordered me back in the end of the car. Another got in."

Hills told about how they placed the little safe on top of the dynamite on the big safe and blew it up, and tried to make him stay in the car when the explosion occurred. He described the explosion, which knocked him flat where he stood by the engine. He said as the robbers left one of them handed him a card.

Prosecutor Reed showed him the card introduced in evidence a short time before, and identified by Lowe. Hills said;

"The leader handed me that card and told me to show it to the newspapers in the morning."

"Describe the leader, the one who got in the car and did so much talking," said Prosecutor Reed.

"He had on a black mask, dark coat like a mackintosh, that came almost to his heels, and he carried a double barreled shot gun when he first got in the car."

"What money did you have in the car that night?"

"One sack of silver with $1,000 in it, a package of $590 in currency, two C.0.D. packages containing $18 and two packages of government war bonds, amounting to $560."

"How much of this was recovered?"

"A11 but thirty dollars of the silver dollars, which were lost. The other packages were recovered intact."

"Did you get a good chance to observe the leader who was in the car with you?"

"The best chance I had was while he was in the rear of the car, where the light was quite dim. He wore a black mask of glazed oilcloth."

Prosecutor Reed showed the glazed mask found in the weeds near the scene of the robbery and identified by Lowe yesterday as very much like the one worn by Jesse James. Hills said it was like the one worn by the leader.

"Describe the leader's appearance."

"He was a small man, five feet six or seven inches tall, weighing one hundred and thirty to one hundred and forty-five or one hundred and fifty pounds. He had very sharp, piercing eyes, and a nose rather prominent."

At the request of Prosecutor Reed, Jesse James stood up and looked, without a trace of nervousness, straight at the witness.

"How did the leader's height compare with the height of the defendant?" asked Prosecutor Reed.

"I should say he was about the same height."

"How does he compare as to breadth of shoulders?"

"About the same. He bore a general resemblance to the man who just stood up."

"You say you noticed the leader's eyes. How does the defendant's eyes compare with them?"

"The robber's eyes were large and piercing eyes, as this man has."

"Is the defendant the man that was there that night and wore the coat and mask?"

"I am unable to state."

Hills then told the following story, giving it with good dramatic gestures, imitations and general effect:

"The next afternoon after the robbery I went to the court house to get a good look at Jesse James and see if he was the man who held me up."

"Who told you to go?"

"Superintendent Moore of the Pacific Express."

"Tell what occurred."

"I went in the court house and Jesse was not there. I strolled around and soon he came in and went behind his cigar stand. I walked up and looked him square in the eye and said:

"I want a cigar."

"I looked square into his eyes and he dropped his eyes and raised them and dropped them again. I found fault with the cigar he handed me and said:

"Young man, I was out late last night and I'm a little nervous. I want a nice, mild cigar to settle my nerves.

"He reached in and got one and I paid him. As he handed me the change he said in a deep tone of voice:

"'Thank you, sir.'"

"Did his voice resemble any you had ever heard before?"

"No; it was not his natural voice even."

MY FATHER   JESSE JAMES

Court adjourned for noon at this point.

After the court adjournment at noon Frank P. Walsh, attorney for Jesse James, was asked what he thought of the testimony of W. W. Lowe. He said:

"The most important thing for the defense is that Lowe now denies positively that he ever made a written confession; that he ever dictated a confession, or that he ever signed his name to any statement whatever. When we showed him his confession published in the Star, October 13, he said it was not his, that he never made it, but we will prove that Lowe did make the confession printed in the Star of that date.

"The reason Lowe denies that confession now is because there are discrepancies between his confession and his testimony now. For instance, there is a discrepancy in the time he says he left the point near the James home to go to the robbery, and there is a discrepancy between his statements with regard to where he met Evans.

"In his printed confession he says he met the big man Evans near the James home. He says he, Jesse and Andy Ryan got in one buggy and Charlie, the 'old man' and Evans got in another buggy, and all drove out together. Now he swears that he and Jesse got in the buggy and drove out and overtook Andy and they drove on and overtook Charlie and the 'old man' in another buggy, and that the first time he saw Evans was after he got to the scene of the robbery.

"Another thing, Lowe denied positively yesterday afternoon that he had been promised anything to confess. I asked him positively yesterday if the police promised to be light on him if he confessed. He said, "No." This morning he admits that this promise was made to him."

Prosecutor Reed was asked today why Lowe denied his confession.

"Why," said Mr. Reed, "he never did make a written confession, and never did sign one. He told the officers, I suppose, the whole truth, and they wrote it down in a condensed form, and that is what The Star printed."

When court met after the noon recess today, Hills, the messenger, was put on the witness stand again and was asked by Prosecutor Reed:

"Did you ever hear the voice of Jesse James at any other time than when you were at his cigar stand?"

"Yes, sir."

"At the Westport police station."

"Where did you ever hear that voice before?"

"The night of the robbery."

"Whose voice was it?"

"The voice of the leader of the gang."

Charles A. Slocum, engineer of the train that was held up, was called next. He said they got to Belt Line crossing about 9:59 or 10 o'clock. The train stopped at the crossing. A man stepped up to the engine cab with a gun. He told them to get down and they did so and held up their hands. The man who ordered them down had an Irish brogue. One of the men on the ground said to another:

"'All right. Bill, get up in the engine.'"

"The man called Bill got up in the cab and blew five blasts on the engine whistle as a signal for the brakeman to go out behind with a flag."

"Had William W. Lowe ever worked with you before, Mr. Slocum?" asked Prosecutor Reed.

"Yes, sir."

"Did you get a good look at the robber who climbed up in your cab?"

"Yes, sir."

"Was he Wlliam W. Lowe"

"Yes, sir; it was William W. Lowe."

Slocum told the story of how the baggage car was uncoupled, and all that was done, his story agreeing in every particular with the testimony of W.W. Lowe and Hills, the express messenger.

"Did you get a good look at the man who marched the express messenger out at the point of a gun?"

"No; I didn't see him closely."

"Describe him as near as you can."

"He weighed about one hundred and thirty-five or one hundred and forty pounds and slim built, and wore a long coat nearly down to his heels."

Jesse James stood up at the request of the prosecutor, but Mr. Walsh objected to Slocum giving his opinion, because Slocum had said all he knew was that it was a slim man. The court sustained this objection.

"What sort of a looking man was the one who guarded you at the engine?"

"He talked with an Irish brogue and had a peculiar way of throwing his head forward, and he talked in a nice, easy tone."

"Have you seen that man since?"

"I couldn't say positively."

Slocum had been taken to Mansfield to see Bill Ryan, under arrest there for robbing a Memphis train. The theory of the state is that Bill Ryan was the Evans of the Leeds hold-up, but Slocum would not say that the Evans of the Leeds hold-up was the man under arrest at Mansfield.

"What is your best judgment about it?"

"I do not know positively."

Prosecutor Reed pressed the question and Walsh objected. The judge finally interfered and asked Slocum:

"Now, sir, if you saw that man again would you recognize him?"

"If I saw him act and heard his voice I could probably say."

"Have you seen the man since?"

"I have seen a man who answers very well the description of that man."

"Did you recognize him as the same man?"

"I wouldn't say positively."

Prosecutor Reed asked: "Where did you see that man?"

"At Mansfield, but I would not swear positively it was the same, but he tallies well with the same man."

Mr. Walsh, in cross examining Slocum, asked:

"Did you know positively that it was W. W. Lowe when he got in the engine that night?"

"I thought it was him."

"Did he call you by name, or you call him?"

"No."

"How long had Lowe worked for you before that?"

"He had fired for me at different times."

"Will you swear positively that it was William W. Lowe who held you up that night?"

Mr. Slocum hit the arm of the witness chair very vigorously with his clinched fist as he answered:

"I made up my mind right then that it was Lowe, and I haven't changed it since."

"When did you first tell that it was Lowe?"

"About two days after the robbery I told it to Del Harbaugh, the detective. I think I told my fireman, too."

"Were you trying to conceal that you recognized Lowe?"

"I didn't want to say anything to hurt him. I didn't want to cause him trouble."

E. L. Weston, fireman of the train, testified next and his story of the details of how the train was held up agree with the stories told by Lowe, Hills and Slocum. Mr. Walsh asked him on cross examination:

"Do you know W. W. Lowe?"

"Yes; I've known him for ten years."

"Was Lowe the man who got into the cab?"

"I don't know."

"Did you see Lowe there that night?"

"I don't know."

Weston testified that he had been to Mansfield and saw the man under arrest there and thought it was one of the men who was at the engine the night of the robbery, but would not say it was the same.

E. M. Hisey, the telegraph operator at Belt Line junction, who was captured by the robbers, was the next witness. He said he was leaning back in his chair in the telegraph shanty and a man came in and with an oath ordered him to throw up his hands. Another man came in and smashed the telegraph instruments with a pair of pliers.

Prosecutor Reed showed him the pliers which were found the next morning on the ground, and Hisey said they were the same. Hisey said the man who held him up had a shot gun and shoved it in his face and cursed and was very fierce, threatening to kill him. There was a man in the office waiting to get a ride on a freight train, and the robbers held him up, too, and marched both of them down to where the rest of the gang had held up the train. One of the two robbers who took him from the shanty called the other Bill.

"The man who held me up had a light hat on, a black mask with the eyes showing and a long rubber coat nearly to his heels. I heard it rattle. I saw his chin. He was a small man, who would weigh one hundred and forty or one hundred and forty-five pounds, a young fellow. He swore nearly every word he said.

"Have you seen the man since who held you up that night?" asked Prosecutor Reed.

"I have seen a man I think is him."

"Who is he?"

Hisey pointed straight at Jesse James and said positively:

"That fellow sitting right there."

"Who, Jesse James?"

"Yes; Jesse James. I think he is undoubtedly the fellow; there is no mistake about it."

This was by all odds the strongest evidence against Jesse James produced at the trial so far. It amounts almost to a positive identification. Jesse James did not flinch under it or show signs of nervousness.

Hisey testified further that he saw Jesse James in the Westport jail after the robbery and he noticed the moment he went in that Jesse watched him. He saw Jesse at the court house and said to him there:

"I have been mistaken about the color of your eyes. It looked to me as if you had dark eyes, but I see now that they are light. It seemed that they were dark when you had that mask on."

Mr. Walsh, in cross-examining Hisey, asked this question:

"Didn't you say in Witte's saloon, in Leeds, a month after this robbery, that it was not Jesse James who held you up?"

"No, sir."

"Didn't you say, in the presence of Murphy, Mason, Miller, Noland and others, in that saloon, that you had seen Jesse James since the robbery, and it was not Jesse who held you up?"

"No, sir; I did not."

The Star of February 25 printed the following:

"The most positive identification of Jesse James as one of the Leeds train robbers was made in the court room this afternoon by William J. Smith of Stotesbury, Missouri, who was a passenger on the Missouri Pacific train the night it was held up. Smith testified that he was riding in the smoking car and got out when the train was held up and walked up among the robbers. One of the robbers put a gun against his breast and ordered him back into the car.

"Did that man have anything over his face?" asked Prosecutor Reed.

"He had nothing over his face. He had something black around his neck, as if it were a mask, slipped down."

"How light was it?"

"It was very light. The light streamed out the mail car door."

"Did you get a good look at that man!"

"Yes, sir; I got a good look at him."

"Do you see that man in the court room?"

Mr. Smith pointed to Jesse James, sitting facing him and said:

"Yes, sir; there he sits right over there."

"You mean the defendant, Jesse James?"

"Yes, sir; it was Jesse James."

Frank P. Walsh began the cross-examination of Smith.

"Where were you born?"

"In Kentucky."

"How long have you lived in Stotesbury?"

"Two years."

"Where did you live before that?"

"On a farm in Cass county."

"How long did you farm there?"

"Eleven years."

Mr. Walsh volleys him with questions about Detective Harbaugh and other detectives. He asked if Harbaugh had been "with you a good deal lately."

Smith said that he first saw Harbaugh a month ago when Harbaugh went to his home in Stotesbury with Detective Bryant to see what he knew. Smith said he was staying here with his brother-in-law, E. T. Bergen, who drives a hack for the Depot Carriage company. He said that detectives were not paying his way here, but he expected his expenses to be paid for coming here to testify. He said Harbaugh was not paying him. Smith said he was working for the Pittsburg & Gulf railroad.

The next day of the trial this fellow Smith was put on the stand and had to admit that he had been in jail for burglary, and that for the sake of his family his friends bailed him out. Scarcely anyone in the court room believed any part of the testimony of Smith.

The Star's account of the rest of the testimony this day was as follows:

"S. M. Downer, a freight conductor on the Missouri Pacific, testified that Sunday, August 28, while his train was coming to Kansas City two men boarded it when the train stopped at the Belt Line crossing. They got on midway of the train and climbed on top of a car. Downer sent his rear brakeman up to tell them to get off. The two men walked back over the top of the train to the caboose. The larger one clambered into the caboose and the other stayed outside. The man who went in said:

"Mr. Downer, I'm a railroad man, I'm switching in the Sante Fe yards. I've been out here to a Dutch picnic in Swope Park and if I don't get in on your train I'll be too late for my work."

Downer asked him his name and he said it was Bill Lowe. That started a conversation, because Downer knew Lowe's brother.

"Who was with Lowe?" asked Prosecutor Reed.

"A young man of twenty-three or twenty-four years, smooth faced, weighing from one hundred and thirty-five to one hundred and fifty pounds."

"Do you think you would recognize him if you saw him?"

"I have seen the young man since, but I won't swear to it," answered Downer.

Judge Shackleford asked Downer: "Could you be reasonably certain of this young man if you saw him?"

"Yes," answered Downer.

"Now, Mr. Reed, you may ask him who it was" said the judge.

"Who was it?" asked Reed.

"I think it was that young man sitting there," pointing to Jesse James.

"You mean Mr. James?"

"Yes, sir; Mr. James."

Mr. Walsh cross-examined Downer:

"Did you get a good look at the young man who was with Lowe?"

"No; I only glanced at him as he was crossing the car next to the caboose."

"On such a slight glance are you willing to swear that Jesse James was the man?"

"I haven't done so."

"You don't want to swear this young man is the one?"

"I answer in this way, to my best judgment. I say he is the one, but I will not swear positively to it."

The next three witnesses were T. H. Hutchison, a grocer and a school director of Leeds, who swore that Sunday, August 28, W. W. Lowe and Jesse James called at his store; Walter Hutchinson, his son, who saw Jesse and Lowe there, and Burt Meyers, a young man who saw them, too.

T. H. Hutchison said he became acquainted with Jesse James last July, when Jesse went to him to try and get a place for his sister to teach school.

"I was in my store August 28 when Jesse and another man came in a little after one o'clock and asked for a drink. I drew a fresh bucket of water. They talked awhile. The big man pointed to a shot gun on the wall and said it was like one his father used to own. When they were leaving Jesse asked me who got the school. I told him and he said it was just as he had expected. They went south in the direction of Belt Line junction."

W. W. Lowe was brought into the court room and Mr. Hutchison pointed to him and said:

"That is the man who was with Jesse."

Walter Hutchison and Bert Meyers swore that they were at the store when Jesse and the other man were there, but they could not say that the other man was Lowe.

Francis McGingan, a coal miner, said he went to the scene of the hold-up the next morning and found false whiskers. He was shown those in the court room and identified them.

The next three witnesses were Will Starkey, Ben Shaeffer and A. J. Theakston. They were working for the Missouri Valley Bridge Company Sunday, August 28, finishing a new bridge for the 'Frisco road near Leeds and near where the train was held up. Starkey knew Jesse James, because Starkey boarded with one of the school directors and Jesse had been out there to try to get a place for his sister to teach school. Starkey testified that Sunday afternoon, August 28, he saw Jesse James and another man walking on the Missouri Pacific tracks near where the hold-up was. He pointed out Jesse to the other workmen on the bridge. Shaeffer and Theakston corroborated this and had their time books in court to prove that they did work on that bridge that afternoon.

There was one witness that the state did not call and he was H. P. Vallee, the brakeman of the train upon which Lowe said he and I rode in from Leeds. Soon after my arrest I secured the following affidavit from Vallee:

"H. P. Vallee, of lawful age, being duly sworn, upon his oath says that he is in the employ of the Missouri Pacific railroad as brakeman on a freight train; that he was acting in that capacity on the freight train on that road known as second No. 208 on the 28th day of August, 1898, when W. W. Lowe and another man rode on that train from the Pittsburg and Gulf crossing to Sheffield on that line; that S. M. Downer was the conductor of the train; that I have seen and conversed with Jesse James today and am positive that he was not the man who was on the train with Lowe on that occasion; nor have I ever said or intimated that he was, but upon the contrary I have at all times since I was first asked to look at James and identify him said that he was not the man. The man who was on the train with Lowe was taller than James and had sandy hair and three or four days growth of sandy beard. I have never seen James on any train at any time."

To show now how the railroad detectives conspired to convict me I wished, of course, to have Vallee as one of my witnesses. He would have been a most important witness in my behalf. His testimony would have impeached Lowe and proven his story to be false. To prevent my getting him as a witness the railroad company took him away from his job in Missouri and gave him another job as brakeman on their line in Kansas, and told him he would lose his job altogether if he came and testified for me. The law is that a man cannot be compelled to come from one state into another to be a witness in a case. So I was utterly powerless to get Vallee to testify for me. Milton J. Oldham, one of my lawyers, tried to learn from the railroad company the location of Vallee but they refused to tell him.

The day that the state closed its testimony against me the Kansas City Star printed the following:

"The past life and character of Jesse James and his general reputation in this community, where he has lived since he was a child, will be shown by the defense before it closes its side of the case in the trial of Jesse James for train robbery, which defense began in the criminal court this morning. It is likely that this testimony about the good habits of Jesse and his devotion to his widowed mother and his orphaned sister will have as much influence with the jury in reaching a verdict as anything else in the case.

"To look at young Jesse James as he sits day after day in the court room it is hard to believe that he is a train robber or a criminal of any sort. He does not look nor carry himself like the men who rob trains usually do. He is boyish in his looks; he is a boy in his actions. He has nothing of a hardened look on his face. He does not seem to take the trial as a very serious matter. He listens to the important testimony and follows it intently, but in the intervals when questions are asked about things of lesser interest he talks, jokes and laughs with the newspaper reporters and with others and seems to take a boyish interest and delight in any kind of a laughable thing that happens.

"This morning when the trial was in progress and a witness was giving important testimony a young man whom Jesse knew very well entered and sat down close to him. Jesse leaned over and whispered:

"How did the Tigers come out at Lawrence?" A whispered reply was made and Jesse laughed and asked again:

"Who played guards? Who played in my place?"
Jesse is a member of the Tigers' basket ball team that played the Lawrence team Saturday.

So far, neither the mother, sister nor grandmother old Mrs. Samuels-of young Jesse James has been in the court room, but they will be there and they will tell what a good boy Jesse has always been. This will be among the most important testimony in behalf of Jesse. It will require strong evidence to convince the average juror that a young man only twenty-two years old, who has been almost the sole support of his mother and his sister since he was eleven years old, who worked through all these boyhood years almost without losing a day, who deprived himself of the things boys love and carried his wages home every payday and gave his earnings to his mother to help pay off the mortgage on the house, and who actually did alone and unaided, pay for this home; it will be hard to make the average juror believe that that boy robbed a train.

When the jurors see the young man's mother on the stand and hear her tell these things; when they hear his sister tell of his love and devotion to her, and that it was his wages that kept her at school and gave her a musical education; when the old grandmother tells how kind and devoted this only son of her bandit son has been, it will go a long way with the jury.

And these things are true. Jesse James has been a model son and brother. The people of this community have watched him grow up and until this charge of train robbery was brought against him there was nothing wrong ever heard of him."

I quote the newspaper account again of my defense, as follows:

Cassimer Welsh, a deputy marshal, was sworn and testified:

"I and Deputy Marshal Leahy went to the scene of the robbery the night of the robbery and talked to Hills, the express messenger. We asked Hills for a description of the men. He said the man who seemed to be the leader and did all the talking was a big man. We asked him to describe him and just then Sergeant Caskey came in with his uniform on, and Hills pointed to Caskey and said the leader was about the size of him. Hills said the leader was over six feet tall."

"How does Sergeant Caskey compare in size with Jesse James?"

"Caskey is almost twice as large."

"Did Hills at any time describe a man who answer to a description of Jesse James."

Deputy Welsh answered very positively:

"No, sir; he did not describe anyone who would answer to a description of Jess James."

Charles K. Bowen of the Kansas City View Company, testified that after the arrest of Jesse James he went with Finis C. Farr, one of Jesse James' lawyers, to the scene of the robbery and talked with Hisey, the telegraph operator who was held up by the robbers.

"I asked Hisey if it was Jesse James who held him up and he told me that it was not Jesse James. He said he had been down to the court house and looked at Jesse, and it was not he who held him up."

Prosecutor Reed, on cross-examination, asked:

"Are you sure Hisey told you it was not Jesse James?"

"I am as positive as that I am sitting here. Hisey didn't have any reservation. He said he could not tell who it was who held him up and hadn't the least idea who it was."

H. B. Leavins of 3341 Forest avenue, secretary of the Lombard Investment Company, testified that the night of the robbery he saw Jesse James at the south end of the Troost avenue car line at 8:15 o'clock, or very near that time.

Mrs. H. B. Leavins testified that the night of the robbery she and her husband were at the end of the Troost avenue car line and saw Jesse help his mother and another woman and two children on the car.

"What time was that?" she was asked.

"Some time between 8 and 8:30 o'clock, as near as I can tell."

Charles W. Hovey, a deputy county clerk, said that the night of the robbery he saw Jesse James at the drug store at the end of the Troost avenue line at 9 o'clock. He was sure it was 9 o'clock because he heard the curfew whistle blow. Mr. Hovey also testified as follows:

"After Jesse was arrested he came to me and asked me to go over to the city hall with him to see S. M. Downer, conductor of a freight train. I am a notary public and Jesse wanted me to take Downer's affidavit. I took my notarial seal with me. Jesse James asked Downer in my presence and hearing if he had said that

he would identify Jesse as the man who rode in with Lowe from Belt Line junction Sunday afternoon, August 28. Downer said he had not said it was Jesse, and he would not say that it was Jesse who was on the train. Jesse asked him to make an affidavit to that effect and Downer said,
'No; he had a good job on the Missouri Pacific road and he was not going to lose it by making affidavits.'"

George TV. Tourtellot, superintendent of the Armour Packing company, was the first witness examined after the noon recess and the first witness to the good reputation of Jesse James.

"How long have you known Jesse James?" was asked him.

"Seven or eight years."

"How long did he work for the Armour Packing company?"

"Six years."

"Are you acquainted with his reputation in this community for honesty, uprightness, truth and veracity?"

"I am."

"What is it?"

"It has been first-class in every respect."

C. E. Jones, a druggist of Thirty-third street and Troost avenue, testified next that Jesse James was in his store the night of the robbery as late as 8:45 o'clock and talked to John Noland, who was playing the slot machine, and that Jesse got some pennies and played the slot machine, too, and was in the store six or eight minutes.

Walter Gaugh, a bookbinder, testified that the night of the robbery he left the junction of Ninth and Main streets at 8:30 o'clock and went on a cable car to the end of the Troost line and got to the end of the line at 9 o'clock or a little after, and saw Jesse James there.

Charles Howard, of Hill & Howard's drug store at the end of the Troost avenue car line, testified that Jesse James was in the store at 8:55 o'clock and took a glass of soda water.

Miss Murray, a stenographer in the New York Life building, was sworn and testified that in November she took the deposition of Hisey, the telegraph operator. She had this deposition with her and said Hisey gave it under oath. The following questions asked Hisey and his answers were read to the jury:

"I will ask you who those two men were that came and held you up, if you know?"
'
"I was not acquainted with the gentlemen."

"Did you know them at any time?"

"Never met them before to the best of my knowledge."

"Have you ever met them since?"

"I could not say positively that I have, and I could not say positively that I have not. That is a pretty hard question to answer."

This testimony is important as tending to impeach Hisey, who says now that one of the men was Jesse James. When Hisey was on the stand the other day these questions and answers in his deposition were read to him and he denied that he gave the answers.

James S. Rice, a watchman at the end of the Troost line, testified that he saw Jesse James in Hill & Howard's drug store at 9 o'clock. Rice said he came out of the drug store just as the curfew whistle blew, and Jesse James entered the store at the same time.

G. W. Daniels, a Wells-Fargo express messenger, testified next that he saw Jesse James in Hill & Howard's drug store at 9:10 or 9:15 o'clock. Daniels said he was driving north on Troost avenue and was passing J. J. Squires' house, six blocks from the drug store, when the 9 o'clock curfew whistle blew. He drove leisurely to the drug store and saw Jesse in there. Daniels said he told his superintendent about it a few days after the robbery.

Dr. T. J. Beatty testified that he saw Jesse James in the barber shop at Thirty-third street and Troost avenue at seven o 'clock. When the doctor told this Prosecutor Reed asked him with a laugh:

"What time did the curfew whistle blow that night?"

"I don't know."

"You mean to say you didn't hear it."

"I didn't hear it."

"What time did the explosion go off?"

"I don't know."

"Didn't hear that either, hey?"

"No."

Joe Gorsuch, a bill clerk for the Kansas City, Fort Scott & Memphis road, testified that he saw Jesse James at 8:30 o'clock at the end of the Troost avenue line the night of the robbery.

Mrs. Ida Foster lived on the other side of the street from Jesse James and a half block south, at the time of the robbery. She sat at the window till 7:30 o'clock with the trees in plain sight to which W. W. Lowe says the horse used by the robbers was hitched. There was no horse and buggy there up to 7:30 o'clock. She could say nothing about it after that time.

Mrs. O.D. Stanley who lived in the same house with Mrs. Foster, testified that the night of the robbery she sat on her front porch from 7:30 until 9 o'clock. The trees to which Lowe says the horse and buggy stood were across the street and in full view, and she was sure there was no rig there. On cross examination Mrs. Stanley said her husband came home at 7:30 o'clock that night, and she poured the coffee for him, and she could not remember whether she did or did not stay with him in the house while he ate his supper.

Mrs. J. M. Bunch lives at 3338 Forest avenue, near the James home. The night of the robbery she and her husband were sitting on the steps of their house when Jesse James passed at 9:10 or 9:20 o'clock. They spoke to him and he answered and went on and into his own home. Mrs. Bunch fixed the time because she heard the curfew blow.

J. M. Bunch corroborated this testimony of his wife.

"How did you fix the time that Jesse James went past your house before anyone accused him of anything?" asked Prosecutor Reed.

"Jesse came to see me seven or eight days after the robbery and asked me if I remembered it. He said officers were suspecting him."

At the end of this testimony, which shows that Jesse James was at Thirty-third and Troost as late as 9 o'clock, one of the lawyers of Jesse James whispered to a friend:

"Now you see why W. W. Lowe repudiated his confession printed in The Star. In that confession, it appeared that they started to drive out to rob the train between 8 and 9 o'clock. After Lowe made that confession, the state took all our witnesses before the grand jury and found out that Jesse was at Thirty-third and Troost avenue after 9 o'clock, and so Lowe had to repudiate that first confession and change his testimony to fit with the testimony of ours."

William Cargill, assistant superintendent of the Armour Packing company was sworn next, and asked:

"How long did Jesse James work at your packing house?"

"Eight years."

"What is his reputation in the community?"

"His reputation was the best. I considered him a model young man while he was in our employ."

Judge John W. Henry, of the circuit court, a former member of the Supreme Court, was the next witness. He said the reputation of Jesse James was good.

E. F. Swinney, cashier of the first National bank, testified next that the reputation of Jesse James was good; there was none better. Then court adjourned.

The Kansas City Journal reported as follows the next day's proceedings in court:

"An old woman yesterday tottered into the court room where Jesse James is being tried on a charge of train robbery. Her steps were unsteady as she tremblingly felt her way over the floor to the witness stand.

She was supported on the one side by a stern-faced, steely-eyed man of middle age, while on the other, guiding her with tender care, was a young woman. The hair of the old woman was whitened with the weight of years and troubles and her failing eyesight had necessitated the use of gold rimmed glasses.

That old woman was Mrs. Zerelda Samuels, the mother of Jesse James, a man who less than a quarter of a century ago was the most noted bandit of the world. Jesse has gone to join the silent majority, shot to death by a treacherous comrade. The young woman who was so solicitous for her welfare was her granddaughter, Mary James, the sister of the defendant.

As the aged woman made her way to the witness chair she was obliged to pass her grandson. He arose, pressed her hand, and was greeted with a soft smile from the grandmother's eyes.

The tension in the court room was great as Mrs. Samuels took her seat. As she sank back in the witness chair she faced the entire assemblage, and five hundred pairs of eyes were fixed upon her.

They noted the tremor of the aged hand, the glossy whiteness of the hair upon which rested a simple and becoming bonnet of black; the plain black silk dress-everything. Every ear was on the alert to hear the words which she would utter.

"Hold up your right hand and be sworn," boomed forth the clerk of the court.

Up went the right arm, but the hand was missing! Nothing but an empty sleeve - empty nearly to the elbow - greeted the vision. The minds of all, unconsciously, instantly reverted to the tragedy in which she lost that hand so many years ago, when Pinkerton detectives are said to have thrown a dynamite bomb into her house, killing an infant in her arms and maiming herself for life.

"You hereby swear that everything you say upon this stand shall be the truth, the whole truth, and nothing but the truth?"

"I do." There was nothing weak about this response. While given in a low voice, it was clear and distinct, and after its utterance the jaws closed with the snap of determination.

"Please state to the court your name, age and residence," said Attorney Yeager, who conducted the examination.

"My name is Zerelda Samuels, I am seventy four years of age, and I live in Clay County."

"Do you know the defendant?" pointing to Jesse James.

"Yes; he is my grandson."

The examination of Mrs. Samuels elicited the fact that she had arrived at the James home the day before the train robbery, from Clay County, and that she had reached the house about noon. She said that upon her arrival Mrs. Allen Palmer, a married daughter, together with her two children, were there, but that they left that night. She testified that Jesse left with his mother, his aunt and the children, to place them on a cable car that night before 8 o'clock. She did not remember when Jesse had got back to the house, but it was some little time. It was moonlight, warm, and they were sitting upon the porch. She said that Jesse had come in the back way, around the house, and joined herself and Mary James on the porch. Some little time afterwards Mrs. James returned, and they were all seated there together when she heard the explosion. She asked Jesse what it was. She didn't remember exactly, but she thought he said it was a blast at the coal mines. They went to bed about 11 o'clock.

"Was there any man there that evening to see Jesse?"

"No, sir; there was no man there at all but Jesse."

"Are you sure?"

"Yes, sir; I am."

"Why did not Jesse go to the depot with his aunt and mother."

"Because I asked him to stay with me. And I didn't think there was any use for both of them to go."

She stated most positively that Jesse did not leave his home after he had returned from the cable car that night.

Mrs. James, the mother of the defendant, was next called. She gave her age as fifty-three. She told of going to the depot with Mrs. Palmer and her children, who took the 9:05 "Katy" for Texas. She left them before the train pulled out and went straight home. When she arrived there she found Mrs. Samuels, Mary and Jesse seated upon the front porch. They remained there until about 11 o'clock and then retired. She did not hear the explosion. She is somewhat deaf. She was positive that Jesse did not leave the house after she had returned that evening.

"Call Miss Mary James," said Mr. Walsh to a deputy. The sister of the defendant came in from the witness room and took the chair. She is a sweet faced young woman of nineteen, was quietly dressed in black and wore black gloves.

"I have lived in the city for sixteen years," she said in response to a question. "I have attended the Woodland, Morse, Linwood, and Central High school."

"You are a graduate of the last?"

"Yes, sir."

She corroborated the evidence of her mother and grandmother. She said that her mother returned from the depot on the night of the robbery between 9:30 and 10 o'clock. They were seated on the porch when she came and Jesse had not been home long.

"We heard the explosion shortly afterward," she said, "and grandma asked Jesse what it was. No, I don't remember what he answered."

"Did any man come up and ask where Jesse was that night?"

"Why, no." surprisedly.

"Was there any man there at all that night?"

"None other than Jesse."

Following is the newspaper account of my testimony given in my own behalf:

On his direct examination Jesse said he was twenty-three years old last August and had lived in Kansas City sixteen years. He went to the Morse, Linwood, Webster and High school. He went to work at the Bee Hive when he was eleven years old. Then he worked for Crittenden & Phister as an office boy for ten months. He next worked three months for the Germania Life Insurance company. He went to work at Armour's packing house June 12, 1891, and quit there January 15, 1898, and opened a cigar stand in the court house.

"Are you acquainted with W. W. Lowe?" he was asked.

"Yes, sir."

"How long had you known him prior to this robbery?"

"Since last May. I met him first in Krueger's court and he came to the court house a few times and bought cigars."

"Do you know Andy Ryan?"

"Yes; he came three or four times to the court house to buy cigars."

"Did you ever ask Lowe how to rob a train?"

"I did not."

"Did you ever plan to rob a train?"

"I did not."

Jesse said that the night of the robbery he was shaved at 7 o'clock, at 7:30 he went home, at 8 or 8:15 he went with his mother, aunt and two cousins to the cable car. He was around Thirty-third street and Troost Avenue till 9 o'clock or a little after, when he went home and stayed all night.

Jesse denied that he was at Andy Ryan's house with Lowe September 21; he denied that he wrote the card which one of the robbers gave to the express messenger. He said he was not the man who rode in on a freight train with S. M. Downer, Sunday, August 28.

"You say you never met Lowe at any other place than you have mentioned; in Krueger's court and at your cigar stand, four or five times?" asked Prosecutor Reed.

"I never did."

"You never had any business with him?"

"Never, except to sell him cigars and tobacco, the same as any one else."

"You never had any other meeting or business or transaction with him at any time or place?"

"I never did."

"Look at the outside of this envelope and see whether or not it is your handwriting."

Reed handed Jesse the envelope of the Lowe letter.

"It looks very much like my writing, but it is not mine," answered Jesse, pronouncing each word distinctly and with emphasis.

"Look at this letter and say if you wrote it."

Jesse looked over the Lowe letter and answered as before;

"It looks very much like mine, but it is not mine."

"Didn't you take that letter to the Sante Fe yards where Lowe worked as a switchman, and didn't you leave it there for him?" asked the prosecutor.

"I did not"

"Did you go to Leeds with Lowe, Sunday, August 28?"

"I did not."

"Were you ever at Leeds?"

"Yes; about two hundred times."

"What was your business there?"

"To get the school for my sister to teach, and bicycle riding."

Jesse said that last summer he tried to induce the school directors of Leeds to give his sister Mary a place, and he rode out there a great many times on his bicycle. He was out there Sunday, August 21, on his bicycle and was in Hutchison's store.

I have given here a summary of the evidence for and against me. The arguments of the counsel to the jury consumed a whole day. The speeches were very eloquent. I have no space here to produce any part of them. The jury retired and took only one ballot, which was unanimous for my acquittal.

After my acquittal the newspapers of the West commented on it liberally. I give here a few of these editorial comments:

"Jesse James may be guilty, but we believe the weight of the evidence was in his favor." - Lexington (Mo.) Intelligencer.

"The acquittal of Jesse James will be heralded with pleasure by all who know his peculiar history. A set of scoundrels were trying to rivet a chain around him and we are glad of their failure." - Pierce City (Mo.) Democrat.

"Jesse James has been acquitted at Kansas City of the charge of train robbery. But no train robber need take any encouragement from that. The people of this state are dead set against this crime. The evidence did not show James guilty. Under the evidence as presented he ought to have been acquitted. No juror who regarded and valued his oath could have voted otherwise. The detectives made the case against Jesse James. They originated it, worked it up, found the witnesses, wrote out their confessions for them, furnished them money for their testimony, had him indicted and had charge of the prosecution, and they were employed to do this by the railroads. The detectives wanted big game. They wanted to make a big show, a spectacular demonstration. The conviction of Jesse James would terrorize train robbers more than would the conviction of twenty ordinary train robbers. So all hands joined in to send him to the penitentiary." - Brunswick (Mo.) Brunswicker.

CHAPTER TWELVE

IN CONCLUSION

In bringing this book to a close, I wish to thank, from the bottom of my heart, those friends who came to my help and support when indeed I needed friends. I know that without the moral and material support those friends gave me the conspiracy of detectives to ruin me might have been successful. I can name here only a few of those friends. Among them were Thomas T. Crittenden, who was governor of Missouri when my father was killed. Mr. Crittenden has taken a deep interest in my welfare since my boyhood, and when I was arrested for robbing a train he was one who came to my support and declared openly that he believed I was innocent. Another friend who stood by me through thick and thin was Tom Crittenden, son of the former governor. When I was arrested Tom Crittenden came to me and said:

"Jesse, I have known you since you were a little boy. I have helped you and watched you closely, and have been very solicitous as to your future. You gained my confidence and I believed in you. I want to know now if you helped to rob this train or if you knew anything about it. I want you to tell the whole truth."

I replied to him: "Tom you are as good a friend as I have on earth. No one ever knew a James to go back on a friend. If I'd lie to you now I ought to be hung like a damned cur. I tell you I am absolutely innocent, and all I ask is a fair trial and I'll prove it."

He said to me then: "I'm going to accept your statement of your innocence as true. I believe you are telling the truth, and I 'm going to stand by you."

At that time Crittenden was a candidate for re-election to the office of County Clerk. The Kansas City World, in commenting on this recently, said:

"The friendship existing between Tom Crittenden, county clerk, and Jesse James, Jr., is quite well known in Kansas City. The newspapers referred to it often during the recent trial of the boy, on a charge of train robbery, and many marveled at evidences of fellowship so staunch as to outlive the effects of evil report against this scion of Jesse James, Sr., the bandit. Mr. Crittenden never doubted the innocence of his protégé. Though the trial occurred in the heat of a political campaign, in which Mr. Crittenden was a candidate for re-election and when to avow sympathy for an accused train robber was to make enemies, still he stood by young James, and helped him with his time, money and influence.

"A political campaign was on. Crittenden was a candidate on the democratic ticket for re-election to take office of county clerk. The campaign was a warm one and the question of train robbery was an issue in it.

"Under those circumstances and in the face of that sort of campaign, it was perilous for a democratic candidate to openly avow his championship of one of the alleged train robbers. But Crittenden made no half way business of it.

"He furnished the bond for Jesse's release. He retained lawyers to defend him, and helped gather evidence to acquit him. He was criticised severely for this, and it was even said that his action would cause the defeat of all the democratic candidates. Then came the acquittal of Jesse, but not before the day of election which brought the re-election of Crittenden.

"After the acquittal, Crittenden assisted Jesse in renting and stocking a cigar store on one of the principal streets, and the young man attends strictly to business and is making money. His best friend is yet T. T. Crittenden, Jr."

Other friends who came to my help were Frank P. Walsh, E. F. Swinney, R. L. Yeager, Finis C. Farr, Milton J. Oldham and Judge John W. Henry. I wish to speak also of the fair rulings made by Judge Dorsey W. Shackleford, who presided at my trial, and by his justness secured for me a fair and impartial trial.

To all of these friends I have this to say, that through no fault of mine shall they ever have cause to regret that they gave me the hand of friendship when enemies had conspired to ruin me. My conduct in the future shall be as it has been in the past. My chief aim has always been, and shall continue to be, to show by my daily life, and by strict attention to the business I have established, that I am worthy of the respect of all good citizens and of the friendship of those who choose to be my friends, and the friends of the family of Jesse James, my father.

I have one thing more to say in conclusion. I bear no ill will or feelings of malice toward anyone. Some of my best friends are men who were Federal soldiers and who fought my father and were fought by him in honorable warfare. I am sure if my father were living to-day he would be the friend of these old enemies and they would be friends of him. I recall that in Lexington, at the close of the war, he and the man who shot and almost killed him became afterward warm personal friends.

I have had an uphill fight. I ask the public to give me the credit of having worthy motives, and of being desirous of succeeding in the world as a business man and a good citizen of the good old State of Missouri, on whose soil my father fought and bled and suffered as few men fought and as few men suffered for

"THE LOST CAUSE"

ALSO AVAILABLE FROM PJM PUBLISHING

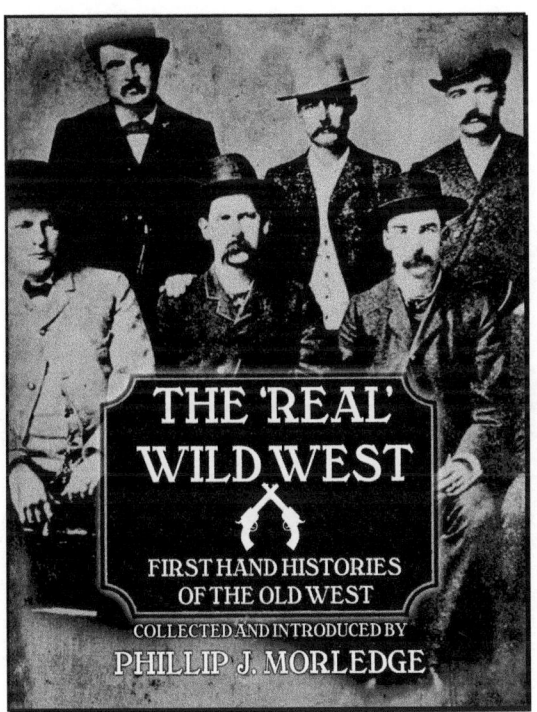

THE 'REAL' WILD WEST

FIRST HAND HISTORIES OF THE OLD WEST

'The 'Real' Wild West' brings together for the first time four legendary first hand accounts of life in the Old West.

Emerson Hough presents a history of the western badman in his 'Story of the Outlaw'. Sheriff Pat Garrett recounts the life and death of a Wild West legend in 'The Authentic Life of Billy, The Kid'. The great showman of the west remembers his early days in 'The Autobiography of Buffalo Bill'. Relive the adventures of the legendary woman of the west, in her own words, in 'The Life and Adventures of Calamity Jane.'

438 Pages

RRP £17.99 / $37.95

AVAILABLE ONLINE FROM AMAZON, TO ORDER FROM ALL MAJOR BOOKSTORES, OR DIRECT FROM

WWW.PJMORLEDGE.COM

www.ingramcontent.com/pod-product-compliance
Ingram Content Group UK Ltd.
Pitfield, Milton Keynes, MK11 3LW, UK
UKHW051256180426
11947UKWH00020B/1738